LOUISIANA STATE UNIVERSITY STUDIES

Max Goodrich, General Editor

*Humanities Series*
Donald E. Stanford, Editor

Number Seventeen
*John Webster and His Critics, 1617–1964*

# John Webster
# and
# His Critics
## 1617–1964

Don D. Moore

*Louisiana State University Press*

**BATON ROUGE**

**MCMLXVI**

*For* CAROL
*and for* RUTH *and* POLK

# CONTENTS

# CONTENTS

vii

# PREFACE

The works of John Webster have had widely varying treatment by literary and drama critics for over three centuries. There is perhaps no other dramatist—Greek, Elizabethan, Jacobean, Restoration, or Modern—whose plays have received a more varied reception and whose critics have been so divided among themselves on whether the writer was due praise or excoriation.[1] While his fellow dramatists Shakespeare and Jonson have nearly always found appreciative critical audiences, despite occasional reservations about "errors" of form and taste, Webster has generated one of the most peculiar critical histories known. In 1617 a contemporary calls him "crabbed," a writer who mangles a poem in the process of creation.[2] Some forty years later, a tribute to his play *The Duchess of Malfi* indicates that it surpasses the work of Sophocles and Euripides.[3] By 1735 another critic says that the dramatist's conceptions were "so eccentric that . . . we cannot trace him";[4] but in 1820 we are told that his two Italian tragedies "come the nearest to Shakespeare of anything we have on record."[5] A little later in the century we hear that one of those tragedies is nothing but an immoral tale of "sin and horror";[6] in the twentieth century, we read that the way in which Webster rose above his fellows was through "intellectual and spiritual insight,"[7] and in the same year that there is, after all, "something a trifle ridiculous about Webster."[8]

The purpose of the following pages is to examine these varying, sometimes violent, responses to John Webster's art, bringing them together for the first time in a comprehensive survey—a service performed previously for Shakespeare and Jonson, but never, at any length, for Webster. Moreover, the book is concerned with the reasons behind the acclamation of a Lamb, the attacks of a Kingsley, the reservations of an Eliot: whenever possible, an effort is made not only to record the critic's impression but also to establish his position in his time. There is included here a survey of Webster's fortunes on the professional stage, a history of drama critics' reactions to *The White Devil* and *The Duchess of Malfi*. It was not simply for the study that Webster wrote—a point neglected by many critics. Lamb in the library and Shaw in row seven are in different critical climes, and this fact will help account for the diversified reaction to Webster.

The general tenor of this entire investigation is predicated at least in part on one of the premises of F. R. Leavis in his *Revaluations:* that the business of the critic is to endeavor, "where the poetry of the past is concerned, to realize to the full the implications of the truism that its life is in the present or nowhere; it is alive insofar as it is alive for us." This survey, then, concentrates particularly on the Webster studies which have considered total meaning and merit, and not on the articles which consider the source of lines in a particular scene. L. C. Knights has written that Shakespearean criticism "has to make the Shakespeare experience available to each reader to the fullest possible extent, and it has to relate that experience to the possibilities of living at the present time. . . ." In this work, the same holds true for John Webster: this study is ultimately concerned with what one Jacobean dramatist has to say of value to the twentieth century, a time thus far not too unlike his own.

# Seventeenth and Eighteenth Centuries

# 1

# EARLY STAGINGS
# AND SCHOLARSHIP

It was once a critical commonplace that many of the Elizabethan dramatists, in the later seventeenth century and throughout the eighteenth, drifted into a hazy, misty oblivion and were mentioned only from time to time as "our old authors" or "the ancient writers." Then, so goes the account, came Charles Lamb's 1808 *Specimens of English Dramatic Poets,* and the old dramatists were recalled to life. Lamb was seconded by William Hazlitt, then Algernon Charles Swinburne and others; and twentieth-century examinations have added to the stature of those dramatists.

But this view is not as widely held today, thanks to twentieth-century scholarship which has uncovered enthusiasm for the Elizabethans during the Restoration and quiet scholarship on the older dramatists which existed during a good part of the eighteenth century. Studies of Shakespeare, Jonson, Beaumont and Fletcher, and Massinger progressed in spite of a certain reticence toward all writing that did not conform and any material that could not be classified and pigeonholed; and Lamb's famous work was in reality an outgrowth of eighteenth-century scholarship.

However, the earlier critical view is true at least in part for one of the Elizabethans. John Webster's greatest plays remained alive throughout the seventeenth century, but after Lewis Theobald's 1735 free adaptation of *The Duchess of Malfi*—which ran for a grand total of two performances—Webster was the subject of no extensive criticism; and his plays, though perhaps read, were cer-

3

tainly not seen again professionally until the mid-nineteenth century. But as we shall see, the eighteenth-century scholars, by continuing their Elizabethan studies, did lead to the more widely read studies by nineteenth-century critics.

Commentary on Webster in his own time is sparse. We gather that he was, for most of his writing days, a hard-working writer, a good man with whom to collaborate. Dekker, Middleton, Massinger, Ford, Heywood—all these at one time or another collaborated with Webster, whose name, according to Thomas Heywood, "of that learned pack . . . was but Jacke."[1] Webster himself salutes his fellow dramatists in the preface to *The White Devil*, and elsewhere calls Anthony Munday his "Kind friend" and Heywood his "beloved friend."[2] More than likely Webster was well thought of by his colleagues.

Reinforcing this probability and providing contemporary commentary on Webster's works are the verses by Middleton, Rowley, and Ford, prefixed to the 1623 edition of *The Duchess of Malfi*. While Rowley's short commentary seems the standard salute for verses of this kind, those of both Middleton and Ford indicate an awareness of the merit of this play and speak accurately of it as a monument to Webster's everlasting fame. Middleton entitles his lines "In the Just Worth Of That Well-Deserver, Mr. John Webster, And Upon This Master Piece Of Tragedy." The phrase "That Well-Deserver" can be interpreted in various ways: perhaps Middleton is implying that Webster's success has not been what it should be; in his preface Webster himself tells us that the first performances of *The White Devil* "wanted . . . a full and understanding auditory"[3] and that his audiences resembled "those ignorant asses (who visiting Stationers shoppes their use is not to inquire for good books, but new books)."[4] Middleton, then, may be stating that the critical appreciation of Webster is overdue, though we can point to the fact that *The Duchess of Malfi*, two years after *The White Devil*, was given a private performance by the leading King's Men's Company at Blackfriars, and later, by the same great company at the Globe Theatre. Shortly before publication of the 1623 quarto there was a revival of *The Duchess of Malfi*; so we remain in the dark as to the implication of Middleton's lines. The phrase may indicate an unusual occasion. Middleton salutes the tragedian in the following fashion:

In this thou imitat'st one rich and wise,
That sees his good deeds done before he dies:
As he by works, thou by this work of fame
Hath well provided for thy living name.
To trust to others' honourings is worth's crime,
Thy monument is raised in thy life-time;
And 'tis most just; for every worthy man
Is his own marble, and his merit can
Cut him to any figure, and express
More art than death's cathedral palaces
Where royal ashes keep their court. Thy note
Be ever plainness; 'tis the richest coat:
Thy epitaph only the title be,
Write DUCHESS, that will fetch a tear for thee;
For who e'er saw this Duchess live and die,
That could get off under a bleeding eye?

In Tragoediam.

Ut lux ex tenebris ictu percussa tonantis,
Illa, ruina malis, claris fit vita poetis.[5]

Middleton's judgment is accurate: Webster's monument is complete in his own lifetime; it is "a work of fame"; and let the simple word "Duchess" serve as his epitaph.

John Ford's comments are equally pertinent. Ford realized the effort Webster had made to write a weighty tragedy, and he refers specifically to the tragic writers of Greece and Rome.

To The Reader Of The Author,
And His "Duchess of Malfi"

Crown him a poet, whom nor Rome nor Greece
Transcend in all their's for a masterpiece;
In which, whiles words and matter change,
      and men
Act one another, he from whose clear pen
They all took life, to memory hath lent
A lasting fame to raise his monument.[6]

William Rowley addresses commendatory verses "To His Friend Mr. John Webster, Upon His *Duchess of Malfi*." Rowley's is the more typical, though complimentary, accolade of the commendatory verse of the day:

I never saw thy Duchess till the day
That she was lively bodied in thy play:

> Howe'er she answered her lowrated love
> Her brothers' anger did so fatal prove,
> Yet my opinion is, she might speak more,
> But never in her life so well before.[7]

Another contemporary reference, however, is not so favorable. This is Henry Fitzjeffrey's sardonic portrait of Webster printed in *Certain Elegies done by Sundry Excellent Wits* (1618), in which Webster is seen in a Blackfriars' audience. The picture is of a man who takes himself most seriously, working slowly to produce material that, alas, no one will understand:

> But h'st! with him Crabbed (Websterio)
> The Play-wright, Cart-wright: whether? either!
>    ho—
> No further. Looke as yee'd bee look't into:
> Sit as ye woo'd be Read: Lord! who woo'd know
>    him?
> Was euer man so mangl'd with a Poem?
> See how he drawes his mouth awry of late,
> How he scrubs: wrings his wrists: scratches his
>    Pate.
> A Midwife! helpe? By his Braines coitus,
> Some Centaure strange: some huge Bucephalus,
> Or Pallas (sure) ingendred in his Braine,—
> Strike Vulcan with thy hammer once again.
> This is the Crittick that (of all the rest)
> I'de not haue view mee, yet I feare him least,
> Heer's not a word cursiuely I haue Writ,
> But hee'l Industriously examine it.
> And in some 12. monthes hence (or here about)
> Set in a shameful sheete, my errors out.
> But what care I (?) it will be so obscure,
> That none shall vnderstand him (I am sure.)[8]

We may derive from this that Webster was one who took himself seriously, so seriously that his speed in composition was not what a Heywood's must have been. He scrubs, wrings his wrists, and scratches his head as he struggles to produce criticism.

That Webster considered himself a serious writer (and also that he was a slow one) is borne out by his preface to *The White Devil*. The play was acted, he writes, in "so dull a time of winter, presented in so open and black a theatre"[9] and before such an audience of boors that it failed. Webster observes that, if it be objected that this play

"be no true dramatic poem," he could write the most sententious
tragedy ever written, full of *Chorus* and *Nuntius*, and still the
"uncapable multitude" would poison it with their reeking breath.
These remarks reflect the 1605 preface by Ben Jonson to *Sejanus* in
which that writer makes essentially the same remarks. He, too, has
omitted certain forms of Aristotelian tragedy, as it is not "needful or
almost possible, in these our times, and to such Auditors, as com-
monly things are presented, to observe the old state and splendor of
Dramatick Poems, with preservation of any popular delight."[10]
Webster goes on to refute the charge that he was "a long time in
finishing this tragedy" with the answer by Euripides to one Alcestides, who accused him of writing only three verses in three days
while he (Alcestides) had composed three hundred. Webster's answer is Euripides': "'Thou tell'st truth . . . but here's the difference,—thine shall only be read for three days, whereas mine shall
continue three ages.' "[11]

Webster's name throughout the seventeenth century was kept
alive, and rightly so, by his two great tragedies, *The Duchess of
Malfi* and *The White Devil*. By 1631 *The White Devil* had been
"divers time acted, by the Queenes Maiesties seruants at the Phoenix, in Drury Lane," according to the second quarto; the second text
of *The Duchess of Malfi* appeared in 1640, "as it was approvedly
well acted at the Blackfriars, By His Majesties Servants."[12]

By 1648, then, Webster's fame was great enough for him to be
mentioned in the same line with Euripides and in the company of
such writers as Sophocles and Shakespeare. In this year "Mercurius
Pragmaticus" wrote an introduction to an effort entitled *The Second
Part of Crafty Cromwell, or Oliver in his Glory as a King,* and
referred to the magnificent lines which are to come in the play. His
lines, he writes, will put other great writers to shame:

> Let the whole crowd of Poets, Seneca,
> Sophocles, Shakespeare, Johnson now in clay,
> Euripides, with famous Webster, and
> Sucklin, and Goffe, leave the Elizian Land.[13]

Webster merits an adjective in the roll call. During this same year,
the anonymous author of *A City Dog in a Saint's Doublet* quotes
briefly from *The White Devil* and alludes to "the famous tragedian
Webster."[14]

The only specific outbursts of enthusiasm for Webster during the later seventeenth century come a few years after these 1648 allusions. The 1651 *Epigrams Theological, Philosophical, and Romantic* includes a full tribute by Samuel Sheppard to Webster and his two tragedies. Again we find the playwright linked with Euripides and Sophocles in this paean of admiration:

> We will no more admire Euripides
> Nor praise the tragick streines of Sophocles,
> For why? Thou in this tragedie hast framed
> All real worth, that can in them be named:
> How lovely are thy persons fitted and
> How pretty are thy lines—Thy Verses stand
> Like unto pretious jewels set in gold,
> And grace thy fluent Prose; I once was told
> By one well skill'd in Arts, he thought thy Play
> Was only worthy Fame to beare away
> From all before it—Brachianio's Ill,
> Murthering his Dutchesse, hath by thy skill
> Made him renowned, Flamineo's such another
> The Devils darling, Murtherer of his brother:
> His part—most strange—(given to him to Act by
>       thee)
> Vittoria Corombona, that fam'd Whore.
> Desperate Lodovico weltering in his gore,
> Subtile Francisco—all of them shall bee
> Gazed at as Comets by Posteritie:
> And thou meantime with never withering Bayes
> Shalt Crowned bee by all that read thy Layes.[15]

Sheppard, who was a poet, journalist, and satirist of decidedly second rank, remains in scholarly history only because of his references to and commentary on greater men of his time. His *magnum opus, The Fairy King,* an imitation of Spenser, came three years after the *Epigrams.* In it Webster is a subject of praise.

Book Five of Sheppard's labored epic has to do with a House of Eloquence, and the sixth canto praises each writer who is included in its hall of fame, the most outstanding ones being More, Sidney, Spenser, Chapman, Wotton, and

> Webster the next, though not so much of note
> Nor's name attended with such noise and crowd
> yet by the Nine and by Apollo's vote
> whole Groves of Bay are for his head allow'd,
> most Sacred Spirrit (some may say Jr. Doate)

> of thy three noble Tragedies, bee as proud
> as great voluminous Johnson, thou shalt bee
> read longer, and with more applause than hee.[16]

Yet the prolific Ben Jonson does not hold a place in Sheppard's House of Eloquence.

John Cotgrave's poetic miscellany, *English Treasury of Wit and Language,* which culled quotations largely from the drama, appeared in 1655.[17] Webster, with 104 excerpts representing him, ranks sixth behind Shakespeare (154), Beaumont and Fletcher (112), Jonson (111), Chapman (111), and Greville (110). *The Duchess of Malfi* is represented with 40 quotations, *The White Devil* following with 36.[18]

In 1661 came the first printed edition of Webster and Rowley's *A Cure for a Cuckold.* The bookseller, Francis Kirkman, writes "to the Judicious Reader" in a preface that during this "tearm" he has printed and published three plays: *The Thracian Wonder, Gammer Gurton's Needle,* and *A Cure for a Cuckold.* "As for this Play [Webster's], I need not speak anything in its Commendation, the Authors names, Webster and Rowley, are (to knowing men) sufficient to declare its worth: several persons remember the Acting of it, and say that it then pleased generally well; and let me tell you, in my judgment, it is an excellent old Play."[19]

With the reopening of the theaters at the Restoration, both of Webster's tragedies enjoyed successful revivals during the latter years of the seventeenth century, our authorities being John Downes, Edward Phillips, Gerard Langbaine, and that well-known playgoer Samuel Pepys.

John Downes writes of the performances in 1662 of *The Duchess of Malfi* at Drury Lane, which starred Thomas Betterton as Bosola and Mrs. Betterton as the Duchess: "This play was so exceedingly Excellently acted in all Parts; chiefly Duke Ferdinand (Mr. Harris) and Bosola: It fill'd the House 8 days Sucessively, it proving one of the Best of Stock Tragedies."[20]

The performance was indeed successful; under William Davenant's guidance the play was acted throughout the decade, its productions bringing about new copies of the 1640 quarto about 1644, "As it was acted by his late Majesties Servants at Black Fryers with great Applause, Thirty Years since." And in 1678 the third quarto appeared.[21] Likewise *The White Devil* had two further editions in

1665 and 1672 because of revivals at the Theatre Royal. Downes lists *The White Devil* with some Jonson comedies, Shakespeare's *The Merry Wives of Windsor* and *Titus Andronicus*, as "Old Plays . . . yet being well Perform'd, were very Satisfactory to the Town."[22]

Satisfactory they must have been, as we read Downes' comment that *The Duchess of Malfi* at first showing filled the house for eight days straight. However, Mr. Samuel Pepys was not often pleased. His first entry in his diary comes on October 2, 1661, when he sees *Vittoria Corombona*: " . . . coming late, and sitting in an ill place, I never had so little pleasure in a play in all my life, yet it was the first time I saw it." Two days later, however, he sees a bit of it again, but it "pleased me even worse than it did the other day."[23] Pepys briefly notes that on September 30, 1662, he saw *The Duchess of Malfi* "well performed, but Betterton and Ianthe to admiration."[24] Four years later Pepys began reading the play. On November 2, 1666, he rode home in a carriage "reading all the way to make end of Massinger's *The Bondman* . . . and begun *The Duchess of Malfi*, which seems a good play." Three days later he sailed to Deptford "reading *The Duchess of Malfi*, the play, which is pretty good."[25] And then, on November 25, 1668, Pepys again saw a production at the Duke of York's Theatre; as Downes said, it proved one of the best stock tragedies. Pepys thus attended, and then wrote that the drama was "a sorry play, and I sat with little pleasure . . . I desire and resolve never to give [his wife] trouble of that kind more."[26] And thus Webster does not reappear in the pages of Pepys' diary; apparently, the man kept his word.

Although *The Duchess of Malfi*, *The White Devil*, and also *Appius and Virginia* were staged frequently during the Restoration, Webster's name is rarely mentioned in the last part of the century. Two references are from the two historians of the stage Edward Phillips and Gerard Langbaine.

Phillips in the *Theatrum Poetarium* (1675) makes but one critical statement. He names the playwright and identifies him as "an associate with Thomas Dekker, in several not wholly to be rejected plays." Phillips then lists the plays, followed by "what he wrote alone, the Devil's Law Case, a Tragi-Comedy, the White Devil, The Duchess of Malfey, Tragedies."[27]

Langbaine in *An Account of The English Dramatick Poets*, published in 1691, is a bit less cavalier in his judgment. Webster was "an author that lived in the Reign of King James the First; and was in those days accounted an excellent poet. He joined with Dekker, Marston, Rowley in several plays; and was likewise author of others, which have even in our age gained applause: as for instance, Appius and Virginia, The Duchess of Malfey, and Vittoria Corombona." Langbaine continues by giving the history and sources of the plays, and observes on *The Duchess of Malfi* that he has "seen it acted . . . at the Duke of York's Theatre."[28] In 1698 Charles Gildon took this material and republished it in his *Lives of the Poets*, adding only that Webster was at one time clerk of St. Andrew's Parish, Holborn, confusing the dramatist with a religious writer of the same name.

Webster was not forgotten in the years following his death; his plays kept his name alive through the end of the seventeenth century.[29] To be sure, the leading Elizabethan representatives in the Restoration are Shakespeare and Jonson, while Beaumont and Fletcher, of course, play a starring role. These writers figure in many books of poetic miscellany, dedications of Restoration plays, and critical works of Dryden, Cowley, Oldham, and others.[30] Nevertheless, Webster follows these writers in appreciation, along with Chapman. And while perhaps not often mentioned, Webster and his blood-tragedies have a significant influence in the Restoration drama. Nathaniel Lee, Thomas Southerne, and Thomas Otway are among the dramatists who often dealt with the similar themes of black lust and faithless kindred. As Professor Allardyce Nicoll notes, "The horrible presentments that are put forward in so many of the Restoration tragedies, heroic and otherwise, make us realize that, if the poetic spirit of Webster and of Ford was in many ways lost, certainly their love of blood and of riotous torment never was."[31]

Webster's fortunes begin to slip somewhat in the eighteenth century, but not until then. The eighteenth century found little use for him, as indeed it found little use for many of the Elizabethan dramatists. The classical critics, believing in an antithesis between art and nature, celebrated Shakespeare as an accidental genius, a wondrous phenomenon above critical laws and rules. Jonson remained fairly intact because of his attention to these "rules"; and Beaumont and Fletcher's relationship to the courtly world of the French and English and their facile plotwork kept them in vogue. But the plays of John Webster, with their bursts and lapses, if they were to be played at all, would have to be revised. And this was

their fate on the two occasions that they were produced. Writes one
critic of the Restoration and early eighteenth century:

It was the balanced, practical, realistic simplicity of matter and of form,
that fascinated an age whose eager, ambitious idealism, nascent imagination, and tingling emotions had brought only confusion, bitterness, and
repletion. In short it was an even proportion, a regular organization, a
perfection of form, which came to be the ideal of the neo classical group.
    All that was strange, unusual, singular, particular, or exotic, apart
from the accepted extravagances of a few genres like the heroic tragedy,
all that could not be brought into harmony with the whole, or catalogued
and classified according to rule, law, and precedent, was to be viewed
with distrust. . . . Conformity, regularity, convention . . . were to be
observed and followed.[32]

We might note that Webster's lack of form (a fault denied by some)
was to plague him through the years. In the twentieth century, in
fact, the *Scrutiny* critics would echo with modification certain
aspects of the criticism of Lewis Theobald in 1733. With Webster,
the view must be all-inclusive.

    Unlike the Romantic criticism, with its emphasis on the organic
unity of the play, eighteenth-century criticism is for three-quarters
of a century an emphasis on unconnected scenes and the greatness
of this or that passage. With only a few exceptions, there is no
serious effort at the overall view, no study of the general movement
or impression of the play. And without such an overall view,
Webster fails to convince. In his preface to *The Fatal Secret*
Theobald comments on Webster's disregard of the unities; he does
not grasp the fact that Webster has instead achieved a unity of tone.
This was left for the nineteenth- and twentieth-century critic to
perceive.

    Webster's stage history for one hundred years can be summed up
briefly: one revival of three performances, and two adaptations with
a total of two performances. On July 22, 1707, at the lavish Queen's
Haymarket, the first playhouse to be constructed in the century, *The
Unfortunate Duchess, or The Unnatural Brothers* was performed.[33]
This is a revision of Webster's *The Duchess of Malfi,* but the identity
of the author remains unknown. We know only the cast, and it was
superlative: Robert Wilks, Barton Booth, Will Bullock, John Ver-
bruggen, and Mary Porter. Webster still attracted some of the finest

and most famous actors of the time. Because of the lack of theatrical criticism in the early part of the century, we are at a loss as to the critical reaction to this Webster showing. All we know is that the play was performed again on July 29, and once more on August 8. The second performance was "At the Desire of several Persons of Quality." This phrase is a common one, sometimes appearing to give the illusion of special request. Yet often it was valid: William Byrd mentions that the play he attended January 18, 1718, was spoken for, or requested, by one Kitty Sambrooke; and Lady Mary Cowper records in her diary in 1715 that *The Wanton Wife* was "a favorite Play, and often bespoke by the Ladies."[34] So, grasping at straws for hints of response to Webster, we find it pleasant to assume that a patron or two of the Queen's Haymarket had a taste for *The Duchess of Malfi*. But this is the best we can do. We are left with the knowledge that in the span of the eighteenth century, as best current research can tell us, there were only three nights that a Webster play was performed under something like its original title.

In the same year, 1707, Nahum Tate, poet laureate and plagiarist *extraordinaire*, favored his public with a newly published play which had never been produced and, in fact, never was. John Genest later lists *Injured Love: Or The Cruel Husband* among his notations of "Plays printed but not acted."[35] The play was printed by Richard Wellington, with the frontispiece reading "Written by N. Tate, author of the Tragedy call'd King Lear."[36] Having reworked Shakespeare, Tate turned to Webster: *Injured Love* is the eighteenth-century *White Devil*.

Nowhere does Tate acknowledge his source by name, although he admits in an epilogue that he "chose a Vessel that would bear the shock / Of Censure; Yes, old built, but Heart of Oak." This is the only definite "critical" comment we have from Tate; for his general feelings we must look at the play itself.

Most adaptations—be they in the eighteenth century or in the twentieth century—leave us troubled. Some, however, are a little less offensive than others. Tate's *Injured Love* is one of the latter. Whereas Cordelia and Lear received the poetic justice of continued life in Tate's mangled *True and Ancient History of King Lear*, Vittoria, Flamineo, Brachiano, and the rest meet their proper deaths in the original Jacobean fashion: poisoned pictures and poisoned helmets. Moreover, many scenes in regular Websterian order follow one upon the other, often line for line. The telling difference,

however, lies in Tate's purification of Vittoria herself and of any line
that might bring a blush to a maiden's cheek.

Vittoria Corombona is innocent of any sin, and thus the trial scene
is a mockery. Instead of the bawdry and lust of the first Vittoria-
Brachiano scene in I, ii, we have the following amazing change after
Brachiano's line (199) "You are a sweet Phisition":

> VITTORIA:   You call'd me your Physician, and I make
> This visit to prescribe your Grief a Cure;
> A certain speedy Cure.
> BRACHIANO:   That's double Charity.
> VITTORIA:   'Tis resolutely at once to quench and
> stifle this hopeless Passion.
>
>            . . . . . .
>
> 'Twas I that purpos'd in this Interview,
> We now are wandered to the brink of Ruin,
> And must turn short, or perish.

Vittoria has had no "foolish idle dream" which leads Brachiano to
murder; her later protestations of innocence are to be believed. Her
"innocence-resembling boldness," as Lamb later described it, in
Tate's handling becomes indeed boldness based on actual purity of
heart! The resultant murders and intrigues all grow out of a nonexistent situation. Vittoria, we gather, has been faithful to Camillo,
though she perhaps has had longing for Brachiano and has been
meeting him from time to time. We are led to believe, however, that
these meetings were only for purposes of discussion and analysis.

With the purification of Vittoria comes the sterilization of
lines. Brachiano's "close pandarisme" becomes "reveling visits"; "I'll
make Italian cut-works in their guts" is re-located ". . . in their
skinns"; "lie with" becomes "visit"; "a pox upon him" is changed to
"let him go"; and often "lust" is translated as "vice." Since Vittoria is
actually innocent, she comes "from thence" not "a notorious strum-
pet" but "with suspected fame." If not altered, profanity is omitted
entirely, irregular lines are regularized, and any taunting of the
clergy is missing in 1707. Apparently, Tate was obeying to the letter
the various laws of Queen Anne concerning behavior at the playhouse.

Yet in spite of all the changes, a good portion of Webster remains,
and Tate's *Injured Love* is at least a better handling of Webster
than his *King Lear* is of Shakespeare. But if we can believe

historians such as Genest in 1832 and the actual title page of the play ("Design'd to be acted at the Theatre Royal"—not "acted," but "design'd"), *Injured Love* never found an audience.

Lewis Theobald writes to Thomas Warburton on December 18, 1731:

. . . I have apply'd my uneasie Summer Months upon the Attempt of a Tragedy. Sit verbo venia! I have a Design upon the Ladies Eyes, as the Passage to their Pockets. . . . I'll indulge myself, in submitting a Pair of soliloquies to you, as a Taste of my poor Workmanship. I lay my scene in Italy. My heroine is a young widow Dutchess, who has two haughty Spanish Brothers, yet enjoin her not to marry again. She, however, clandestinely marries the Master of her Household on the morning I open my scene. . . .[37]

There follow two soliloquies from his play with lines from John Webster freely interspersed. The name of Webster is never mentioned, and the scholar Warburton seems quite ignorant of any piracy. Such was the state of Webster scholarship.

Theobald's adaptation was called *The Fatal Secret* and was acted twice at Covent Garden on April 4 and 6, 1733.[38] The brief run is explained by Theobald in the preface to the play:

The Importunity of some Friends, whom I could no means disobey, has drawn from me the Publication of this Piece at a Disadvantage. . . . Such was its fate . . . that appearing at a Season when the Weather was warm, and the town in a political Ferment, it was praised and forsaken; and I had the choice Comfort left me, of hearing everybody wonder that it was not supported. . . . Though I called it *The Fatal Secret*, I had no Intention of disguising from the Public that . . . John Webster had preceded me, above a hundred years ago, in the same story.[39]

Theobald goes on to supply us with our only real piece of neoclassic Webster criticism:

If I have borrowed Webster's Matter freely, I have taken it up on fair and open Credit; and, hope, I have repaid the Principle with Interest. I have nowhere spared myself, out of Indolence; but have often engrafted his Thoughts and Language, because I was conscious I could not so well supply them from my own Fund.
. . . As to our countryman Webster, though I am to confess Obligations to him, I am not obliged to be blind to all his Faults. . . . He had

a strong and impetuous Genius, but withall a most wild and undigested one: he sometimes conceived nobly, but did not always express with clearness; and if he now and then soars handsomely, he as often rises into regions of bombast: his Conceptions were so eccentric, that we are not to wonder why we cannot trace him. As for Rules, he either knew them not, or thought them too servile a Restraint. Hence it is, he skips over Years and Kingdoms with an equal Liberty. (It must be the Unities were very sparingly observed at the Time in which he wrote: however, when any Poet travels too fast, that the Imagination of his Spectators cannot keep pace with him, Probability is put quite out of Breath.) . . . He makes mention of Galileo and Tasso, neither of whom were born till near half a Century after the Dutchess of Malfy was murther'd. . . . If *The Fatal Secret* has any Praise, it is, in my opinion, that it had Pow'r to draw Tears from fair Eyes. The Poet who writes for the Stage, should principally aim at pleasing his female Judges.

In the prologue, one Philip Frowde versifies Theobald's thoughts:

> The rude old Bard, if critick Laws he knew,
> From a too warm Imagination drew;
> And, scorning Rule, should his free Soul confine,
> Nor Time, nor Place, observed in his Design.

Earlier, in referring to Theobald's task, Frowde grew metaphoric:

> A waste, uncultivated Soil he found
> O'er-run with Weeds, yet in the fertile Ground
> Some Flowers, almost impervious to the View,
> Fragrant and fair, irregularly grew.
> These was [*sic*] the Modern's Labour to display
> In Comely Order, open'd to the Day;
> With decent Grace arrang'd before your Eyes,
> He bids them in their genuine Lustre rise.

The result of this neoclassic regulation of Webster is one of the great—and fortunately, little-known—literary disasters of the eighteenth century. *The Fatal Secret* might well be called *The Duchess of Malfi for the Little Christian Child:* Theobald expurgates, simplifies, and then manages to elaborate his simplifications so that we will be in no danger of missing his moral point. Compared with Theobald, Nahum Tate becomes a minor offender.

Only fragments of Webster remain. The play barely begins to move; whereas Antonio and Delio appear briefly at the raising of Webster's curtain, and then give way to Bosola and the Cardinal (who then leaves the stage to Bosola and Antonio), Theobald has his

Delio and Antonio stay on and on, talking, talking, and talking. A little of this verbiage describes characters yet to appear; most of it, however, is pious moralizing on proper court behavior: a little of Webster, usually expurgated, followed by an oppressive amount of Theobald.

General changes are laughable. There are no wax works figures, no dead man's hand. But the supreme moment occurs at the end: Bosola and Antonio—both very much alive—are at the Duchess' tomb, along with others. While Antonio mourns, others enter the tomb:

*(Shouts heard within.)*

ANTONIO:   Amazing transport!

It is the Duchess who emerges, looking as if nothing really serious has occurred. How was she spared? Theobald has had Ferdinand look in her coffin, after all. It is through the efforts of Bosola—none other:

BOSOLA:                     . . . I cheated
Her credulous brother with a waxen Image;
That beauteous Waxen Image so admir'd,
Framed by Vincentio di Lawreola
When her Grace married first.

There is proper joy. Antonio, enraptured, cries:

ANTONIO:   Oh Bosola! My Brother!
Still wear that title and divide in all,
My Wealth, All Joys but One,
The Summ of All!

Antonio takes over as Lord Protector; Bosola, we gather, becomes a sort of roving court advisor, and everyone expresses great gladness —all save the Duchess. Theobald leaves her with some proper moralizing curtain lines:

DUCH.:   Some tears are due
T'appease the offended Pow'rs. Had I not
      breathed
A guilty Vow, my brothers had not bled.
Till Pentinence [sic] shall erase that Debt
      of Sorrow,
I must not yield to joy.

But the play is not completely over: there is an epilogue, with the speaker cheerfully trebling the joys of marriage, with the central thought being how shameful indeed it is for a widow not to remarry. Theobald's purpose is finally summed up:

> His lesson, then, is Each fair Offer seize,
> While you have beauties, and the Pow'r to please.

Theobald's more specific changes result, as stated, in expurgated lines and oversimplifications. The description of the Cardinal becomes, instead of Webster's irregularly lined but powerful account (I, i, 160–83), watered-down in this manner:

> ANTONIO:  What appears in him Mirth, is meer Outside.
> He speaks with others Tongues, and hears Men's
>     Suits
> As oft with others' Ears; will doom to Death
> By Information, and rewards on Hearsay.

The "spring in his face" being only "The ingendering of toads" is omitted, along with the line "If he laugh hartely, it is to laugh/All honesty out of fashion," plus many other short, pithy descriptive lines. Bosola, upon Ferdinand's first ambiguous offer of employment, states tersely (I, i, 265ff.):

> BOSOLA:   So:
> What followes? (Never rained such showres as
>    these
> Without thunderbolts i' the tail of them) Whose
>    throat must I cut?

Theobald's "corrections":

> What follows? Never rained such Showr's as these
> But Thunderbolts succeeded.
> What Achievement must buy
> This Golden Bribe? Whose Throat be cut?

Theobald has an uncanny ability to ruin a line by merely tinkering with it. The great and famous line "Cover her face; Mine eyes dazzle; she died young" (IV, ii, 281) emerges in *The Fatal Secret*: "Cover her face. My eyes begin to dazzle." Theobald rewrites the warning speeches of the brothers to the Duchess and gives us such dialogue as this:

FERD.:  Swear by our Father's Soul, you will not
          marry,
        That if you do, in justice to our House,
        He may solicit Heaven for righteous Vengeance.
DUCH.:  Why must I swear? (*Weeping*)
FERD.:  Ha! Is it then too late?
        These guilty tears proclaim your hot Blood
        And curst licentious Youth have stooped to
          Frailty.
DUCH.:  Your Violence and Suspicions doubly wrong me
        By Virtue and my Father's soul I swear
        I ne'er will marry more till you command
        And give me to a Husband.

Here is Theobald's simplification. He states the issues so explicitly that even the poorest informed will see the conflict.

Theobald delves on into the play, and it gets worse. Lines are redistributed: It is Bosola who reports to the Cardinal the Duchess' own famous line: Bosola tells him she is a woman indeed, "she is Flesh and Blood,/ And not the Figure cut in Alabastor/ Kneels at her husband's tomb." Lines are rewritten: the Duchess' cry concerning Antonio—that it would be mercy "If they would bind me to that lifeless Truncke/ And let me freeze to death" (IV, i, 80)—becomes ". . . That they would bind me to that lifeless trunk/ Till I'm a corpse like him." And so it goes.

At the risk of losing comic relief, we must pass from Theobald, not without noting that the production had its share of well-known actors: James Quin as Bosola, Lacy Ryan as Ferdinand, Thomas Walker as the Cardinal, and Mrs. Hallam as the Duchess. But unlike Tate's *Lear*, which held the boards for considerable time, *The Fatal Secret* after two performances was not seen again. We may assume that Webster (rather, Webster-Theobald) was not to the audience's liking, not only from Theobald's comments in the prologue but also from a letter written to the *Grubstreet Journal* on April 25. The author, signing himself "Nobody," writes to protest the refusal of his own tragedy by the manager of the theater, who instead has staged such atrocities as *The Fatal Secret*. The latter, he reports, "met with the fate it deserved. . . . Let the town now judge if this man deserves their encouragement: let authors consider if this is the man to be apply'd to or even trusted with their performances."[40] And upon this note Webster's plays left the professional English stages, not to return for over a hundred years.

After Theobald, Webster criticism, like Webster's plays, lapses for the remainder of the century. His name is kept alive by a few anthologies and brief mention by scholars.

Samples of Webster's writing were kept on public view by the publication of *The British Muse* ("A Collection of Thoughts, Moral, Natural, and Sublime, of our English Poets; who flourished in the Sixteenth and Seventeenth Centuries") in 1738. A work of three volumes, this was a commonplace book made up of quotations from many of the older English prose writers and dramatists, and stands as the first important collection of samplings from old English drama before Lamb. The book was put together by Thomas Hayward, culled from the remarkable library of Edward Harley, Second Earl of Oxford, and with the advice of Harley's librarian, William Oldys. Two hundred plays furnished proper comment on subjects listed in alphabetical order: Adversity, Adultery, Chastity, Cruelty, Dignity, and on into the Y's. Webster is represented with excerpts from *The White Devil, The Duchess of Malfi,* and *The Devil's Law Case.* Although it was not a popular work, *The British Muse* nevertheless represents an important antiquarian effort, and merited a republishing later in the century (1777) under the title *Beauties of the English Drama.* Much of the rather windy editorial comment was eliminated, but many of the quotations were preserved without change.

Webster's *The White Devil* is included in the great collection of earlier drama published first in 1744 by Robert Dodsley. Drawing on the Earl of Oxford's extensive library, Dodsley published an inexpensive work which put into the hands of the public plays rarely read outside an exclusive library. Webster's play goes unannotated, but later editions in 1780 and 1825 include the erroneous "parish clerk" biography (first given by Gildon in his *Lives of the Poets,* 1698) and list his plays and their dates. The 1825 edition by Reed, Collier, and Gilchrist makes use of Henry Fitzjeffrey's sardonic portrait and Theobald's introduction to *The Fatal Secret.* Thus, in 1744 there was a Webster play for the world to read—but why bother when Tate's *King Lear* was playing at the Garden?

David Erskine Baker's *Biographia Dramatica, or a companion to the playhouse* was originally compiled in 1764, and is important likewise for its preservation of the names and dramas of the earlier playwrights. Webster is again listed as a clerk of St. Andrews, Holborn, and is said by Baker to have been "accounted a tolerable poet, and was well esteemed by his contemporary authors, particularly Dekker, Marston, and Rowley, with whom he wrote in conjunction."[41] His plays are listed with their earliest production plus brief commentary: *The Devil's Law Case* is "a good play, and met with success"; *A Cure for a Cuckold* "was acted several times with applause"; and *The Duchess of Malfi* is a story "well known in history and was acted with success." Previous stage dictionaries had seldom given so much attention to the old English dramatists.

Scholarly study of the earlier English dramatists continued quietly throughout the century. While specific criticism of Webster is almost nonexistent, a new kind of criticism slowly made inroads: the historical method. By Edmund Malone's time, many scholars had realized that the complete study of Shakespeare depended in part upon a knowledge of his contemporaries. In his definitive article, "The Scholarly Origin of the Elizabethan Revival," Earl Wasserman notes that it was the mangler of Webster and erstwhile King of Dunces who could be credited with beginning scholarly historical interest: "If the Revival, then, is to be traced to any one factor, it is to the transference of the method employed in editing classical texts to the editing of the English classics. The modern scholarly method . . . was established for English literature with the work of Lewis Theobald."[42] Following Theobald's 1733 edition of Shakespeare, the regular procedure in editing Shakespeare came to include 1) collation of texts, 2) explanation of passages and works by comparison with other portions of Shakespeare plays and 3) comparison with the works of his contemporaries.

More generally, Alexander Pope, while paying little heed to Shakespeare's fellows, had written as early as 1725 of the futility of judging Shakespeare by neoclassic standards and helped to open the way for a fresher approach to the Elizabethans:

. . . not only the common audience had no notion of the rules of writing, but few even of the better sort piqued themselves upon any great degree of knowledge or nicety that way, till Ben Jonson getting posses-

sion of the stage brought critical learning into vogue. . . . Till then our
authors had no thoughts of writing on the model of the ancients. . . .
   To judge therefore of Shakespeare by Aristotle's rules, is like trying
a man by the laws of one country, who acted under another.[43]

Pope's common sense preface to Shakespeare's works includes his
metaphor of the building: the neat modern building as opposed to
the Gothic structure. The Gothic building (Shakespeare) has much
the greater variety and much the nobler apartments, though we may
be conducted to them by dark, odd, and uncouth passages.

   Thomas Warton and Bishop Richard Hurd took a firmer stand
concerning this approach in mid-century. Spenser's *Faerie Queene*
came under the scrutiny of both critics, and each man strongly
affirmed Pope's dictum of looking at the writer in his own age.
Warton wrote in 1754, "In reading the works of an author who lived
in a remote age, it is necessary, that we should look back upon the
customs and manners which prevailed in his age, that we should
place ourselves in the writer's situation, and circumstances."[44] He
notes that it is absurd to think of judging Ariosto or Spenser by
precepts which they did not attend to because of the relativity of
taste, and adds that

Spenser . . . did not live in an age of planning. His poetry is the careless exuberance of a warm imagination and a strong sensibility. . . . Ex-
actness in his poem, would have been like the cornice which a painter
introduced in the grotto of Calypso. . . . If The Faerie Queen be
destitute of that arrangement and economy which epic severity requires,
yet we scarcely regret the loss of these while their place is so amply sup-
plied by something which more powerfully attracts us, something which
engages the affections, the feelings of the heart rather than the cold
approbation of the head.[45]

   Bishop Richard Hurd reflected these ideas in similar fashion in the
1762 *Defense of Romantic Literature:*

When an architect examines a Gothic structure by Grecian rules, he finds
nothing but deformity. But the Gothic architecture has its own rules, by
which when it comes to be examined, it is seen to have its merit, as well
as the Grecian. . . . The same observation holds of the two sorts of
poetry. Judge of The Faerie Queene by the classic models, and you are
shocked with its disorder: consider it with an eye to its Gothic original,
and you find it regular. The unity and simplicity of the former are more
complete; but the latter has that sort of unity and simplicity which results
from its nature.[46]

For both of these historical critics, then, there exists in the older writings not a unity of action but a unity of design. While Warton and Hurd appear to be critical outcasts on this point, for certain later critics this unity of design is responsible for Webster's greatness.

Eighteenth-century scholarly interest in the past continued in slow, steady progress. Bishop Percy's famous *Reliques of Ancient Poetry* (1765) soon followed Hurd's commentaries on earlier literature; Hurd's study was preceded a year earlier by a study of early Welsh poetry by Bishop Evan Evans. There was Thomas Gray's work with Welsh and Scandinavian literature, and the furor over James MacPherson's *Ossian*. Although studies of the Elizabethan dramatists were parasitic, usually accompanying an edition or a study of Shakespeare, an interest, if not general, is there.[47] John Upton's *Critical Observations on Shakespeare* (1746) reflects a favorable attitude toward the Elizabethan dramatists; George Colman's preface to Thomas Coexter's edition of Massinger (1761) calls upon David Garrick to investigate Shakespeare's contemporaries, to whom he might turn his talents. Thomas Hawkins emphasized the merits of Kyd and Peele in his three-volume *Origins of the English Drama* in 1773, and George Steevens' edition of Shakespeare in 1778 made many detailed references to the Elizabethan playwrights. Edmund Malone's 1790 edition of Shakespeare further stressed Christopher Marlowe, Robert Greene, and others in his "Historical Account of the English Stage" and included a page of Webster-Shakespeare parallels. Richard Farmer had earlier noted the need for study of Shakespeare's allusion in his essay (1748) on Shakespeare's learning; and Walter Whiter anticipated the later work of Caroline Spurgeon and Wolfgang Clemen in his effort in 1794 to describe Shakespeare's unconscious associational patterns of imagery (*An Attempt to Explain and Illustrate Various Passages of Shakespeare, on a New Principle of Criticism*).

Thus, while John Webster's name is not found often in the writings of the eighteenth century, we can see the inroads made by the new historical approach which would have its culmination in the writings of Lamb and Hazlitt in the early nineteenth century. Perhaps Oliver Goldsmith best summed up the attitude of a great many toward an Elizabethan revival. In 1759 he wrote of recent stagings of Shakespeare, Jonson, and Massinger:

Old pieces are revived, and scarcely any new ones admitted. The actor is ever in our eye, and the poet seldom permitted to appear; and the public are again obliged to ruminate over those hashes of absurdity, which were disgusting to our ancestors even in an age of ignorance; and the stage, instead of serving the people, is made subservient to the interests of avarice. . . . Let the spectator who assists at any of these newly-revived pieces specifically, of Shakespeare only ask himself whether he would approve of such a performance written by a modern poet? I fear he will find that much of his applause proceeds merely from the sound of a name and an empty veneration of antiquity.[48]

Yet, in spite of Goldsmith's protest, Shakespeare survived; and through a new Romantic approach, Shakespeare's contemporaries soon would have lives of their own. And for some critics would come a later conviction that of these contemporaries, the greatest was John Webster.

# Nineteenth Century

# 2

# WEBSTER'S REPUTATION
# RE-ESTABLISHED

At the same time that certain Shakespeareans were realizing the value of the historical approach to their subject, certain other critics were realizing that the Augustan belief in a steady rising in the arts from a barbaric state to early eighteenth-century neoclassical heights had led to an unfortunate extension: as literary progress could rise, so it could decline. Some writers and critics began to see the rise of reason as the death of imagination. For many, the Augustans had grown precious, over-refined. Thomas Warton's *History of English Poetry* (1744–81), for instance, is permeated with the idea that the growth of intellectual analysis and Newtonian physics stifles the great forces of inspiration and that the Augustan Age of wit is a falling off from earlier, greater ages. Correspondingly, Shakespearean critics, in their efforts at a historical approach to the past, brought forth a doctrine of which many an eighteenth-century writer was ignorant: a creative writer should be seen in the light of his own time, and not judged by the standards of today. The rules, regulations, and correctness of a Lewis Theobald need not serve as yardstick for the evaluation of a John Ford. This revaluation of the past—not merely the classical past of the Augustans—and new inroads in criticism mark the beginning of a new movement. The age of Romanticism brought back strongly the age of the Elizabethans.

Dissatisfied with the "correctness" of contemporary writing, theorists looked back for a less theoretical, more imaginative age, just

27

as poets searched for new and more personal subjects, new ways of expression. As "incidents and situations from common life" became the best poetical subject for one great poet, so the unfettered Elizabethans and their age became eminently suitable for Romantic criticism. As early as 1759 Bishop Hurd wrote:

> There is, I think, in the revolutions of taste and language a certain point, which is more favorable to the purposes of poetry than any other. . . . It lies somewhere between the rude essays of uncorrected fancy, on the one hand, and the refinements of reason and science, on the other.
> And such appears to have been the condition of our language in the age of Elizabeth. It was pure, strong, and perspicacious, without affectation. At the same time, the high figurative manner which fits a language so peculiarly for the uses of the poet, had not yet been controlled by the prosaic genius of philosophy and logic.[1]

The "pure, strong, and perspicacious" language of the Elizabethan, without excess of refinement, goes hand in glove with the primitivistic Romantic doctrines and the idea of the "spontaneous overflow of powerful feelings." The total impression, the pulsing, organic whole, became the objects of nineteenth-century criticism. Rousseau had praised the natural impulse over strict discipline; the Romantic poets took this to heart; and critics discovered that the Elizabethans and Jacobeans often wrote in such a fashion. We could forget about the Duchess of Malfi's missing children and the time problem of *Othello*—we must realize instead what a profound impression each play makes.

Webster, after Lamb's *Specimens of English Dramatic Poets* in 1808, leads a curious life in the criticism of the nineteenth century. Travis Bogard has called it "schizo-critical."[2] Webster is praised on the one hand, damned on the other. Swinburne ranks him next to Shakespeare; Sir William Watson would have him reinterred. The reason for this lies in the difference between the organic view and the close view, a carry-over from the Augustan years. Viewing Webster is like looking at an impressionistic painting. From a distance, the whole can be magnificent. A close examination with a magnifying glass can be disastrous. This is why Webster's plays often fail when acted, as we shall see in the reviews of the revivals of *The Duchess of Malfi* which began in 1850. Paraded live before us, the play is revealed in all its majesty of verse and magnitude of sins. The fifth act carnage is impressive to read but, if we can believe the stage reviewers, sometimes embarrassing to watch. And with the revival of Webster plays in the nineteenth-century theater, the study of Webster criticism takes on an important new aspect.

The first year of the nineteenth century brought Charles Dibdin's *History of the Stage*. Dibdin did not particularly profit from late eighteenth-century approaches to the Elizabethans, although he gives Shakespeare and Jonson proper accolades. Webster, however, is written off briefly, linked in a significant heading: "Webster, Rowley, and the Inferior Dramatic Poets." Webster merits only the following erroneous report: "Webster, however, does not appear at any time to so much advantage as in those pieces when he labored with others, his best knack being more to find out materials for his associates than to give form to them, for he was a parish clerk, and an assistant at a school, neither of which occupations seems very much calculated to give his genius scope, whatever talents he might possess."[3] To this is added the list of Webster's plays, including *The Thracian Wonder*.

On November 10, 1805, Charles Lamb wrote to William Hazlitt:

You send me a modern quotation poetical. How do you like this in a play? Vittoria Corombona, a spunky Italian lady, a Leonardo one, nick-named the White Devil, being on trial for murder, etc.—and questioned about seducing a duke from his wife and the state, makes answer—

> "Condemn you me for that the duke did love me?
> So may you blame some fair and crystal river,
> For that some melancholic distracted man
> Hath drowned himself in it."[4]

Since around 1796, according to his letters to Coleridge, Lamb had been enthusiastically reading the Elizabethan and Jacobean dramatists; and in 1808 he published the work generally credited with "restoring" these writers, *Specimens of English Dramatic Poets who lived about the time of Shakspeare*. The book was not, as could be expected, a tremendous popular success; nevertheless, Lamb took the Elizabethans out of scholarly hands and revitalized them with his impressionistic, if not overly learned, criticism. George Saintsbury, in his *History of Criticism*, put it accurately: "Everything necessary to unite Lamb's critical excellence united here—actual merit, private interest, for though the study of the minor as well as

the major Elizabethans had been progressing steadily, and "Dodsley" had gone through several editions, yet the authors were caviare
to the general still."[5]

When confronted with the question of *why* Lamb's interest in the
Elizabethans, we can only return to the statements of Bishop Hurd
and again to the general idea of the Romantic movement away from
the sharp neoclassic distinction between the general and particular
in art. We might also find a clue in Lamb's own personality:
William Watson, in attacking Webster in 1893, attributed Lamb's
interest in the often dark and murky world of the minor dramatists
to the fact that always "the world as seen by a picturesque torchlight
rather than by candid sunlight attracted his gaze."[6] He would have
Lamb retreating from his prosaic world of the East India Company
into the past. Watson overstates his case; yet Lamb's temperament
was one which could indeed embrace the picturesque world of
writers past. At any rate, Lamb took the whole view of the Elizabethans, a view which had not previously been taken. And hence his
importance. (It is unfortunate that Coleridge, by far the greater
critic and also one who stressed totality of vision, seems never to
have written on Webster.)

Lamb's method of criticism, later reflected by Hazlitt, was new.
With large extracts from the poets and not merely single passages
and what he calls "detached beauties,"[7] he writes what are little
more than marginalia. His critical expressions are usually exclama-
tions and enthusiastic commentary. Like Hazlitt's in 1821, his criticism is evocative, metaphoric, and extremely personal. At one point
he reminds us of A. E. Housman's remarks on the danger of
thinking on great poetical lines while shaving: writing on *The
Revenger's Tragedy,* he states, "I have never read it but my ears
tingle, and I feel a hot blush spread my cheeks."[8] This impressionistic method seems new to his time, though critics on the continent
were also dealing in similar forms. In Germany Johann Joachim
Winckelmann, Johann Gottfried von Herder, Jean Paul, and often
August and Friedrich Von Schlegel utilized impressionistic study, as
did François Chateaubriand in France. As best we can tell, Lamb
and Hazlitt are responsible for its introduction into nineteenth
century England.

This impressionism represents the great Longinian influence on
Romantic criticism by its emphasis on appreciative ecstasy in the
reaction of the reader, instead of the Augustan emphasis on analytic,

judicial inquiry into the subject. Written probably in the first century, Longinus' *On the Sublime* foreshadowed the thoughts which underlay the critical writings of Hazlitt, Lamb, and other romantics. For Longinus, the sublime is a spell thrown over the reader: "For, as if instinctively, our soul is uplifted by the true sublime, it takes a proud flight, and is filled with joy and vaunting, as though it had itself produced what it has heard."⁹ Sublimity is derived usually from the short outburst, the inspired electric moment often comprised in a single thought:

The legislator of the Jews, no ordinary man, having formed and expressed a worthy conception of the might of the God head, writes at the beginning of his Laws, "God said"—what? "Let there be light; and there was light; let there be land, and there was land."¹⁰

The sublime passage flashes forth at the right moment and "scatters everything before it like a thunderbolt." This thunderbolt bursts about the head of the reader, leaving him in a period of *ekstasis*, unconcerned as to how the author has done what he has done. For many romantic theorists this intensity, the creation of great imaginative moments, became the criterion for poetic value. Poetry at its highest was the incandescent passage which could be written no other way. "When composition begins," wrote Shelley, "inspiration is already on the decline."¹¹ Thus, Lamb and Hazlitt, in place of penetrating analysis and inquiry into the causes of intensity, undertook to show the reader the aesthetic effect of John Webster on their own minds. Like Longinus' reaction to the sublime quality of *The Odyssey*, a reaction expressed in terms of sense impression through similes of the setting sun and the ebbing tide, Lamb and Hazlitt similarly tried to express their reactions to Webster in terms of critical responsiveness and enthrallment.

Lamb truly sees the greatness of Webster, and his marginalia seem more sincerely enthusiastic than those appended to other writers. He quotes from *The Duchess of Malfi* the Duchess-Antonio love scene, the tortures and death of the Duchess, two of the fables (the Salmon, III, v; Reputation, Love, and Death, III, ii), and the "Fie upon this single life" speech, III, ii. He copies Vittoria's trial scene, Marcello's death, Francisco's account of Cornelia's grief, Marcello's funeral dirge, and various sententia, and reproduces IV, i, of *Appius and Virginia*. (He makes an effort to record as much of Webster's borrowing from Shakespeare as possible.)

His commentary was quoted by many others throughout the nineteenth century and on into the twentieth. Of *The White Devil:*

> This White Devil of Italy sets off a bad cause so speciously, and pleads with such an innocence-resembling boldness, that we seem to see that matchless beauty of her face which inspires such gay confidence into her; and we are ready to expect, when she has done her pleadings, that her very judges, her accusers, the grave ambassadors who sit as spectators, and all the court, will rise and make proffer to defend her in spite of the utmost conviction of her guilt. . . .
>
> I never saw anything like the funeral dirge in this play, for the death of Marcello, except the ditty which reminds Ferdinand of his drowned father in the "Tempest." As that is of the water, watery; so this is of the earth, earthy.

Lamb is equally enthusiastic concerning the fate of the Duchess, and again, his comments have been echoed through the years. Particularly fixed by Lamb for many nineteenth century critics to come was the idea of Webster as master of gothic horror, though some would later deny his mastery. Of her tortures:

> As they are not like inflictions *of this life,* so her language seems *not of this world.* She has lived among horrors till she is become "native and endowed unto that element." She speaks the dialect of despair, her tongue has a snatch of Tartarus and the souls in bale. . . . To move a horror skillfully, to touch a soul to the quick, to lay upon fear as much as it can bear, to wean and weary a life till it is ready to drop, and then step in with mortal instruments to take its last forfeit—this only a Webster can do. Writers of an inferior genius may "upon horror's head horrors accumulate," but they cannot do this. They mistake quantity for quality, they "terrify babes with painted devils," but they know not how a soul is capable of being moved; their terrors want dignity, their affrightments are without decorum.[12]

The sale of the book was not large, and the great quarterlies allowed it to pass unnoticed, with the exception of the *Monthly Review:* to that journal, there was "nothing very remarkable except the style, which is formally abrupt and elaborately quaint."[13] Furthermore, the critic resented some of Lamb's eulogies on certain dramatists. Yet selections from the critical notes reappeared in Lamb's collected works in 1818, receiving high critical praise, and from Lamb's reassessment of the dramatists came the *Blackwood's Magazine* articles in 1818 on various writers, the *European Magazine's* 1820 study, and, most important, Hazlitt's lectures in November and December of 1819 at the Surrey Institute.

Following Lamb's tributes, Webster's plays next came under the scrutiny of *Blackwood's Magazine* in its series of studies on the Elizabethan dramatists. This magazine's approach represents one aspect of nineteenth-century criticism: there is a limited appreciation of those writers who, for this group of critics, could not even begin to approach the stature of Shakespeare. Time and again *Blackwood's* would pay great tribute to a Marlowe or a Webster, but shortly would emphasize that writer's limitations and his inferiority to the master. These critics did not always have the long view of Lamb or Hazlitt; their criticism often dwelled upon the individual scene as separate from the rest of the drama. To be sure, Lamb reproduced only scenes, but his impressionistic comments, though brief, sometimes capture the spirit of the whole play.

The *Blackwood's* series began with an examination of Marlowe in January, 1818; then came two studies of Webster's tragedies by "H. M.," in March and August of the same year. The first, on *The Duchess of Malfi*, sums up the entire attitude of the series: ". . . none of the predecessors of Shakespeare must be thought along with him."[14] Few of the other dramatists, says the critic, have ever conceived a consistent character, and an air of incompleteness hangs over their compositions. And so it is with Webster:

Some single scenes are to be found in his works inferior in power of passion to nothing in the whole range of the drama. He was a man of truly original genius and seems to have felt strong pleasure in the strange and fantastic horrors that rose up from the dark abyss of his imagination. . . . But our sympathies suddenly awakened, are allowed to subside. There is nothing of what Wordsworth calls "a mighty stream of tendency" in the events of his dramas, nor in our opinion, is there a single character that clearly and boldly stands out before us like a picture.[15]

Of the torture scene, H. M. remarks that "the peculiar genius of Webster bursts forth into a strange, wild, fantastic and terrible grandeur," but "the interest of the drama expires with the fourth act." (This problem of the fifth act will prove to be a popular object of debate among later critics.) The great bulk of the article is taken up with extensive quotation from the play, in the manner of the *Specimens;* and indeed H. M. closes, rather abruptly, with Lamb's remarks on the play.

Five months later the same critic turned to *The White Devil,* and we have even more of the neoclassic approach: "The play is so disjointed in its action, the incidents are so capricious and so involved, and there is, throughout, such a mixture of the horrible and absurd—the comic and the tragic—that we find it impossible, within our marrow, to give anything like a complete analysis of it."[16] Again, H. M. records long excerpts. Of the Brachiano death scene, he observes that it is distinguished by the extravagant horror in which the strength of Webster lies and admits that "in spite of ourselves, the scene strikes us with the same feelings that are produced in real life by some strange and unnatural murder."[17]

Summing up, after considerable quotation, he states that

there is great power in this drama and even much fine poetry, but . . . it shocks rather than agitates and the passion is rather painful than tragical. There are, in truth, some scenes that altogether revolt and disgust, and mean, abandoned, and unprincipled characters occupy too much of our attention throughout the action of the play. . . . scene follows scene of shameless profligacy, unredeemed either by great intellectual energy, or occasional bursting of moral sensibilities.[18]

He admits that although Vittoria is sketched with great spirit and freedom, "we feel that she is not fit to be the chief personage of tragedy, which ought ever to deal only with great passions and with great events. There is, however, a sort of fascination about her . . . and something like admiration towards her is awakened by the dauntless intrepidity of her death."[19]

Following the lead of *Blackwood's*, the *European Magazine* in 1820 began its own series on the Elizabethan dramatists, observing in the October issue that "the elder English dramatists are those authors to whom our national literature is more indebted than any others, and there are no parts of our early poetry which deserve to be cherished with more fervent veneration."[20] The anonymous writer finds the dramatic authors equal in their own way to the more classical French dramatists: "The spirit of English tragedy is of too severe and mighty a character, to bend down to any rules but its own."[21] He laments the sorry situation of the present day, which is "as barren of dramatic talent as it is ungrateful in its encouragement of the small number of authors who write for the stage."[22] Then for those who would honor the founders of poetic excellence, he introduces the first subject of the *European Magazine*'s new series on the older dramatists, John Webster.

The *European Magazine* offers little criticism but certainly further popularization of Webster by reprinting long excerpts from two dramas, *Appius and Virginia* and *The White Devil*. A possible neoclassic preference for the former play rounds out the October discussion by way of several lengthy quotations from Webster's one carefully "unified" drama. A month later the series continued with *The White Devil*, credited as being Webster's best play, possessing "all the faults and all the excellencies of our early dramatists. . . . the irregularity of the fable . . . the lofty and pathetic spirit of the poetry. . . ."[23] The article tells the story in much detail, quoting liberally from the play. The trial scene is not included, being in "Mr. Lamb's elegant work . . . that book being as well known, and as much in common use, as it so justly deserves to be."[24] The writer at length salutes Webster not so much for his dramatic incidents as for his verse: "Horror on horror's head accumulates throughout this tragedy, blood and crime are its springs, and their punishment bitter and proportioned to their enormity, fill up the details. Monstrous as the incidents are, they all tend to virtues side; and if we do not yield the praise of good taste to the author in his selection and arrangement of them, we must not withhold the meed from his impassioned and inspired verse."[25]

We may note that the *European Magazine* and the *Blackwood's Magazine* critics seem to stand somewhere between the neoclassic and the nineteenth-century impressionistic approach to criticism. While not grasping a unity of tone, they often utilize Lamb's metaphoric approach. A complete triumph of the Lamb impressionistic method—and with more substance—came in 1819 with the lectures of William Hazlitt on the dramatic literature of the age of Elizabeth. The journals had further popularized the Elizabethans, and Hazlitt's treatment more firmly established the place of these writers—and John Webster—in literary history.

Hazlitt's method in dealing with the Elizabethans in his lectures at the Surrey Institute derived in part from Lamb, and ultimately from Longinus: "I say what I think and I think what I feel," observed Hazlitt. "I cannot help receiving certain impressions from things and I have sufficient courage to declare (somewhat abruptly) what they are." In his public lectures, he read over "a set of authors with the audience, as I would do with a friend, to point out a favorite passage, to explain an objection . . . neither to tire him nor puzzle myself with pedantic rules and pragmatical formulas of criticism that can do no good to anybody." All this, wrote Hazlitt, is because "in art, in taste, in life, in speech, you decide from feeling, and not from reason; that is, from the impression of a number of things on the mind, which impression is true and well-founded, though you may not be able to analyze or account for it in the several particulars."[26]

His attitude was summed up early in the lectures (published in 1820 as *The Literature of the Age of Elizabeth*). It was not the attitude of the *Blackwood's* critic:

Shakespeare's contemporaries are a mighty phalanx of kindred spirits closing him round, moving in the same orbit, and impelled by the same faults and the same excellences. . . .

Shakespeare tower'd above his fellows in shape and gesture proudly eminent; but he was one of a race of giants—the tallest, strongest, the most graceful and beautiful of them; but it was a common and noble brood.[27]

Hazlitt's approach to Webster is through historical, comparative criticism combined with evocative tribute:

Webster would, I think, be a greater dramatic genius than Dekker, if he had the same originality; and perhaps is so, even without it. His *White Devil* and *Duchess of Malfi*, upon the whole, perhaps come the nearest to Shakespeare of anything we have on record; the only drawback to them . . . is that they are too like Shakespeare, and often direct imitations of him, both in general conception and individual expression. . . . Dekker has . . . more truth of character, more instinctive depth of sentiment, more of the unconscious simplicity of nature; but he does not . . . clothe his subjects with the same richness of imagination, or the same glowing colors of language.[28]

For Hazlitt, Webster gives greater scope to his characters, brings them into dramatic play by contrast and comparison, and "carries both pity and terror to a more painful and sometimes unwarrantable excess." Turning to his full-blown metaphoric mode of criticism, he finds Vittoria "made fair as the leprosy, dazzling as the lightning. She is dressed like a bride in her wrongs and revenge. . . . Nothing can be finer than the whole conduct and conception of her trial scene. The sincerity of her sense of guilt triumphs over the hypocrisy of their affected and official contempt for it. . . . In the closing scenes with her cold blooded assassins . . . she speaks daggers. . . . Every word probes to the quick."[29] Hazlitt quotes extensively from this scene, and remarks on the graces of this forgotten poet.

He is more critical of *The Duchess of Malfi*, though he does credit it with many flashes of greatness. And although this play is more profound, it is to Hazlitt "more laboured, and the horror is accumulated to an overpowering and insupportable height." The madhouse scenes seem to exceed "the just bounds of poetry and tragedy." Such exhibitions tend to "stupify and harden, rather than exalt the fancy or meliorate the heart." Here Hazlitt anticipated the criticism of later writers, particularly of the stage critics. He admires greatly, however, the Duchess' instructions about her children, her last word, "Mercy," and her famous reply, "I am Duchess of Malfy still": ". . . as if the heart rose up, like a serpent coiled, to resent the indignities put upon it, and being struck at, struck again. . . . This is not the bandying of idle words and rhetorical commonplaces, but the writhing and conflict, and the sublime colloquy of man's nature within itself!"[30]

Such criticism has to a large extent passed from the scene. But this impressionistic rhetoric of Hazlitt and Lamb served to re-establish Webster as a writer of consequence. Possibly it was the right kind of criticism at the right time: through Lamb and Hazlitt's colorful phraseology one could not help noticing the Elizabethan writers. Their judgments were not always entirely accurate—Hazlitt seems to have difficulty placing Webster over Dekker—but they were all-inclusive and spectacular, sometimes, of phrase. In reviving an author, close or textual criticism will not suffice.

For a considerable period following Lamb and Hazlitt's work, Webster criticism was not particularly impressive. As many critics were slow to perceive the merits of the younger Romantic poets, so a great many critics failed to share Lamb and Hazlitt's view of John Webster. Webster seems definitely re-established, though there is seldom any outbreak of complete enthusiasm. "Webster is great—but" seems the trend. Yet in this period following Hazlitt's lectures there were no critics who vigorously attacked Webster as later there would be. Not until Canon Charles Kingsley's outburst in 1856 was there any complete renunciation of the dramatist.

The journals paid more heed to Webster following Hazlitt's lectures. In 1823 the *Retrospective Review* devoted an anonymous article to Webster, full of unimpressive and frequently erroneous judgments, but definitely favorable. The article begins with a tribute to his dramatic form: his dramas "are much better calculated for representation than most of our early dramas. . . . This characteristic is the excellence which most peculiarly characterizes Webster."[31]

This seems only speculation on the part of the anonymous critic, since, as far as we know, Webster had been off the public stages since 1733. And when he reappeared, he did not always meet with success. But to the *Retrospective Review*, Webster was the rare specimen whose plays were fine literature and, at the same time, actable. Later in the century critics would divide over the idea of literature *vs.* theatricality.

Webster "possessed a strong mind, which kept the object steadily in view, and to the accomplishment of which he proceeded at as sober a pace as he probably did in the performance of his duties as a parish clerk. . . ."[32] Our critic makes the questionable observation that "in the integrity and consistency of character, he generally fails, and in poetic imagery he seldom indulges."[33] But in Vittoria's trial, we never for a moment doubt the probability and consistency of the scene. The tortures of the Duchess are "consummate art. . . . measure is heaped up to the brim without being over-full . . . a fearful and terrible effect."[34] Although its scenes are not as powerful, *Appius and Virginia* is the most finished and regular of the canon; and finally, Webster is hailed as a "great dramatist, who was minute without being trivial, elaborate, without being dull; and whose power in touching the passions was equalled by few of his contemporaries."[35]

The *Edinburgh Review* furthered the name of Webster that same year when it published a review of Sheridan Knowles' *Virginius* and Thomas L. Beddoes' *The Bride's Tragedy*. Prefacing the review itself is a discussion of earlier English dramatic authors, a discussion in which Beaumont and Fletcher are ranked next to Shakespeare and above Jonson and Massinger.

Nevertheless, Webster receives favorable recognition. He was sometimes harsh, sometimes dull, "an unequal writer; full of gloomy power, but with touches of profound sentiment and the deepest pathos. . . . A common calamity was beneath him, and ordinary vengeance was too trivial for his Muse. His pen distilled blood. . . . There are few passages in Shakespeare, which have so deep a sentiment as the following: The fourth act scene of Bosola and Ferdinand over the body of the Duchess."[36] The writer compares him with Marlowe: while Marlowe's imagination was soaring, Webster's was penetrating and profound. "The one rose to the stars, the other plunged to the centre."[37]

In 1830 the Reverend Alexander Dyce, the noted Elizabethan

editor, brought out the first edition of Webster's plays. It included the two major plays plus *Appius and Virginia, The Devil's Law Case, Northward Hoe, The Thracian Wonder, The Famous History of Thomas Wyatt,* and *The Malcontent.* Dyce later edited numerous other dramatists, but Webster was one of his first choices.

His introduction, as criticism, is not particularly valuable. It is primarily concerned with Webster's life, and Dyce can be given credit for first dismissing J. P. Collier's continued claim that Webster was the parish clerk of St. Andrews. His actual criticism is an appreciation of Webster similar to Lamb's. Noteworthy are this clergyman's ideas on the bawdry in the plays with Dekker as collaborator:

Public taste has now reached the highest pitch of refinement, and such coarseness is tolerated in our theatres no more. Perhaps, however, the language of the stage is purified in proportion as our morals have deteriorated, and we dread the mention of the vices which we are not ashamed to practise; while our forefathers, under the sway of a less fastidious but a more energetic principle of virtue, were careless of words and only considerate of actions.[38]

In the midst of evocative praise for Vittoria we find bits and pieces of critical acumen:

I admire the dexterity with which Webster has discriminated between that simple confidence in their own integrity which characterizes the innocent under the imputation of any great offense, and the forced and practised presence of mind which the hardened criminal may bring to the place of accusation. . . . never, in a single instance, has the author ascribed to Vittoria in the trial scene one word which was likely to have fallen from an innocent person under similar circumstances.[39]

Dyce is greatly affected by *The Duchess of Malfi;* he points out the delicacy of the wooing scene and the painful reality of the suffering and death of the Duchess. He champions the almost forgotten *Appius and Virginia:* "When I consider its simplicity . . . pathos . . . the easy unimpeded march of its story, I cannot but suspect that there are readers who will prefer the drama to any other of our author's productions."[40]

An important contribution in the firm re-establishment of Webster's reputation, the edition—and Webster—received a good notice in the London *Literary Gazette:* "Webster, forming himself with Marston is unquestionably one of our best painters of manners. . . . When we consider that, independently of his vivid local traits, he abounds in poetical beauties (not debased by any of the very gross coarseness of his age), we shall find more reason to commend Mr. Dyce's labours to the favour of all literary persons."[41]

From Dyce's edition comes a tribute to Webster by Sir Walter Scott, who, writing Dyce in 1831, speaks of the possibility of reviewing Dyce's edition of Robert Greene: "I shall be inclined to include Webster, who I think, is one of the best of our ancient dramatists."[42]

An early critical trend—if really critical—was the emphasis on horror in Webster. Certainly nearly every critic mentions the terror in Webster, but possibly not so much as the 1820–40 critics, following, perhaps, Lamb's emphasis. Though the articles from the quarterlies have appeared above in excerpts only, there is much dwelling on the terrors of Webster and his proficiency at depicting them.

So it is in part with the article (a review of Dyce's edition) by J. M. in the *Gentleman's Magazine* for May, 1833. Webster is inferior to Jonson in humor, Fletcher in sentiment, Massinger in handling of plot. However, "he far, very far, surpasses them all in the depth of his pathos, his tragic powers, and his command over the sublime, terrible, and the affecting. . . . An epitaph to him is a joke, and a sexton is his bedfellow and friend. He has a dagger more often in his hand than a knife; and a phial of poison in his pocket."[43] This writer reflects one aspect of later criticism of *The White Devil* when he speaks of its plot as disjointed and not well conceived, with characters seen in parts and fragments rather than consistently developed. He further criticizes the play on the grounds that "there is a strange, unnatural mixture of levity and wretchedness . . . that seems to feed upon the despair and hopelessness of the human heart."[44] He is perhaps the only critic who thinks Vittoria's trial too long in getting to the point, and surely the only one dismayed by Webster's injured Isabella. Of her renunciation by Brachiano: "We confess, as we read, the pages were wet with our tears."[45]

Nathan Drake in the 1838 *Shakespeare and His Times* assigns rank in the "school" of Shakespeare. Webster is fourth behind Fletcher, Massinger, and Ford. (Jonson, Drake says, should be considered separately.) Again, the horrors of the writer are emphasized: "He has introduced touches of expression which curdle the very blood with terror, and make the hair stand erect." Drake belongs to the school of Shakespeare's idolators; while he can sincerely appreciate Shakespeare's contemporaries, they remain pygmies beside a giant. Yet for all Webster's faults his tragedies "are, most assuredly, stamped with, and consecrated by, the seal of genius."[46]

Henry Hallam's long *Introduction to the Literature of Europe* (1839) is in general a better piece of history than of literary criticism. Hallam was an historian and not a critic of dramatic literature. He, like so many others, sees Webster only as a writer of horror: "The deep sorrows and terrors of tragedy were peculiarly his province. . . . Webster was deeply tainted . . . with the savage taste of the Italian school, and in *The Duchess of Malfy* scarcely leaves enough on the stage to bury the dead."[47] Hallam also has a tendency to rank writers. In the Elizabethan period he puts Shakespeare first, Jonson second, Beaumont and Fletcher third, then Massinger, and "at a considerable distance below Massinger we may place his contemporary John Ford."[48] And only then comes Webster. It is Massinger who "as a tragic writer, appears second only to Shakespeare."[49] *The Duchess of Malfi*, however, receives just tribute: "The scenes are wrought up with skill, and produce a strong impression. Webster has a superiority in delineating character above many of the old dramatists; he is seldom extravagant beyond the limits of conceivable nature; we find the guilt, or even the atrocity of human passions, but not the incarnation of evil spirits which some more ordinary dramatists loved to exhibit."[50]

In a review of George Darley's edition of Beaumont and Fletcher, the *Edinburgh Review* for April, 1841, links Jonson and Fletcher as following Shakespeare in importance, the former two attempting to found a new school of drama. "The next place after them belongs to Webster and Middleton."[51] Robert Chambers, selecting poetical excerpts for his 1844 *Cyclopedia of English Literature*, quoted the funeral dirge for Marcello and the death scene of the Duchess, making little critical comment. Generally, he feels that Webster's plays are powerful though filled with horrors.[52]

Thomas B. Shaw in his 1847 *Outlines of English Literature* compares Webster's mind to a Gothic cathedral "with its arches soaring heavenward, but carved with monsters and angels, with saints and fiends, in grotesque confusion." In his summary of

Renaissance literature Shaw represents a welcome effort to state what the writers had to say. Webster dwelled "ever on the vanities of earthly glory, on the nothingness of pomp, not without many terrible hints at the emptiness of our trust, and many bold questionings of human hopes of a hereafter."[53] Unfortunately Shaw has no more to say.

In mid-century at the Sadler's Wells Theatre came the first production of *The Duchess of Malfi* in over a hundred years. In the R. H. Horne version the heroine is named Mariana, the role of Julia is cut entirely, and the strangling scene takes place off stage, with the Duchess staggering in to cry "Mercy" at the moment of her death. This adaptation was to hold the stage—if infrequently—until William Poel's version in 1892, with Isabella Glyn, Mrs. Emma Waller and Miss Mariott finding personal success in Horne's treatment of the Duchess. The producer-director was Samuel Phelps, who, having taken over Sadler's Wells Theatre in 1844, determined to make it a "temple to the dramatic muse"[54] after many years of maudlin melodramas. Tremendously interested in the Elizabethans, he produced during his eighteen years as manager thirty-four plays of Shakespeare and revived long dead plays of such writers as Massinger, Beaumont, and Fletcher, Marston, Jonson, and Otway. Since Sadler's Wells was located several miles from the London theatrical center, Phelps seems to have felt that his mission was one of bringing fine old plays to the hinterlands. His efforts made Sadler's Wells quite well known, and his resignation as manager caused great regret.

The reaction to his production of *The Duchess of Malfi* on November 20, 1850, begins a new kind of Webster study and Webster reaction: stage criticism. And as noted earlier, Webster on the stage is something other than Webster in the study. We may dismiss Lamb's indictment of *King Lear* as a theater piece because of previous outstanding *Lear* productions. But in Webster's modern stage history, the theater critics (even allowing for the extra-sensitive Victorian) have often been less than kind to the various productions. Flesh and blood representation of Webster's horrors and terrors, and human beings enacting his problems of logic and causation, often obscure the thought of a play like *The Duchess of Malfi;* and later ideas (see David Cecil, Irving Ribner) that the play is a dramatic symbol of a quest for moral order can lose force when we consider the harsh fact that the Cardinal looked absolutely ghastly spattered with stage blood (1892) and that Ferdinand died standing on his head (1919). Only in the mid-twentieth century—and then infrequently—has Webster on the stage been acceptable. Even then, much cutting has been employed, sometimes to Webster's detriment. Reading Webster is immensely profitable; staging his plays has proved to be immensely difficult.

In reviewing the Sadler's Wells production, the London *Literary Gazette* commended the generally good performances of Isabella Glyn as the heroine, Manager Phelps as Ferdinand, and George Bennett as Bosola. But the play as staged, it said, was "old and barbarous. . . . Mr. Horne has sought to soften the features of the old play, but even what remains is unnatural harrowing. The various physical terrors which the Duchess is made to suffer are intensely barbarous; and indeed the whole tissue of the drama is repelling. . . . There is throughout a seeking for the horrible, but the poetry is distinguished by immense power and affluence of language."[55] The *Illustrated London News* admitted that "in this celebrated drama there are, perhaps scenes not to be equalled out of Shakespeare; but, in its general conception, it is more like *Titus Andronicus*. . . . The action in the fourth act is imprudently prolonged after the death of the Duchess. The curtain should fall immediately on her execution. All beyond that not only impairs the situation, but lengthens our horror into disgust."[56] The critic closed by paying tribute to an honorable experiment and observed that "the house was crowded and the curtain fell to immense applause."[57]

The weekly *Athenaeum* reported: "We have here indeed the tragedy of the churchyard; the fetid atmosphere of the charnel that is breathed by the stern old poet. . . . Mr. Phelps struggled hard to overcome the inherent difficulties of the part of Ferdinand. . . . But no genius could have achieved a triumph in such a part: the utmost that talent . . . could effect, was to render it endurable."[58] Miss Glyn was majestic in the later scenes, lively in the first. The writer speaks of Horne's adaptation and says that no pains could have eliminated the original clumsy structure. At times, however, "we have here not even Webster."[59] Indeed, "for the purpose of restoring one of our old dramatists, there is no argument for this reproduction, and the alterations made to render the reproduction possible, prove that Webster cannot be restored. . . . The house was crowded. Though evidently somewhat puzzled by the horrors of the situation, the beauties of the dialogue seemed to be appreciated by the pit; and at the conclusion the applause was loud."[60]

The most famous critic of the 1850 production was George Henry Lewes, who was, perhaps, the William Archer of his day. In his own terms, he called for the well-made play with a consistent, logical characterization and a unified plot. Oblivious to any metaphoric significance in the older drama, he stated at one point that "the greatest injury yet sustained by the English drama was the revival of admiration for the old English dramatists."[61] To paraphrase his argument on the older dramatists in *The Leader* for August 3, 1850: a drama should be a reflex of the writer's own life, issuing out of the atmosphere of the time. The Elizabethans, in spite of their clumsily prepared situations and sketchy characterizations, did indeed do just that: their age lives in their pages. But for Lewes, too many mid-nineteenth-century dramatists merely copied the older Elizabethan form. They should reflect their own day, as did the earlier cruder writers. Shakespeare, he notes, succeeds in 1850 not because of his form but in spite of it. Thus the 1850 writer should "shun the old writers as they would the plague":[62] they were sloppy dramatists, and the atmosphere of 1850 is that which needs expression.

One is not surprised, therefore, at his report of Phelps' production. Horne had lessened the horrors of the piece, but "the irredeemable mediocrity of its dramatic evolution of human passion is unmistakable. The noble lines of manly verse which charm the *reader* fail to arrest the *spectator*, who is alternating between impressions of the wearisome and the ludicrous."[63] Lewes attacks vigorously the motives of Ferdinand, a charge to be renewed later in the century by William Archer. He dwells at length on the lack of reasons for the persecution of the Duchess and what he terms "clumsy ignorance. The *Duchess of Malfi* is a nightmare, not a tragedy."[64]

Lewes admits the play to be "terrific melodrama" that "delights the pit."[65] Horne, however, he says, "would write a better play himself and his labour would be better employed."[66] He is impressed by Miss Glyn, though he has several reservations about her voice. Phelps as Ferdinand seemed as confused to Lewes as he did to the *Athaeneum* critic; Bennett in the role of Bosola pleased him. With that he terminates his account.

A systematic thinker and philosopher, Lewes was unable to enter the world of Webster, to share the symbolism and the tragic vision of a world where the dignity of the human condition is its only value. But this world on theater boards is difficult to portray. When we see it, we must surrender ourselves to it, and the stage critics and most general viewers are too solidly oriented in their own realistic time. Shakespeare succeeds; but he is a greater writer than Webster.

In 1852 we return to the stream of impressionistic, general criticism of Webster-as-literature which ran so strong in the nineteenth century. Edwin Whipple speaks enthusiastically and at length of the Italian tragedies as "among the grandest tragic productions of Shakespeare's contemporaries":

Few dramatists, indeed, equal him in the steadiness with which he gazes into the awful depths of passion, and the stern nerve with which he portrays the dusky and terrible shapes which flit vaguely in its dark abysses. . . . Vittoria's conduct at her arraignment is the perfection of guilt in all its defying impudence. . . . Webster seems to have imitated the spirit of Shakespeare more directly than any of his brother dramatists.[67]

Whipple's remarks serve as a mid-century summary of preceding Webster criticism; his five-page appreciation of the dramatist, after several years of only brief mention in journals and books, served to send Webster into the second half of the century entrenched in a strong position in the history of literature.

# 3

# LATER VIEWPOINTS

The first serious attack on Webster by a non-stage critic came three years later, in 1856, in the May issue of the *North British Review*. The critic was the great Victorian moralist, Canon Charles Kingsley, author of *Westward Ho!* and possibly the last of the practicing Puritans.

The lengthy essay is a defense of the closing of the theaters by the Puritans. Kingsley undoubtedly felt a close kinship with the Puritans, being himself an active Christian Socialist and greatly interested in the idea of reform. His early novels, *Alton Locke* and *Yeast*, reflect this enthusiasm and the idea that reform will not come about through revolution but through the awakening of the higher classes to the higher things of life—and to a realization of their responsibilities to the masses. Thus, the literary philosophies behind the 1850's Christian Socialist movement naturally reflected the idea that literature without a moral purpose of uplifting the masses was the work of the devil. Kingsley's essay is a notable example.

"We believe," wrote the Canon, "that . . . dramatic art had been steadily growing coarse from the first years of James; that instead of the arts advancing to perfection under Charles I they steadily deteriorated in quality though the supply became more abundant."[1] Adultery, he writes, is never a subject for a comedy, never a subject for laughter. Thus, why blame the Puritans for their actions? And the tragedies: though there are a few noble plays—and there are a few good comedies—

as the staple interest of the comedies is dirt, so the staple interest in the tragedies is crime. Revenge, hatred, villainy, incest, and murder upon murder, are their constant themes and (with the exception of Shakespeare, Ben Jonson in his earlier plays, and perhaps Massinger) they handle these horrors with little or no moral purpose, save that of exciting or amusing the audience, and of displaying their own power of delineation in a way which makes one but too ready to believe the accusations of the Puritans.[2]

One can predict how Webster will rate after this.

"The whole story of Vittoria Corombona is one of sin and horror. . . . There is no trace of that development of human souls for good or evil which is Shakespeare's especial power."[3] Kingsley attacks what he considers Webster's static characterization: "Webster's characters, be they young or old, come on the stage ready made, full grown, and stereotyped; and therefore, in general, they are not characters at all, but mere passions and humors in human form. Now and then he essays to draw a character: but it is analytically by description, not synthetically and dramatically, by letting the man exhibit himself in action."[4] The trial scene of Vittoria only indicates "a general acquaintance with the conduct of all bold bad women when brought to bay. . . . the strength of Webster's . . . scene lies simply in intimate acquaintance with vicious nature in general."[5] As for *The Duchess of Malfi,*

What he was thinking and writing of was not truth, but effect; not the Duchess, but her story; not her brothers, but their rage. . . . we must take the liberty to doubt whether the Duchess is "a person" at all. General goodness and beauty, intense though pure affection for a man below her in rank, and a will to carry out her purpose at all hazards, are not enough to distinguish her from thousands of other women, but Webster has no such purpose at all. . . . She would have appeared more noble had Webster taken half as much pains with her as he has with the madmen, ruffians, ghosts, and screech owls in which his heart really delights.[6]

With this remarkable Victorian stricture from his earlier paragraphs, we will turn from Canon Kingsley's critical comments: "The matter is simple enough. We should not allow these plays to be acted in our own day, because we know that they will produce their effects of sin. We should call him a madman who allowed his daughters or his servants to see such representations. Why, in all fairness,

were the Puritans wrong in condemning that which we now have
absolutely forbidden?"[7]

Once again we have had the hard eye of realism turned on
Webster. While much of the above criticism may seem hardly worth
recording, it points out again that for the strict-minded realist,
Webster and his characters will not hold up. Travis Bogard in the
twentieth century was to say similar things about Webster's so-
called static people, but with different effects. As for Kingsley's
Philippics as to the morality involved, we note only that he undoubtedly missed a great deal of the joy of literature, and also
something of Webster.

For several years Webster received generally favorable comment,
Kingsley's sermonizing having had no palpable effect. The Elizabethan group in its entirety was subject of an 1865 appreciation—
perhaps in delayed rebuttal to the statements of Kingsley and
Lewes—in the Cornhill Magazine. Renaissance drama was "universal by right of its commanding interest, of its insight into nature, of
its freedom from any prejudice . . . of the liberality with which its
wealth was cast unreckoned on the world. . . . The poets beheld
the world in its youth, and we still ponder on their words."[8] In
speaking of their courage and nerveless attitude toward death, the
anonymous author quotes Bosola: "We cease to grieve, cease to be
fortune's slaves,/ yea, we cease to die by dying." The fourteen pages
of this article serve somewhat as a mid-century supplement to Lamb
and Hazlitt's early appreciations.

The second edition of Charles Knight's popular Pictorial Shakespeare in 1867 briefly saluted Webster's "power of approaching the
terrible energy of Shakespeare's passion, and the profoundness of his
pathos in the characters which he took out of the great muster roll of
humanity. . . ."[9]

A period of literary histories, cyclopedias, and dictionaries began
in 1871 as critics seemed to feel more and more secure in pigeon-
holing various writers. Henri Van Laune's translation of the French
critic H. A. Taine's History of English Literature in 1871 recognized
only the murky atmosphere of Webster, as so many nineteenth-
century works do: "A sombre man, whose thoughts seem incessantly
to be haunting tombs and charnel houses. . . . No one has equalled
Webster in creating utterly desperate characters . . . in blackening
and blaspheming human life, above all, in depicting the shameless
depravity and refined ferocity of Italian manners."[10] In the United

States, Austin Allibone's *A Critical Dictionary of English Literature and British and American Writers*, appearing in 1872, simply terms Webster "one of the greatest of English dramatists"[11] and quotes brief excerpts from favorable comment by Hazlitt, Hallam, and Drake.

Thomas Campbell's observations on the dramatist could easily have come from the early eighteenth century. His *Cyclopedia of English Poetry* (1874), not overly enthusiastic about many of the Elizabethans, takes note of Webster's preface to *The White Devil*: "In the same preface Webster deprives himself of the only apology that could be offered for his absurdities as a dramatist, by acknowledging that he wrote slowly; a circumstance in which he modestly compares himself to Euripides. In his tragedy *The Duchess of Malfi*, the Duchess is married and delivered of several children in the course of five acts."[12]

A. W. Ward's extensive *History of English Dramatic Literature* appeared in 1875. Here is our first "modern" history of the English drama, and his pronouncements on the various dramatists affected many later critics. He unequivocally places Jonson as "greatest of Shakespeare's contemporaries among the dramatists,"[13] doubts seriously "whether Marston deserves to be remembered among those of genius,"[14] and draws strong attention to Chapman, who "has no superior or equal among our Elizabethan dramatists in the beauty of individual passages."[15] He does his best to remove Beaumont and Fletcher from a place near Shakespeare, thrusting sharply at their facile playmaking which, "though often attractive and often justly admired, never fully satisfies the mind or harmonizes the feelings brought into tumult. . . . Beaumont and Fletcher will never take deep root in the national heart."[16]

He sees Webster, as many later critics were to do, as a genius with many imperfections. *The White Devil*, to summarize Ward, is essentially imperfect. In an ill-proportioned whole, Webster has included highly effective touches of detail. But the catastrophe follows at too great a distance from the climax. Though the characters are often impressive, "there is no relief to the almost sickening combination of awe and loathing created by such characters and motives as this drama presents."[17] (Ward at times speaks for Victorian morality.) The powerful effects come from single touches, "flashes of genius which seem to light up of a sudden wide horizons of emotion."[18] *The Duchess of Malfi* is of a more mature workmanship, and the fourth act terrors are magnificent, "though the dance of the madmen superfluous."[19] While the Duchess seems to be drawn artlessly, she perhaps is designed to contrast with the diabolical craft of her persecutors. Looking back over the Webster canon, Ward emphasizes the great intensity of Webster and the fact that he has

true insight into human nature, and is capable of exhibiting the operation of powerful influences upon it with marvelous directness. He knows that men and women will lay open the innermost recesses of their souls in moments of deep and sudden agitation; he knows that unexpected contrasts . . . will offer themselves. . . . All this he knows, and is able to reproduce, not continually or wearisomely, but with that perception of supremely fitting occasions which is one of the highest . . . rarest powers of true dramatic genius.[20]

However, Ward is not a symbolist of the twentieth century, and cannot see a total tragic vision in Webster:

What Webster in general so admirably reproduces amounts to situations only; in construction he is far from strong . . . and in characterization he rarely passes beyond the range of ordinary types. There seems little moral purpose at work in his most powerful efforts, nor is it conceivable that his imagination, so occupied with the associations of the law court and charnel house, should have been able to wing his genius to freer and loftier flights.[21]

Closing his study of the Elizabethans and Jacobean's, Ward refuses to rank the writers in order of importance, as had often been the case with earlier critics, and calls for the whole view of the period, not simply isolated inspection of separate dramatists.

In the later nineteenth century, Webster the dramatist had a great champion in Algernon Charles Swinburne the poet. Swinburne strove diligently to be the Charles Lamb of his day: writing various studies of the Elizabethans, he tried to introduce the minor poets to a new audience and to continue and broaden Lamb's work. Unfortunately the general public still had little taste for his subject, and, not having read the dramatists, paid little heed to Swinburne's efforts. The scholars who had indeed read the writers often disapproved of the poet's eulogies, tributes not accompanied by the proper scholarship. Thus his efforts, culminating in the 1908 *Age of Shakespeare,* had a mixed reception, and in a large segment of the public no reception at all. Nevertheless, a certain amount of renewed attention in journals and newspapers resulted; Webster and his company had found a new spokesman.

According to biographers, Swinburne at age twelve was introduced to the Elizabethans by Campbell's *Specimens of English Poetry* and the selections from *The Duchess of Malfi*. The following year he was presented with an edition of Dyce's Marlowe, and later, Webster and Ford. From then on, the Elizabethans and their vigorous poetry constituted, for Swinburne, history's greatest age. Later in his life he wrote several studies of the dramatists which were reprinted in the 1908 collection of his Elizabethan studies. His essay on Webster appeared first in 1886.

His criticism belongs solidly in the Lamb-Hazlitt metaphoric, impressionistic tradition. A romantic himself, Swinburne charges through the writers, often praising to the heavens, governing solely on an esthetic basis: the artist's milieu, his sources, any authorship problems, and general scholarship are usually ignored. His aim, like Lamb's, is to convey his own enthusiasm to the reader. Generally speaking, he is at his best when dealing with a dramatist he does not care for, *i.e.*, Dekker and Massinger; with his favorites, he often loses control. And Webster is ranked second to Shakespeare.

Writing in the *Nineteenth Century* for June, 1886, he eulogizes thus: "The crowning gift of imagination, the power to make us realize that thus and not otherwise it was, that thus and not otherwise it must have been, was given—except by exceptional fits and starts—to none of the poets of their time but only to Shakespeare and to Webster. . . . And there is no third to set beside them."[22] Swinburne looks briefly at *The Devil's Law Case, Appius and Virginia* (he finds Virginia nobly drawn) and gets on to the Italian tragedies, which entitle their author to the "station at Shakespeare's right hand."[23] Only in Aeschylus, Dante, and Shakespeare can Swinburne find passages which in sheer force of noble and tragic horror can be set beside the sublimest Websterean passages. Remarking on Webster's introduction to *The White Devil*, Swinburne finds the writer far superior to Euripides, the latter being to Webster "as a mutilated monkey to a well made man."[24] He takes us through the play, pointing to this and that great scene, observing, for instance, the similarity between Vittoria's trial and Mary Stuart's.

Before looking at *The Duchess of Malfi*, he gives us a bit of

questionable information regarding the "vulgar tradition which represents this high-souled and gentle-hearted poet as one morbidly
fascinated by a fantastic attraction towards the violent delights of
horror. . . . The great if not incomparable power displayed in
Webster's delineation of such criminals as Flamineo and Bosola
. . . is a sign rather of his noble English loathing for the traditions
associated with such names as Caesar and Medici and Borgia."[25]
The "gentle-hearted" Webster with his "noble English loathing"
might have been surprised by this.

Swinburne admits Antonio's defects as a character, and further
acknowledges that Webster had a difficult time giving life to the
Duchess, a figure of passive endurance. Though powerful, "she
hardly stands before us as distinct from others of her half angelic
sisterhood as does the White Devil from the fellowship of her
comrade in perdition."[26] Yet compare, he urges, the figure in
Painter's story with the Webster derivation, and realize the purify-
ing and exalting power of Webster's imagination. But even Swinburne cannot escape the problems of the fifth act:

A weightier objection which can be brought against the conduct of the
play . . . is the sudden vehemence of transformation which in the preceding act seems to fall like fire from heaven upon the two chief
criminals who figure on the stage of murder. It seems rather a miraculous
retribution, a judicial violation of the laws of nature, than a reasonably
credible consequence or evolution of those laws, which strike Ferdinand
with madness and Bosola with repentance.[27]

However, Swinburne adds, the thunder-charged atmosphere con-
verts us and we believe. He closes his article noting again that
Webster ranks second to Shakespeare and that he is the cleanliest—
as Marston is the coarsest—writer of his time. Swinburne was to
write further on Webster, a sonnet, and a shorter essay in *Studies in
Prose and Poetry* published in 1894. In the latter, he primarily
repeats his enthusiastic commentary of 1886, save for the observation that *"The Duchess of Malfi* is the most tragic of all tragedies
save *King Lear*."[28]

*The Age of Shakespeare*, Swinburne's last published work, was
composed of his earlier Elizabethan essays in sometimes revised
form. Illustrating the general attitude of the public were many
reviewers who wondered if Swinburne had not overestimated
Webster and his company. The *Times Literary Supplement*, for

instance, decried Swinburne as the last of the Romantic poets and critics, and as one whose enthusiasm for Shakespeare's contemporaries was unreasonable. This reviewer felt that since Swinburne's own poems were episodic he naturally felt inclined toward the plays of Marlowe and Webster, which, for the writer, were made up entirely of episodes. Swinburne's ranking of Webster on a higher level than the supposedly degenerate tragedian Euripides, scoffed the *Times*, represented "romantic criticism at its worst."[29]

In Swinburne we have the last of the eloquent Romantic impressionists. Other critics would utilize the evocative method still, but none so thoroughly as he. Webster would not find again so enthusiastic a reader even among his most ardent supporters. And we say "reader" in Swinburne's case, and not "viewer" or "playgoer." While Swinburne makes many a reference to Webster as "this noble poet," nowhere is Webster called a noble dramatist. It seems never to have entered his mind that the plays of Webster were designed to be played upon a London stage. For Swinburne, as for Lamb, *The White Devil* and *The Duchess of Malfi* were not plays, but poems.

George Saintsbury's *History of Elizabethan Literature* in 1887 stands as another important survey of the Renaissance dramatists. Again we have Webster characterized as the great writer of dramatic flashes. The distinguishing mark of Saintsbury's study is that of all the plays he prefers *The White Devil*. The sequence of events is intelligible, he writes, and the presentation of the character is complete. He objects to some unnecessary detail and questions the reality of Flamineo and Monticelso. However,

When these criticisms and others are made, *The White Devil* remains one of the most glorious works of the period. Vittoria is perfect throughout, and in the justly lauded trial scene she has no superior on any stage. . . . But the real charm of *The White Devil* is the wholly miraculous poetry in phrases and short passages which it contains. . . .
*The Duchess of Malfi* is to my way of thinking very inferior—full of beauties as it is. In the first place, we cannot sympathize with the Duchess, despite her misfortunes. . . . She is neither quite a virtuous woman (for in that case she would not have resorted to so much concealment) nor a frank professor of "All for love." Antonio . . . is an unromantic and even questionable figure. Many of the minor characters . . . would be much better away. . . . By common consent, even of the greatest admirers of the play, the fifth act is a kind of gratuitous appendix of horrors stuck on without art or reason. . . . Nevertheless the dramatic flashes in the play would save it.[30]

Saintsbury brings up the favorite problems of the realistic critics, the lack of motivation of the Cardinal and the hesitation of Ferdinand in the execution of his revenge. For Saintsbury, as for others, these constitute grave errors.

A separate edition of Webster's Italian tragedies appeared in 1888 in the Mermaid series, edited by J. A. Symonds, along with Cyril Tourneur's *The Revenger's Tragedy* and *The Atheist's Tragedy*.

Symonds' introduction furthers the fast-growing popular idea of Webster's plays as mosaics. In his introduction he first notes that Webster is writing within the revenge play tradition of the tragedy of blood, but has advanced possibly beyond *Hamlet* in that he does not need the vulgar machinery of revenge and ghosts. But Webster "views human fates and fortunes with despair" and leaves us "at the last without a prospect over hopeful things."[31] He is Shakespeare's greatest pupil in the art of tragedy; his forte, according to Symonds, lies not in the construction of plot or creation of characters, but in a great sense for dramatic situations. His plots "are involved and stippled within with slender touches; they lack breadth and do not rightly hang together. Their characters though forcibly conceived tend to monotony, and move mechanically."[32] And in an important paragraph he speaks of a blurred total impression:

We rise from the perusal of his Italian tragedies with a deep sense of the poet's power and personality, an ineffacable recollection of one or two resplendent scenes, and a clear conception of the leading characters. Meanwhile, the outlines of the fable, the structure of the drama as a complete work of art, seem to elude our grasp. The persons who have played their part on the stage of our imagination stand apart from one another like figures in a *tableau vivant*. . . . The plays lack the breadth which comes from a master motive.[33]

As for his scenes of horror, "his profound pity for the innocent who suffer shipwreck in the storm of evil passions not their own, save him, even at his gloomiest and wildest, from the unrealities and extravagance into which less potent artists—Tourneur, for example —blundered."[34]

The criticism of William Minton, lecturer at Aberdeen, was published in 1889 in his volume *Characteristics of English Poets*. Written originally around 1885, his commentary is interesting in that it deals in part with Webster as dramatist.

Minton is firmly on Webster's side. His characters are all excellent:

even Appius and Romelio are unsurpassed. "In following these masterpieces the student of character is kept in an ecstasy of delight by stroke after stroke of the most unerring art."[35] Of Webster as dramatist: "Mark how studious Webster has been that his actors shall never go lamely off the stage: they make their exit at happily chosen moments and with some remark calculated to leave a buzz of interest behind them. When we look closely into Webster's plays we become aware that no dramatist loses more in closet perusal: all his dialogues were written with a careful eye to the stage."[36] The impelling forces of the great plays are passionate love, avarice, and bitter repentance; even the villains, Flamineo and Bosola, are "invested with a certain dignity."[37] Minton approves of the violence of the death scenes and observes how tame they would be should a *nuntius* be allowed to relate the tragedies.

Edmund Clarence Stedman's *The Nature and Elements of Poetry*, published in 1892, speaks briefly of Webster and the fact that *The Duchess of Malfi* teaches both the triumphs and the dangers of dramatic poetry. His is a middle view: "The construction runs riot; certain characters are powerfully conceived, others are wild figments of the brain. It is full of most fantastic speech and action; yet the tragedy, the passion, the felicitous language and imagery of various scenes are nothing less than Shakespearean. To comprehend the good and bad qualities of this play is to have gained a liberal education in poetic criticism."[38]

Writing in the *Library Review* for October, 1892, of the unfortunate cuts made in *The Duchess of Malfi* in its 1850 production, Arthur Dillon states that "any labor spent on the presentation of Webster's masterpiece is well spent. . . . for when we come to the heart of the story, from the arrest of the Duchess to her death, what a play it is!"[39]

The play had not been staged in leading London theaters since 1850. Miss Mariott had portrayed the Duchess at Sadler's Wells in 1864; Isabella Glyn had appeared with some success in the Horne version in suburban theaters, and the *Illustrated London News* reported in April, 1868, "This is a performance superior to any now extant in London."[40] But not until October 21, 1892, at the Opera Comique was *The Duchess of Malfi* produced in London. The Independent Theatre Society, formed to preserve by staging various old masterpieces, got William Poel to adapt and stage the play.

Poel's version consisted of some scene rearrangements and, happily, few additions. His cutting of lines, on the other hand, brought criticism from one reviewer. In the majority of the reviews we are confronted again with the problem of whether Webster is totally effective when seen.

The Poel production starred Mary Rorke as the Duchess and Murray Carson as Bosola. The next morning the *Times* reported that

The play, as now performed, can only be considered attractive by reason of its nightmare-like scenes enacted in the prison, where the Duchess is put to death. Slowly and deliberately performed on what, for the most part, is a darkened stage, its long drawn out intrigue would be found oppressive and tiresome by an ordinary audience. . . . If the play were put up for a run, further excisions of the text would be advisable, three hours and a half of its horrors, native and imported, being a too liberal allowance.[41]

The *Graphic* critic was disgusted with all of the actors save Miss Hall as Cariola, and complained about the horrors. (Poel had luminous skeletons painted on the backs of the costumes of the madmen.) All that this revival had done was remind this critic that the play was powerful, but primitive.[42]

The writer for the *Nation* made interesting observations. He had anticipated with great interest this revival, it being a worthy effort. But: "scene followed scene and incident succeeded incident with an irrelevancy and a suddenness that left one fairly bewildered."[43] He states that we simply cannot seek solution for Bosola's motives, for the hatred of the Duke and Cardinal, for the Duchess: like "the screen in the modern society play or the convenient arrangement of doors in the modern farce,"[44] they must be accepted. This anonymous critic is the only writer of his era to come close to a twentieth-century approach to this situation. He goes on to say that the only way out is to have the play consummately well rendered for a modern audience. "But to read a drama in the library is a very different thing from seeing it performed on the stage. If the beauty and power depend upon the lines rather than the construction, then, when these lines are cruelly murdered in the mouths of second rate or inexperienced actors, . . . tragedy degenerates into burlesque."[45] Miss Rorke, for this writer, imitated Ellen Terry; out of charity, he does not identify the actor playing Ferdinand; and Carson as Bosola "spoke with his eyes, his nostrils, his forehead; he writhed and grimaced so unrestrainedly that by the time he reached the end of the first act he had exhausted his resources and could but begin and go through the same tricks over again."[46] He concludes by noting, as does another critic, the unfortunate laughter of the audience: "At moments when the audience should have wept, they tittered, and this, too, in the fourth act where horror crowds upon horror in the long ingenious torture. . . . I, for my part, would rather never have seen Webster's *Duchess of Malfi* on the stage than to have allowed the sad parody presented on the boards of the Opera Comique Friday last."[47]

The *Athenaeum* was on the fence: "Amateurish as was the rendering in many characters, the play proved stimulating. Its horrors were less repulsive than had been anticipated and it was possible to understand how Shakespeare's epoch found them impressive and awe-inspiring."[48] Nevertheless, the *Athenaeum* critic disliked the fact that "people wander on and off the stage in a manner that seems fitful, unworthy, and capricious."[49] He also notes, as did the *Nation* critic, that the audience was given to humor and not purgation during the fourth act: "Some irreverence in the public is pardonable when so complete a holocaust is exhibited, and a tendency to risibility manifested itself when the madmen were brought on the stage."[50] This critic found Carson's Bosola speaking his lines "with commendable precision, if in a style a little monotonous."[51] After the report given by the *Nation's* reviewer, one wonders just how Carson played Bosola.

Clement Scott, an enthusiastic playgoer, wrote a brief but favorable account for the *Illustrated London News*. He rejoiced in hearing poetry once again in the theater; the end result was interesting and complete (a kiss-of-death criticism today), and as for Carson as Bosola, he was "head and shoulders above all the rest."[52]

Finally, Francis Wedmore, writing for the *Academy*, looked at the play more as a literary critic, observing that "an audience without imagination, without historical knowledge, versed only in the commonplace and the cockney, titters, it may be, or becomes indifferent."[53] The poetry of the playwright is "lost upon a public and upon players who account inflation to be poetry and familiarity to be wit."[54] However, Wedmore remains in the camp of the realistic critics, admitting that "the relation of character to character, the why and wherefore of minor events—these things are not invariably made plain: Webster himself, perhaps, could hardly have passed creditably through a searching examination of them."[55] Wedmore, the literary critic at the theater, pays little heed to the staging and states that if the play does not continue to be presented, it is not because of the horrors but "on account of the limited measure of interest which [the stage] displays in the achievements of writing."[56]

Perhaps the most important result of the 1892 staging of the play was the first outburst from Webster's most vigorous detractor, the theater critic William Archer, early in the following year. Before examining the Archer attacks, however, we may note the general dramatic trends of the late nineteenth century as a partial explanation of both Archer's vitriol and the failure of the 1892 revival of *The Duchess of Malfi*.

The period of the last decades of the nineteenth century is generally headed in drama anthologies under "The Rise of Realism and Naturalism" or some similar title. Up to the 1870's most of the drama had clung to the stale romanticism against which the earlier critic George Henry Lewes protested, while such novelists as Balzac and Tolstoy were facing the modern realities of the time. John Mason Brown writes that the time finally came for playwrights to end the cleavage "between the grotesque and the commonplace, the picturesque and the factual, the Gothic revival and the scientific spirit, the cloak and swords of yesteryear and the slums of today."[57] Realism became the idea of a theater. The late nineteenth century, with its rise of the middle and working classes, psychological theorems, and mechanistic philosophies, was not the era for a symbolic, poetical drama. There were, to be sure, exceptions to this rule—we are faced with such works as Ibsen's *Peer Gynt*, Strindberg's *Easter* and *The Dream Play*, Maeterlinck's *Pelleas et Melisande;* yet generally the drama was far more prosaic than poetic. The environment itself, used heretofore as dramatic background, came to stage center in such plays as Hauptmann's *The Weavers* and Gorki's *The Lower Depths*. And with the rise of a social outlook, the protagonists of the drama changed. Although Cyrano de Bergerac thrilled many in 1898, the dashing Count of Monte Cristo had become the little man, the old Baumert of *The Weavers;* while the highborn Duchess of Malfi had to make way for the lowborn peasant women of *The Lower Depths*.

It would be difficult to chart the rise of realism and the "well-made play" chronologically.[58] While one could go back to Elizabethan middle-class drama and farther for realistic effects, a more specific beginning would be in the early nineteenth century with the French workaday-world characters of Eugene Louis Scribe (1791–1861). His people were involved in tricky intrigues, discoveries, and highly contrived plot denouements. The situations were artificial, but they held Scribe's audience, the middle-class world of Louis Phillippe and Louis Napoleon. Here then was the "well-made play" technique, imitated later by Emile Augier, Alexandre Dumas *fils*, and Victorien Sardou. Their plots dealt with life in their own time and with ordinary people of the streets. There was the Russian Nikolai Gogol and his satires, the naturalistic Emile Zola and his adaptation of *Therese Raquin*, and his German antecedents George Buchner and Friedrich Hebbel. For Hebbel, modern tragedy dealt with the lowly individual up against an impersonal society, a theme expressed in his 1845 tragedy of the middle-class *Maria Magdalene* and one we would later find in 1949 in Arthur Miller's *Death of a Salesman*. In England, T. W. Robertson stood alone in the 1850's as a playwright who, though a crude dramatist, seriously looked at his own time. Finally, and most important, there were Strindberg, Chekov, Arthur Pinero, and William Archer's idol, Henrik Ibsen, who had served as stage manager for numerous productions of Scribe's plays.

Here were great writers, writing for a new audience, the audience of the middle class. This society, beset with scientific advancement, European political corruption and failures of revolution, industrial gains, and hundreds of other forces, looked to the stage for well-knit plays that reflected the rapidly changing world that they knew. Archer and Bernard Shaw were late nineteenth-century products of these times, and their reaction to the Elizabethan dramatists was vigorous and violent.

Both Archer and Shaw were enthusiastic Ibsenites. Archer helped introduce the realistic Norwegian dramatist in 1880 with his translation of *Pillars of Society*, published in 1888. The following year brought his translation of *A Doll's House* and its production at the Novelty Theatre. Shaw delivered his lecture on Ibsen in 1890 before the Fabian Society; it became his lengthy essay *The Quintessence of Ibsenism* in 1891. Meanwhile, Archer was championing Ibsen in the journals. And thus, with his immersion in the problem-social-realistic play, came Archer's first article on John Webster in the January, 1893, issue of the *New Review*. Archer was the parttime drama critic for this journal; and when Webster came under his scrutiny, the results were predictable.

On the whole, Archer's first writing is not as vituperative as his later criticism. Titling his article "Webster, Lamb, and Swinburne," he states as the central thesis simply that great literature does not necessarily make great drama. We are told that Lamb and Swinburne did not look at Webster on the stage; they examined him in the study. Archer says early that Lamb "regarded the Elizabethan drama too much in the light of absolute literature, making it a law unto itself. . . . Poetry, pure beauty, force, dignity, perfection of utterance, is in reality one and eternal. . . . Drama on the other hand is a thing of convention, of fashion. . . . and the conventions of one period must not be mistaken for everlasting canons of art."[59] For Archer, the whole Lamb tradition should be revaluated. He and his followers were not at the right point of view for estimating the Elizabethan drama *as* drama.

Archer then tells the story of the play, and a bare recounting of *The Duchess of Malfi* plot never looks particularly good. He stops to linger over the fourth act. He wonders first why the Duchess makes no effort to touch the wax figures of her children as any normal mother would; he then recounts tersely the rest of the proceedings in Act Four. And Act Five does look bad when Archer states flatly,

The Cardinal's mistress Julia is poisoned; Bosola kills Antonio, mistaking him for the Cardinal; then he kills the Cardinal's servant, the Cardinal himself, and Ferdinand, who, by the way, is still raving mad; and Ferdinand, before he dies, kills Bosola. . . .
    In this tragedy, then, five men, three women, and two children come to violent ends, the children and two of the women being strangled on the open stage. Yet, says Mr. Swinburne, ". . . there can be discovered no falsehood more foolish or more flagrant than the vulgar tradition which represents this high souled and gentle hearted poet as one morbidly fascinated by a fantastic attraction towards the violent delights of horror, and the nervous or sensational excitements of criminal detail."[60]

Archer admits that in his narrative, he excludes the great verbal felicity of Webster, which is indeed powerful. "What is certain is that the writings of Webster are full of 'literary power, poetic beauty, and charm of passionate and pathetic fancy,'" he writes, quoting from Swinburne. But, he adds, might not Lamb and Swinburne "have mistaken a low form of drama for a high, and even the highest, because they found it robed in regal purple of pure poetry?"[61]

Anticipating the argument that Webster does not deal in horrors for their own sake but to illustrate the development of character, Archer asks why the resignation and fortitude of the Duchess cannot be made clear without the dead hand and wax corpses. He questions the idea that Cariola's screaming death is designed to contrast with the dignity of the Duchess': "Who can fail to perceive that if this were the intention, the death of the maid must of necessity precede that of the mistress, not follow it, as in Webster?"[62] He protests the strangling of the children after the Duchess is dead: this is more piling of horror on horror. (Had they been strangled in front of their mother, the effect might have been intolerable, but nonetheless dramatic.) Archer's point is that despite Lamb's remark about moving a horror skillfully, "in *The Duchess of Malfi* (and, to a minor degree, in *The White Devil*) the horrors are *unskillfully* moved—that they are frigid, mechanical, brutal."[63]

Archer closes with brief remarks about the motivation for the brothers' virulent opposition to their sister's remarriage, the two years' delay of vengeance, the excrescence of Julia, and the rapidly changing scenes. He admits that Bosola was almost "one of the most complex and most human villains in drama."[64] But in the long run, "Webster was not, in the special sense of the word, a great dramatist; he was a great poet who wrote haphazard dramatic or melodramatic romances for an eagerly receptive but semi-barbarous public."[65]

Several years later Archer would take up the cry again, and even more vigorously. But this article alone gave impetus to Shaw's more general attacks, and was supported by William Watson later in the year. While we may dismiss much of Archer's criticism as the work of a hard-headed man blind to symbol, it makes certain dramaturgical points which are valid. The nineteenth-century reaction had set in.

Watson followed Archer's opinions in the 1893 *Excursions in Criticism*. Staying away from the dramatic aspects of Webster, he went back to the early idea that Shakespeare's greatness can be seen by comparing him with his contemporaries. Of the Swinburnian ranking of Shakespeare first and Webster second, Watson scoffs that the atmospheric changes are telling: "Cynicism, disgust, and despair were the brief and casual refuges of Shakespeare's spirit. These moods are the permanent and congenial dwelling places of minds like Webster's. . . . We turn to Webster and it is like exchanging the breath of morn for the exhalations of the charnel."[66] The critic grasps only that in Webster "life seems a chance medley, a rendez-vous of bewildered phantoms; virtue in this disordered world is merely wasted, honour bears not issue, nobleness dies unto itself."[67] Watson feels that the fatalism in the Italian tragedies lacks the force of that in Greek tragedy, "from which a certain tonic and astringent philosophy of life may be extracted."[68] He then conjectures as to the reasons for Lamb's interest, conjectures noted earlier, and closes his essay with a plea for cooler reappraisal of the Elizabethans. He admits that Jonson, Massinger, and Beaumont and Fletcher had sporadic merit, but as for the likes of Webster and Ford, they were better left un-rediscovered.

To round out a trio of Webster's enemies we might look briefly at an example of George Bernard Shaw's reactions to the Elizabethan dramatists. Shaw, of course, had his own dramatic theories, derived in part from Ibsen. For Shaw, a play should be formed on three components: exposition, complication, and discussion. Ultimately, the social effect of a drama was more important than its literary brilliance. The following gems from his reviews from 1895–98 serve as indication of his feelings toward the school of Shakespeare:

> What Shakespeare got from his "school" was the insane and hideous rhetoric which is all that he has in common with Jonson, Webster, and the whole crew of insufferable dullards whose work stands out as vile even at the beginning of the seventeenth century, when every art was corrupted to the marrow by the orgy called the Renaissance, which was nothing but the vulgar exploitation in the artistic professions of the ter-ritory won by the Protestant movement. . . .
> When one thinks of the donnish insolence and perpetual thick skinned swagger of Chapman over his unique achievements in sublime balder-dash, and the opacity that prevented Webster, the Tussaud laureate, from appreciating his own stupidity . . . it is hard to keep one's critical blood cold enough to discriminate in favor of any Elizabethan whatever. Nothing short of a statue at Deptford to the benefactor of the human species who exterminated Marlowe and the condemnation of Mr. Swin-burne to spend the rest of his life in selling photographs of it to American tourists, would meet the poetic justice of the case.[69]

Possibly the only way to deal with such a great outburst as this is to leave it alone in all its sarcastic splendor, realizing that probably a good portion of it was written to call attention to its author. Taking this into account, however, it remains difficult to understand how Shaw could be so completely out of tune with dramatists such as Jonson, Marston, and others who dealt with their own times (if in their own way), often in the same sarcastic, upbraiding spirit which Shaw manifested three centuries later.

Webster criticism-in-the-study rounds out the century. In America James Russell Lowell's lectures on the old English dramatists, given originally in 1877, were revised and published in 1893. Lowell does not see the Elizabethans as Hazlitt's race of giants, but he does see their sporadic, formless greatness. For Lowell, not only Webster but the entire group outside of Shakespeare and Jonson lacked form: "With the greater part of the secondary dramatists, the characters seem like unpractised people trying to walk the deck of a ship in rough weather, who start for everywhere to bring up anywhere, and are hustled against each other in the most inconvenient way."[70] Of Webster's portrayal of evil: "Crime becomes . . . tragic when it merely furnished the theme for a profound psychological study of motive and character. The weakness of Webster's two greatest plays lies in this—that crime is presented as a spectacle and not as a means of looking into our own hearts and fathoming our own consciousness."[71] Yet Lowell can say that "both these plays are full of horrors, yet they do move pity and terror. We feel that we are under the control of a usurped and illegitimate power, but it is power."[72] On the whole, Webster, for Lowell, is similar to Victor Hugo: "There is the same confusion at times of what is big with what is great, the same fondness for the merely spectacular, the same insensibility to repulsive details, the same indifference to the probable or even to the natural, the same leaning toward the grotesque, the same love of effect at whatever cost; and there is also the same impressiveness of result."[73]

One more mention of Webster in 1893 came in J. W. Cunliffe's *The Influence of Seneca on Elizabethan Tragedy.* We learn that Webster was influenced by Senecan violence and Stoicism; but Cunliffe says little else, devoting his time to dramatists other than Webster.

Edmund Gosse, a leading critic of the late nineteenth century, did much to keep Webster's name alive during this period. He wrote of him first in his 1883 *Seventeenth Century Studies,* which went through five editions, and later in *The Jacobean Poets*, 1894. Gosse proved to be, actually, in the Archer-Shaw line: later, as an enthusiastic Ibsenite, he often made a distinction between literature and dramatic literature. He knew the theater, and he knew poetry. Happily, however, he is more clear-eyed than Archer and Shaw. In *The Jacobean Poets* he admits of *The Duchess of Malfi* that "dramatic, in the acceptable sense, it may scarcely be called," but it is nevertheless "the finest tragedy outside Shakespeare."[74]

For Gosse, writing in 1894, the movement of the whole of *The Duchess of Malfi* has been sacrificed to an extraordinary brilliance in detailed passages. He admires both the Duchess and Antonio, believing that the latter has been "simply and wholesomely drawn."[75] Disagreeing with Lamb and Swinburne's ideas on Webster's skillful introduction of horrors, Gosse finds certain aspects of the fourth and fifth acts "blots on what is notwithstanding a truly noble poem, and what, with more reserve in this respect, would have been one of the first tragedies of the world."[76] Notice the use of the term "poem": this, for Gosse, is the genre of *The Duchess of Malfi*. It is "a tragic poem to be enjoyed in the study."[77]

He is not quite as pleased with Vittoria and her company as he is with *The Duchess of Malfi*: "*The White Devil* reads as though the writer had put in only what interested him and had left the rest for a coadjutor who did not happen to present himself and fill up."[78] Nevertheless, this play "is not less full than *The Duchess of Malfi* of short lines and phrases full of a surprising melody. In the fabrication of these jewels, Webster is surpassed only by Shakespeare."[79] Gosse states, in a questionable summary, that "if it were not certain that the playwright flourished between 1602 and 1612 we should be inclined to place the period of his activity at least ten years earlier. . . . as a romantic poet of passion he takes a position in the very first rank of his contemporaries."[80]

Gosse's original approach differed from that of the 1894 *The Jacobean Poets*. Writing earlier in *Seventeenth Century Studies* he praised Webster in ponderous phrases, in the manner of his friend Swinburne. Inferior to Jonson in scope, learning, invention, comedy, and ease of dialogue, nevertheless Webster, "like Shakespeare, is transcendental; his strong muse wings itself out of the common world and sees things with the eye of a visionary."[81] Gosse takes us through *The White Devil*, relishing most of the characters, and saluting the "vigorous and often musical"[82] versification. Among his impressionistic notations stand two worthy points: he disagrees with Lamb over the effect of Vittoria's "innocence-resembling boldness," pointing out that "Monticelso's altogether extravagant abuse has as much to do with the favour we feel for her as her own rather brazen confidence."[83] More important, he sees a Shakespearean restoration of order at the end of the play in the brief appearance of Giovanni, "rising like the morning star"[84] and indicating a new life to come. While Gosse's phraseology may be extravagant, certain later critics would agree with him.

Although waxing most enthusiastic over the portrayals of the Duchess, Ferdinand, Bosola ("the cleverest male invention of Webster"[85]), and even Antonio, Gosse does regret the two-year delay of Ferdinand's revenge; and while he can see a symbolic return to order in The White Devil, he cannot find it in The Duchess of Malfi. The fifth act comes in for its now traditional criticism: "we can hardly account for the want of taste and art shown in the fifth act. . . ."[86] unless with the loss of the Duchess came a loss of interest. It is odd that the critic could see the restoration of order in The White Devil and miss the same reestablishment in the later play. Gosse closes his chapter with a sentimental vision of Melpomene laying a wreath on the statue of Webster at dewy dawn in the garden of the gods. Only Shakespeare and Webster receive her tribute in this "delicious terrace that overlooks the western sea."[87] We can only wonder what Shaw's reaction was.

Gosse's criticism, as we have seen, runs from impressionistic literary enthusiasm to praise with considerable qualifications as to dramatic force. Writing finally in his 1897 Short History of Modern English Literature, he regrets Webster's lack of a grasp of style and want of a happier architecture.[88]

The year following The Jacobean Poets brought a totally different kind of study from Gosse's. In 1895 Frederick Carpenter published Metaphor and Simile in the Minor Elizabethan Drama, a work which was almost out of place in its time. Carpenter examined closely the language of the dramatists, their imagery, and their style. While his study is greatly overshadowed by twentieth-century "New Critics," it remains one of the earlier, important first steps away from nineteenth-century impressionism.

Carpenter writes that Webster worked consciously, deliberately, and with a thorough command of his materials. The pages are filled with tropes, and though profuse, they seldom seem forced or out of

keeping. (The *Scrutiny* group and other later critics find this statement completely erroneous.) He remarks accurately on Webster's
biting intensity of language, and unfaded and unusual imagery—
animals, mists, and birds. While Webster "errs if anything on the
side of the bizarre, or even of the grotesque,"[89] his poetry is great.
The sardonic character of Flamineo, for example, "is heightened by
the irony of his incessant similes. . . . Antonio's rather colorless
virtues are artfully depicted through his fondness for sententious
comparisons." Carpenter says little; but his efforts in the direction
of imagery study are carried on by later writers who were not long
in following this approach.

The year 1895 brought two more references to Webster. John
Corbin's *The Elizabethan Hamlet* studied the mad scenes of Shakespeare's play in an effort to prove their comic purpose. His feeling is
that during the tortures of the Duchess, "the jests of the madmen are
precisely of a nature to amuse the audience."[90] In the same year, a
selection of Edwin Whipple's *Atlantic Monthly* essays was published
under the title *The Literature of the Age of Elizabeth*. As in his
remarks of almost fifty years earlier, Whipple remains the impressionistic Webster enthusiast; he celebrates the intense power of
Webster's steady vision of the blackness in life:

He is such a spendthrift of his stimulants . . . that he would render the
mind callous to his terrors, were it not that what is acted is still less than
what is suggested, and that the souls of his characters are greater than
their sufferings or more terrible than their deeds. . . . Webster lifts the
wickedness at once from the region of the senses into the region of the
soul, exhibits its results in spiritual depravity, and shows the satanic
energy of purpose which may spring from the ruins of the moral will.[91]

We are almost at the end of the century; and it would be pleasing
to be able to give Mr. Whipple's affirmative remarks as the closing
word from the century's critics. But there remain two entries which
fail to agree with Whipple's feeling that Webster was, underneath it
all, a moralist interested in showing the "ruins of the moral will." We
take especial note of these not because they are of monumental
importance, but because, through their reservations concerning John
Webster, we realize that we can resolve very little about nineteenth-
century Webster criticism. It has a see-saw effect; and the century
ends on the "down" scale with Sidney Lee's biography of Webster

for the *Dictionary of National Biography* and an account of Webster in a journal published at Wellesley College.

Lee wrote his biographical account of Webster in 1899; it still stands as official in subsequent editions. After giving us the history of Webster's life as best we know it, and listing his collaborations with other dramatists, Lee writes that at an uncertain date between 1607 and 1612 Webster "for the first time wrote a play single-handed, and there evinced such a command of tragic art and intensity as Shakespeare alone among Englishmen has surpassed."[92] But Lee tempers his praise quickly. While admitting along with others the now famous dictum that "Webster approaches Shakespeare nearest in tragic power," Lee hastens to add, "But his power is infinitely circumscribed when it is compared to Shakespeare's."[93] For this critic, Webster lacked Shakespeare's touch in developing character; Lee contends that many of Webster's characters are far too elaborate. And at length we have the dignified Victorian attitude: "With a persistence that seems unjustifiable in a great artist, Webster, moreover, concentrated his chief energies on repulsive themes and characters; he trafficked with an obstinate monotony in fantastic crimes."[94] Having delivered himself of this, Lee closes the biography more affirmatively, speaking of his vigorous and musical blank verse, and his achievement of a dignified reticence in spite of his unfortunate subject matter. For the lay reader, Webster today emerges from the *Dictionary of National Biography* as a good man, but with odd quirks which should have been looked after.

Finally, we turn to an article by Grace Cook in the *Wellesley Magazine* for February, 1899. Miss Cook, the journal's editor, writes on "English Tragedy in the Reign of King James I"; and generally, she is shocked by it. (And she would have found allies in both America and England.) For her, "Jacobean tragedy stands forth not in the robust, wholesome, and gigantic vitality of its immediate predecessor, but unstable, unsymmetrical, unlovely, often impotent and puny when stripped of its gorgeous trappings."[95] *The White Devil* of Webster is typical of all the Jacobean drama in which the "tragic action appears either violently forced or wholly inadequate, because its fitness for the occasion is more obvious than its intrinsic necessity to the character uttering it."[96] In *The Duchess of Malfi*, "Webster has not made clear the reactionary influence of her own experience upon the Duchess. . . . there is wanting an essential motivating power to acting or suffering."[97] However, the writer does see some impression of retribution and justification at the end of the play: "The sorrowing Duchess dies, but she triumphs. In very few tragedies of the period is the sense of victory through death so complete."[98]

Like William Watson in 1893, Miss Cook celebrates great tragedy and the joy inherent in the form: there is joy in man's divine nature and joy in our inheritance of struggling divinity. But "joy such as this is denied in Jacobean tragedy. Disheartened, we turn away from the endless striving after nothing, from the emptiness and the futility of passionate raving."[99]

To sum up: the impressionistic long view or the close realistic examination—these are the chief nineteenth-century approaches of those Webster critics who are emphatically pro or con. Claimants for Webster's greatness emphasize throughout the century his power in creating a dark and terrible poetic vision. Less whole-hearted critics, to speak very generally, fall into three broad categories. First, there are those in the first half of the century who emphasize the horror of Webster. For many magazine critics, particularly, Webster is decidedly gifted in the ability to create the terrible scene; but he overdoes it, and we are repelled. Second, there are the critics who, in the second half of the century, emphasize the spottiness of Webster. For critics such as Ward, Saintsbury, and Symonds, the dramatist is a creator of superb flashes only; his plays, as Symonds wrote, "lack the breadth which comes from a master motive." Webster is often decidedly great; but he is a writer of great imperfections: there is a lack of characterization (the Duchess is often pointed out as static), and a total meaning is blurred. The third critical group is dominated, of course, by Archer, and represents the tough, realistically minded critic who cares little for simile and metaphor and more for logic and probability. Archer is practically the whole group itself, but we can add Lewes, his spiritual father; William Watson; and Shaw, who of course directed most of his tirades against Shakespeare himself. This is the critical segment which makes manifest the impossibility of staging Webster, a theatrical approach which so many nineteenth-century critics seem to overlook. These divisions are very broad, and overlap considerably, but they are there.

Thus we may derive the nineteenth-century composite of John Webster, Jacobean dramatist: he was a genius, but a very imperfect one. Many of his dramatic flashes are comparable only to Shakespeare, and his scenes of terror are the greatest known; but he is a dramatist of great lines and occasional scenes only. He understood human nature, but often a sense of character failed him. There is defiant courage displayed by the Duchess and Vittoria, but there is certainly no moral purpose in his plays and no totality of tragic vision. Act IV of *The Duchess of Malfi* is one of the greatest acts ever written; it is absurd that Act V was written at all. We enjoy reading Webster any evening when we find ourselves with a penchant for the dark and the terrible; but we cannot endure seeing what we read presented on a stage. In the study there is horror; in the theater there is laughter. Second only to Shakespeare in the power of creating an occasional mighty scene, Webster often falls behind Jonson's and Beaumont and Fletcher's consistency of presentation.

Finally, let us add a very general comment regarding Webster's reception by many critics and the reading and viewing public. The darkness, the bleakness of Webster—even looking at the play as a poem to be read in the study—was simply not the general mood of most of the nineteenth century. We see what one writer has just said in 1899—man's nature is partially divine; let us have the tragedies which leave us with a sense of truth and justice. Until the later years of the century, for many people (Matthew Arnold excluded) it was a period in which a Tennyson was seemingly assured of meeting his Pilot face to face when he had crossed the bar; and a Browning never turned his back but marched breast forward and greeted the unseen with a cheer.

But science was slowly cutting man down to size; and the world was getting larger and more impersonal. William Ernest Henley might proclaim that he was the master of his fate; yet some thinkers reflected Thomas Hardy's wish that the oxen *might* be kneeling down in reverence on Christmas Eve, though the occurrence was not likely. In America the "good years" of 1880–1910 would give way to a world war, and man's divine nature would be called into serious questioning. The world of the twentieth century would be for many quite similar to the dramatic world (albeit "empty and futile") of Webster. And thus would one poet turn to Webster's wasteland for his own re-creation of the meaningless world of the twentieth century.

# Twentieth Century

# 4

# WEBSTER IN THE STUDY

Criticism of John Webster is almost a perfect mirror of the changing critical trends in England and America. Looking back over the nineteenth century, we see in Webster study the critical methods which prevailed: the impressionistic ramblings of Lamb and Hazlitt, culminating in the romantic studies by Swinburne, and the urbane writings of Saintsbury, Gosse, and others in the "gentleman-and-scholar" tradition, *litterateurs* perhaps affected by the art-for-art's-sake movement, who specialized not in acute analysis but in the art of appreciation. Bradley's lectures on Shakespeare probably influenced the rare Webster critic interested in the psychological understanding of Vittoria Corombona; and we find further the biographical-historical method of Morley's *English Men of Letters* series in some of the Victorian critics' appraisals of the playwright. What is not, however, reflected in nineteenth-century Webster criticism is the critical teaching of Matthew Arnold. Arnold and his important emphasis on reasonable classical order and morality is not felt in Webster criticism until the twentieth century with T. S. Eliot and his followers.

And with the twentieth century comes new and important criticism. The art of praise gives way to the art of close analysis. Instead of a Saintsburian effort to enjoy or admire nearly everything produced in the past, the modern critic more often concentrates on the work of the past by judging it for its timeless appeal and value in the light of definite standards. And the standards for Webster (and many others) are set in the twenties and thirties by T. S. Eliot and the complementary doctrines of F. R. Leavis' *Scrutiny* magazine. Eliot and *Scrutiny* come to play the most influential roles in Webster critical history: the most important commentaries up through 1960 grow at least in part out of their critical precepts.

To bring order out of sixty years of important Webster criticism, we will examine only the leading critical documents, particularly those making the larger critical assessments. For the twentieth century, the study will be in very general critical groupings and not wholly chronological.

We will end with a review of the modern stage history of Webster, for it was for the stage and not the study that Webster wrote. But his plays lead a tenuous life still, though there have been, at last, some successful presentations of the two tragedies. The important fact is that certain producers are interested in doing Webster, and the success of London revivals in 1945 and 1947, for instance, indicates that at least the British public will accept him when done well. The review of the stage history is limited to the professional productions of the two main tragedies, and the criticism is usually from accounts in the next day's newspapers or that week's periodicals. For better or worse, these reviews most directly affect the fortunes of any playwright.

Interest in Webster is strong in the twentieth century, whether he is dismissed or praised. Part of the renewed interest is the result of Eliot's attention to the Elizabethans and metaphysicals, and his placing of them in the main line of English thought and writing. Eliot bears a slight kinship to Lamb in this respect, whether he would have admitted the relationship. But another reason for the revival—encompassing the general public's occasional acceptance of stage presentation of Webster—is that we in the present-day world of uncertainty and fear are more in tune with the Websterian universe than was the nineteenth century. In a world which has been torn by two world wars and where nuclear annihilation seems a terrifying possibility, we can more freely sympathize with the Duchess of Malfi in her own private Hell. Eliot's Wasteland—our twentieth century—is remarkably similar to the charnel house atmosphere of Webster; and the equation follows through. The following excerpt is from an article by Edmund Wilson called "Notes at the End of a War." He had recently seen a 1945 revival of John Webster:

Implausible though it may appear, *The Duchess of Malfi* . . . is probably the most fascinating show to be seen in London. . . . You would think that this old tragedy of blood, with its grotesque horrors and highly wrought speeches is the kind of thing of which a revival would be sure to turn out dreary or comic. . . . No, *The Duchess of Malfi* was not funny. You understood what Gertrude Stein meant when she said that she had reread in France, during the war, Shakespeare's tragedies and historical plays and had realized for the first time that human life could be like that. . . . one saw the scene of the released lunatics in which the Duchess is told her doom, just at the moment of the exposé of the German prison camps.[1]

❦

During the first years of the century, Webster study progressed at a steady pace. Nearly every year the dramatist was mentioned—usually at some length. Although some of the criticism in this first period carries over the Victorian legacy of impressionism and urbane academicism, efforts are made to break through with sound scholarship. We must admit, however, that quite often this sound scholarship is also soundly dull. One comes to rejoice over the Webster critic who is scholarly but who can write: one reason for the permanence of Rupert Brooke's study is its style.

Heralding the coming of more acute analysis of Webster is an important document in the first year of the new century, W. W. Greg's "Webster's *White Devil*: An Essay in Formal Criticism," appearing in the English *Modern Language Quarterly*. Greg turns his scholar-bibliographer talent to the sixteenth-century sources for the story—the first time such a systematic study had been made. He examines the sources, observes the changes made by the dramatist, and makes the flat statement that Webster knew what he was doing at all times: " . . . we are dealing with a conscious and careful artist whose work is the outcome of leisure and thoughtful consideration, very different from the promiscuous blotching of Henslowe's hacks."[2]

Webster's greatest change, according to Greg, is in the treatment of Isabella. She becomes a loving wife, and her death coincides with Vittoria's husband's. Her goodness, along with Cornelia's, provides a foil for the evil of Vittoria and Brachiano. Of Vittoria and the world she represents, Greg observes that she is "not so much a violator of the moral order as one to whom moral considerations convey no meaning. . . . Terrible and fascinating in the consistency of character into which no moral misgiving can find entrance, she fights ruthlessly, desperately against fate."[3]

The last part of Greg's essay makes another new contribution to Webster scholarship: a study of the general construction of the play. He takes the scenes in order and discusses the relation between them regarding time and place. He sees the scenes in Act I as providing the exposition and introduction; the events in Act II, the complication; Act III provides the obstacles; Act IV, triumph and reversal; and Act V, retribution and catastrophe. The climax, for Greg, is not the trial, but the scene in the house of convertites. Here is the turning point of the plot: fortune begins to change as Brachiano's jealousy grows. In all, Greg's essay lacks the sweeping generalities of the Victorians; it is quiet and to the point. Underlying his approach is the conviction that Webster in this play is a finished artist, a portrayer of a world which is not moral or immoral, but amoral.

Historical criticism, fairly strong in the early years of the century, makes further progress in Clayton M. Hamilton's 1901 article on *The Duchess of Malfi* as a tragedy of blood. Although the genre was mentioned from time to time in the previous century, Hamilton stands as the first critic to subject Webster to an analysis under that particular heading. His account is inferior to that of the later and more nearly complete study by Fredson Bowers, but the beginning is made. We are given what become familiar ingredients—the idea of a tragedy of revenge, including the ghost, the scheming villain, and the hired rogue. Webster's treatment is the supreme climax of this genre, for Webster "admits of no peer but Shakespeare himself."[4] The great change Webster makes, according to Hamilton, is the reformation of the traditional "hired rogue," in this case, of course, Bosola. Thus Act V is not an afterthought, but for Hamilton, "a tempestuous climax."[5] The author sees Webster as a learned dramatist and the creator of a gloom which nevertheless does not include hopeless despair. Lightening the gloom of the darkest depths is a lyric eloquence. The tradition of the tragedy of blood called forth Webster's greatness, says Hamilton, and when he died, the species died with him.

J. E. Morris, writing the following year in the *Fortnightly Review*, contributes an article that still belongs in the modern Webster bibliography. He is the first writer to take note of the schizo-critical approach to Webster criticism: he writes that there is too much individual prejudice in recent criticism which is satisfied with a rhetorical triumph and the maintenance of a thesis. Swinburne overlooks all blemishes; Watson vigorously criticizes all errors without noticing any merit. "There is, however, reason for believing, in a complete and final survey, that Webster is infinitely the greatest of that fascinating brotherhood of playwrights."[6]

Morris anticipates studies to come by noting the Websterian imagery: "He exhibits throughout a singular fondness for illustrations drawn from nature, and especially from bird life."[7] He points out, as he notes the many bird images, that Webster uses the lark and nightingale differently from most poets. In his hands, the birds of traditionally pleasant associations take part in grim utterances, his examples lead to a discussion of Webster's "unhealthy" imagination: "He cannot say the simplest thing without giving it a sinister turn."[8] Often the sinister images are just disgusting; elsewhere they create a legitimate effect in deepening the horror and darkness. "Cursed with a kind of perpetual second sight, he sees the potential death-cloth clinging round every living person."[9]

Morris' conclusions are similar to those of some later critics: his first impression is that of "embarrassed and uncertain plots, overcharged with incident and unnecessary episode; of separate scenes of extraordinary power, which yet do not seem to hang rightly together, of a complete absence of what we are accustomed to look for in a well-managed tragedy—of the evolution, that is, of a single interest up to final and overwhelming catastrophe."[10] But the second impression is that of a genius who has probed to the bottom of "the muddy wells of pessimism" and "cynical self-contempt," and "who has seen the human soul still master of itself, though racked by the last imaginable horrors of terror, grief, and hopelessness."[11] He "clings instinctively to what is righteous."[12] He is limited severely in scope, but in brevity and passion is the Tacitus of poets; he condenses terror into the finest of brief phrases. Although his halting blank verse is hardly the work of a great natural artist, in Webster's own narrow sphere, "he speaks with an utterance . . . second only to the utterance of Shakespeare."[13]

The widely used Chamber's *Cyclopedia of English Literature* was revised in 1902, and the general public learned that Webster was occasionally great in spite of himself: "In the elements of pure tragedy he comes nearest to the master himself, and *The Duchess of Malfi* is unquestionably the most elevated tragic poem in the language not written by the pen of Shakespeare."[14] However:

His plays are exceedingly ill-constructed; most of them are mere clusters of scenes, violently put together and eked out with a dumb show, in a manner so primitive that we seem to have gone back a generation. . . . A bewildering quality of execution is characteristic of every play of Webster's. . . . He was perhaps a poet who by force of circumstances was forced on to the stage, rather than a born dramatist. . . .[15]

At length, "Webster is the highest expression we possess of the sinister pursuit of moral beauty in the literature of crime and horror."[16]

Thomas Seccombe and J. W. Allen's 1903 *The Age of Shakespeare*, like so many other appraisals, gives Webster second place ranking in the dramatic scale of the time, and, again as usual, compliments his rare and intense dramatic power. One observation made by the editors is that there is no moral involved in either tragedy: "Insensate pride, insensate lust and cruelty, destroy good and evil alike in a common ruin, and the curtain falls upon the massacre. There is no moral, or if one stands in the text, it is perfunctory and irrelevant."[17] The authors condemn the playwright, as seems to be part of the fashion in this time, for a complete lack of constructive skill, but they make an interesting observation on the characterization involved: "Webster has little sense of character. When he elaborates, as in Bosola, he becomes unintelligible: ordinarily he is content to express mood and passion. . . . His characters are creatures of the moment, and we can hardly imagine them at all apart from the situations in which they are presented."[18]

Possibly the high point in the historical method of criticism at length is W. J. Courthope's *History of English Poetry*, published from 1895 to 1910; the fourth volume on the Elizabethans appeared in 1903. The main thesis is that the creative imagination is always influenced by the prevailing political institution, and the Renaissance period, with its great queen, made for a correspondingly healthy creative climate. Generally, however, the brotherhood of Shakespeare's contemporaries is handled rather roughly because of their commercial interest in making a living. Shakespeare, according to Courthope, always endeavored to turn the public taste and the traditions of the theater to the service of fine art.

But Webster, too, though dealing in melodrama, brought "an elevating and refining influence which raised this kind of play as nearly as possible to the level of genuine tragedy,"[19] although for this writing he did not completely purge it of all the imperfections of bad taste of his contemporaries and his spectators. And Webster remains still the writer of parts, who disregarded a unity of action. Of *The Duchess of Malfi*:

. . . the plot is too slender to bear all the machinery applied to it. . . . Sixteen persons are employed to work out this simple action, with the necessary result that at least ten parts in the play are superfluous. . . . Where there is so little organic unity of action, it is of course not to be expected that there will be much consistency of character: Webster is content to make his speeches effective for the moment, without considering whether the words are probable and appropriate. . . .[20]

With a certain vehemence he shows us that Webster used and re-used axioms through a listing of many similar lines. "Such self-repetitions, extremely characteristic of the laborious and economical art of Webster, should be remembered when that is spoken of as almost worthy to be compared with the boundless affluence of Shakespeare's genius."[21] Courthope, while failing to find any unity of tone or atmosphere, presages the *Scrutiny* critics in his distaste for extraneous aphorisms and fragmentations.

Courthope's criticism is specifically reflected in Barrett Wendell's 1904 *The Temper of the Seventeenth Century in England*, lectures given at Trinity College in 1902–1903. This Harvard teacher's re-appraisals of tradition and the processes of composition possibly influenced his student T. S. Eliot. Wendell feels that Webster labored too long in order to recreate the world of Renaissance Italy. One section of his remarks is worth particular attention as we look forward to Eliot's decrees about a writer's self-criticism during creation of his work ( see "The Function of Criticism"):

A sense of . . . complexity seems to have weighed down on Webster until it became benumbing: he always seems aware of how very much he has to tell, afraid lest he shall unduly simplify deeds and characters which simplicity would belie. He never appears to have unconscious ease; he never relaxes into sympathetic humor; there are no Nurses . . . no Mercutios. . . . His work is full of isolated situations, and phrases, and touches of character which seem almost ultimate in their combined power and truth to life. What makes the total effect of them bewildering is that he could never quite fuse them into organic unity. . . . His fragments of tragedy are like some unfinished mosaic needing a flash of electric fire to melt their outlines into the intelligible unity of painting.[22]

Webster rises above all of his contemporaries except Shakespeare and Marlowe. But in neither of his great tragedies does he approach the lucidity of either dramatist because of what ultimately is a "crushing sense of fact."[23]

The first close study of Websterian borrowing began in 1904 with Charles Crawford in *Notes and Queries;* it was later reprinted in his series *Collectanea* in 1906–1907. In several articles Crawford notes the close relation between Webster and Sir Philip Sidney, the conclusion being that Webster was never far away from the text of the *Arcadia.* Particularly, some of the most moving incidents in *The Duchess of Malfi* are taken from or are based on events in Sidney's book. Besides some specific passages, there is an inspiration for the waxworks in Pyrocles' anguish at the supposed "execution" of Philoclea, and there is a similar love parallel in the love of Queen Erona for the untitled Antipholus. Crawford's listing of parallel after parallel does not make for the liveliest of reading, but his study remains invaluable as the first real effort to see Webster at work. Besides Sidney's influence, Crawford found incidents and only slightly altered phrasings taken from Marston, Montaigne, and Donne.

In 1905 E. E. Stoll, later to gain fame for his Shakespeare studies, published the first book devoted exclusively to John Webster. As in his later *Art and Artifice in Shakespeare,* Stoll in *John Webster* utilizes all he can gather about the history of the time, as evidenced by the subtitle "The periods of his work as determined by his relations to the drama of the day." It is historical criticism; its laborious, sometimes tedious method was possibly influenced by German scholarship which at that time was making great impressions on American scholars. It is poorly printed, but it is an impressive work.

Stoll's method is to divide Webster's life into three periods: his years of apprenticeship under the influence of Dekker, 1602–1606; the great period of the revenge plays and Marston's influence, 1611–12, 1617; and his final period of the Fletcher era, 1620–27. Stoll studies each period in detail; he is chiefly concerned with what Webster uses from the drama of his time and its tradition. There is seldom any sweeping, overall criticism relative to impressions or themes; instead, Stoll's is a close scholarly view of Elizabethan and Jacobean play writing.

We may note the section on the middle years: for "only in this middle period does he rise above his models and his mediocrity and get on his feet and use his own voice."[24] Stoll finds three great debts to other revenge tragedians. From Marston, Webster makes use of the malcontent's meditation, the cold simile, the brevity of axiom, the careful placing of bodies (cf. Piero's exhibition in *Antonio's Revenge*), the use of omens, and especially the use of satiric remarks. From Tourneur, Webster may have found the ideas of poisoning and torturing, the mental conflict in a tool villain, the taunting of a victim. And from Shakespeare, he takes the idea of madness. However, Webster's imagination is greater than Marston's or Tourneur's. Their poetry harrows and startles; Webster's has a lighter, more artistic touch. Webster's general style is more meditative than dramatic. "The greatest contribution of Webster to characterization, however, is stern, true moral sense. . . . most of his victims have themselves to acknowledge, at the last, that they have pulled their fate down upon their own heads. . . . His cynicism rises from a far humaner and sincerer sort than that which like Marston and Tourneur arises from a dogmatic and hypocritical spirit."[25] Stoll further notes the changes in *The Duchess of Malfi* which Webster makes in the revenge play tradition: the rearranging so that the victim is now the hero(ine), and the revengers—Ferdinand and the Cardinal—are the villains. Drawing perhaps on C. M. Hamilton's *Sewanee Review* article, Stoll also makes note of the amazing change in the tool villain's role, the conversion of Bosola in Act V.

Webster, writes Stoll, was completely dominated by the thought of his day, and by his fellows, Marston, Tourneur, Fletcher, and others, although in his great period he gave more than he took. Here is Stoll's conclusion:

No one so strong ever leaned harder on the staff of tradition; no one ever looked about him more narrowly for material or studied more closely others' methods. The truth may be, that he had no spring of invention welling within him: that he had profound insight, subtle taste, and a zeal to toil, but that he had not within him which of itself would change and make new—make his own—all that he touched. His works are few, follow at long intervals, and show the marks of the file; the materials in them he culled from afar . . . but what determined his choice, or his change, was less some inner necessity than the model he, as a student, then held before him, the influence he then obeyed. These changed, and Webster's work—laborious, discriminating, artistic, but not spontaneous—changed with them.[26]

Stoll's work remains valuable for his scholarly researches. He is not particularly concerned with overall evaluation of any meaning within Webster, but is more interested, obviously, in influences. Today, we are generally interested in evaluating results as much as methods. For one reason, when we concentrate specifically on Webster's borrowing, as do Stoll and Robert W. Dent (*John Webster's Borrowing*, 1960), we tend to come to the conclusion that more than anything else, Webster was an artistic thief. As this is not a particularly pleasing conclusion, we grant him pardon and judge instead his rearrangements. Meanwhile, Stoll's important pioneer work gathers dust on shelves (few recent articles refer to it at all), and the work in fact is not obtainable in many libraries.

The distinguished scholar-critic-philosopher Herbert Grierson turned his attention briefly to Webster in the 1906 with *The First Half of the Seventeenth Century* and continued the line of evaluation by academic critics. He adds little that we have not seen before in the way of adverse criticism. Of Webster's style: "Even the most imaginative touches smell a little of the lamp. . . ."[27] Of his characters: only a few fine poses are etched. "Could the poet have carried Vittoria through the play as Shakespeare does Cleopatra . . . not Shakespeare himself would have produced a greater character."[28] (The Duchess is the greater, more sustained character.) And Grierson is one of the many who fail to see a unity of vision in Webster. Of the plot of *The White Devil*:

. . . the studied care with which Webster endeavored to make it include the crime and punishment has prevented his obtaining the concentration and proportion which give to Shakespeare's plots essential unity. That essential unity is to be sought in the spiritual history of the protagonists. A tragedy achieves artistic unity when every incident is subordinate and auxiliary to the vivid presentation of what these said and did as they passed through some great and fatal crisis. . . . Webster's division of the tragedy into the story of a crime and the story of its avenging has interfered with this concentration and proportioning of the interest.[29]

Grierson's swift appraisals do not permit a longer look at Webster, a look taken by later critics who find precisely a "spiritual history" bringing forth a definite tragic unity in *The Duchess of Malfi.*

Martin W. Sampson found a fairly good reception for his editing in 1906 of the two tragedies in the early Belles-Lettres series. As we might expect from an editor, Sampson takes pains to refute certain charges levelled at his dramatist for many years. Portions of his introduction are good:

> The most obvious mark of our playwright's work is not, I take it, his most characteristic quality. The gruesome imagery, the scenes of blood and horror . . . by no means constitute the whole of Webster: that which is still more characteristic is the intensity with which he conceives and presents a situation, and to emphasize his meaning utilizes horror where another poet would employ something else. To regard Webster's gruesomeness as purely ancillary would be to go too far; but it is assuredly needful to discount the censure of those who see this gruesomeness only. . . . It is not the presence of a crime, but the use made of it, that determines its significance. . . .

> no one who has mastered the essential spirit of Webster will hesitate to think that much of that spirit passed on to Milton—not to Swift the satirist, but to Milton the lover of truth.[30]

Noting one failure, however, Sampson writes that "a real hero Webster has not succeeded in portraying. . . . he seems not to have apprehended the dramatic value of a strong and active man who follows righteous things."[31] This critic prefers *The Duchess of Malfi* to *The White Devil.* The poetic appeal of the former is more permanent than that of the latter, with its repellent story, although *The White Devil* is saved by its technique of dazzling evil and vigorous characters. Webster's greatest power, ultimately, is to put into one utterance something that leaves little else to be said; and "Webster fixes a termination to the drama whose power is in the expression of intense moods."[32] What remains longest with us is Sampson's defense of Websterian horror—it is not the presence of it, but the use made of it. The Webster enthusiast might feel that later critics in attacking Webster for his horrors failed to read Sampson's introduction, which remains worthy.

In 1908 came A. A. Thorndike's *Tragedy* and F. E. Schelling's *Elizabethan Drama,* both to become well-known works. Neither adds anything of particular importance to Webster criticism, though Webster comes off quite well in both treatments. Schelling celebrates the intensity of Webster, while Thorndike discusses Webster in the light of the revenge tradition.

A brief, close reading of Webster's poetry came in 1909 from J. Le Gay Brereton in *Elizabethan Drama*. In the process of making textual comments on Sampson's edition, he notes accurately that

Webster's verse is full of difficulties because he never forgot that it was to be spoken on the stage. He habitually makes more than the usual allowance for natural pause, gesture, and intonation. What a modern writer might suggest by italics, he effects by organic change in his verse. Study, for example, the acting value of the pauses in these lines:

> Yeeld, Yeeld! I give you the honour of armes,
> Shake my sword over you; will you yeeld?

CARD. Helpe me, I am your brother![33]

Volume VII of the *Cambridge History of English Literature* was published in 1910, and chapter seven on Webster and Tourneur, by C. E. Vaughan, gives a more or less official stamp to Webster's greatness. Vaughan draws on several sources previously noted and adds very little to our store of knowledge, except for some well-phrased impressions and one of the few early linkings of Webster to "Donne, greatest lyric poet of the period."[34] He remarks with finality on the debt Webster owes to Shakespeare: "It appears in many turns of thought and phrase; in the portrait of the boy, Giovanni; in the haunting beauty of Cornelia's dirge; in the consummate art, bold yet unostentatious, with which the figure of the heroine is painted; above all, in that union of imaginative reflection, pure poetry, and dramatic genius which brings him nearer than any of his fellow dramatists to the author of Hamlet."[35] Vaughan is one of the first critics to see any real point in the famous last act of *The Duchess of Malfi*. The whole of the last suffers from a lack of dramatic interest, but the intention of Webster, for Vaughan, is clear. Here is the nemesis which falls on the avengers, and growing out of the whole play is a unity of tone which "surpasses all others of the period, save those of Shakespeare."[36] (Later, however, some reversal of this attitude comes with the statement that had the play "ended with the fourth act, the tragic impression would have been yet deeper and more harmonious than it is."[37])

For the most part, the important article maintains that Webster does little wrong. His great sense of tragic issues links him finally with the greatest of the dramatists: "Shakespeare found the deepest tragedy in the resistance of unborn heroism to all assaults from without; in the triumph of the inner self, when all outward happiness is dashed in pieces. So it is in *Hamlet, King Lear,* and *Othello.* And something of the same is attained in *The White Devil* and *The Duchess of Malfi.*"[38] For many undergraduates Webster is forever fixed by this widely used survey.

Between 1913 and 1917 H. D. Sykes, writing in *Notes and Queries,* carried on the type of work done by Crawford in that journal. In several notes (later published in his 1924 *Sidelights on Elizabethan Drama*) Sykes dealt with the date of *The White Devil,* Webster's share in *A Cure for a Cuckold,* his contributions to the Overbury *Characters,* and the date of *Appius and Virginia.* During the period 1914–15 A. F. Bourgeois in the same journal considered Webster's contributions to the *Characters.* His thesis generally is that Webster stole from himself, injecting some of the set pieces into *The Devil's Law Case* after having borrowed some from his own two tragedies to supply Overbury.

C. V. Boyer's *The Villain as Hero in Elizabethan Tragedy* (1914) takes one of the closest looks yet at *The Duchess of Malfi* and finds a sketchy moral unity therein. Years later, several critics wrote that the Webster vision was not clear; Boyer maintains that this is a valid criticism of Tourneur, but not of Webster. In Tourneur, he writes, the fate of the guilty is no more inevitable than the fate of the innocent. But Webster sees things clearly and relates them to each other with no confusion of right and wrong. Perhaps the first of the "moral critics," Boyer sees in Webster that good has its effect as well as evil: "The innocent may suffer from the heartlessness and ambition of the wicked, but they can die heroically, and keep alive the good in others, while sure retribution awaits the violator of moral law."[39]

In line with his title, Boyer devotes most of his attention to Bosola. The tragedy is not with the Duchess. Her end is pathetic, not tragic. In an argument later to be challenged, he maintains that the Duchess had a perfect right to marry and that she bears no tragic guilt. Bosola's death, on the other hand, constitutes the tragedy: with no moral standard to guide him, but with an underlying courage and goodness, it is his tragedy "that when once reformed, he should kill the one man he is trying to save, and be killed himself by the villains whom now he seeks to punish."[40] His is the work of divine vengeance; his resolution to tear himself loose from his evil moorings, according to Boyer, restimulates our exhausted emotions and points to reconciliation.

Unfortunately, the death of the Duchess is, as stated, only pathetic; it reveals no law of human destiny connecting action and suffering. This connection is attempted with the villains, but they lack our sympathy. Though we have a moral unity of outlook, the unity of plot is broken. After the fourth act, "the fifth act might not unreasonably be called Bosola's Revenge! Such a change mars the unity of the play."[41] Further: Bosola is not such stuff as tragic heroes are made on. His struggle with moral law is not of sufficient magnitude; he has goodness within him but no grandeur of soul. Unlike Barabas or Richard III, whom Boyer discusses earlier in his study of the villain-hero, Bosola lacks a daring, a courage, an unscrupulousness which brings on a great struggle with moral law. "We applaud what he does . . . but his previous conduct has been too wicked for us to lament his fall as that of a morally good man."[42]

Here is Boyer's interesting conclusion: "The faults of the tragedy are the result of Webster's limited and cynical view of the world. He attempts to depict characters and a situation as universal which human experience refuses to accept as anything but exceptional. . . . We are not carried out of ourselves and thrilled with awe."[43] In his study of Bosola and the moral unity of the tragedy, with the emphasis taken from the Duchess, Boyer's 1914 writing bears a definite kinship with the critical accounts of the 1940's and 1950's. As for his conclusion, we may note that it was written before two world wars.

> But the best I've known,
> Stays here, and changes, breaks, grows old,
>    is blown
> About the winds of the world, and fades from
>    brains
> Of living men, and dies.
>                         Nothing remains.

These lines, similar to the poetry and central thought of John Webster, are not his at all; they come from the pen of Rupert

Brooke, the Byronic figure of the late Georgian years who flashed like a meteor across the English heavens and then disappeared; his early death in World War I cut off his lyrics in what was surely the early stage of his song. Because of his early death, Brooke remains for us a writer who might have been great had not fate intervened. But while many critics of today sadly dismiss him as but the promise of a poet, Brooke lives on in scholarship as the author of one of the better books on Webster, *John Webster and the Elizabethan Drama*, published in 1916, one year after his death.

Whenever—or if ever—we think of Rupert Brooke, we think of such poems as "The Great Lover" and "Grantchester" and Brooke's celebration of life with its wonders, sights, and sounds, a feeling not unlike that of Webster's fiery spirited protagonists. But not unlike Webster is another aspect of Brooke's poetry, a haunting note of pessimism and mutability which creeps into his later poetry as the war clouds lowered. Add to the above lines these:

> So lightly I played with those dark memories,
> Just as a child, beneath the summer skies,
> Plays hour by hour with a strange shining stone,
> For which (he knows not) towns were fire of old,
>     And love has been betrayed, and murder done,
> And great kings turned to a little bitter mould.

And in many other poems Brooke, the erstwhile patriotic idealist, indicates the coming *Zeitgeist* by his poetic efforts to find solitude, flight and escape, and relief from a pressing, sometimes dirty world. So it is not improbable that a spirit like Brooke's could find deep interest in the kindred spirit of Webster.

His book was actually written in 1911–12 and was the essay with which Brooke won a fellowship at King's College, Cambridge, in 1913. He was a spirited youth of twenty-four; the charm of the book is that it reflects this very youth and spirit. It amuses; it probably outrages some scholars in its sarcastic, effective dismissal of certain tenets; it reflects Brooke's own temperament by being at one moment absurdly colloquial and at the next, stylistically brilliant; and finally, it entertains and instructs. It indicates the coming taste for the Jacobean dramatists among certain major postwar poets, poets whose careers were not ended on board a French hospital ship in the Aegean Sea.

Although Webster is the main subject of the book, eighty-three of one hundred sixty-two pages are devoted to the progress of the Elizabethan drama and its traditions, and to the theater itself. A lengthy appendix contributes the real scholarship, which centers mainly on linguistic and metrical evidence to prove that Heywood, not Webster, was the chief author of *Appius and Virginia*. But in his fourth chapter Webster study begins, and Brooke begins by stating what we are sometimes led to believe by reading of Webster's problems upon the stage: " . . . he emerged from Henslowe's stable with so little facility in writing, and so little aptitude for a good plot (in the ordinary sense), that one must conclude that his genius was not best fitted for theatrical expression, into which it was driven."[44] He would have been more effective untrammelled by dramatic needs: "One can see, almost quote from, a rather large grey-brown novel by John Webster. . . ."[45] Of interest is Brooke's commentary on the revenge play, pertinent because of the disparaging remarks of later critics such as Edwards and Jack in *Scrutiny*. There we read of one of Webster's great flaws: that of limiting his vision to the close confines of the revenge play tradition. One wonders if they had read these lines of Brooke closely:

There is something in the idea, but not much; and it has been over-worked. . . . The truth is that there was a certain type of play, the plot of which was based on blood-for-blood vendetta, and the atmosphere of which had a peculiar tinge. . . . later, the atmosphere became indistinguishable from that of a good many plays of the period. . . . Webster used it in one of two plays that in other ways resemble the work of other people who used the revenge plot. That is all. To call *The Duchess of Malfi* a revenge-play is simply ridiculous. If it is raked in, you must include *Othello* and a dozen more as well. . . . It would be much more sensible to invent and trace the "Trial-at-law" type, beginning with the *Eumenides* . . . till you ended with Galsworthy's *Justice*.[46]

Before moving on to general Websterian characteristics, Brooke lingers briefly on each Webster play, telling the story and making observations. Though *The White Devil* admittedly is not told very skillfully from a dramaturgic point of view, the characters, he writes, should not be castigated for improper motivation: "Characters in a play gain in realism . . . if they act unexplainedly on instinct, like people in real life, and not on rational and publicly-stated grounds, like men in some modern plays."[47] *The Duchess of Malfi* is a greater play: "Webster's supreme gift is the blinding revelation of some intense state of mind at a crisis, by some God-given phrase. All the last half of *The Duchess of Malfi* is full of them."[48] And in this play, even more so than in *The White Devil*, Webster is most triumphant at the moment of death: "Webster, more than any other man in the world, has caught the soul just in the second of its decomposition in death, when knowledge seems transcended, and the darkness closes in, and boundaries fall away."[49]

In his chapters on characteristics, Brooke adds little that we have not learned, but his flair for phrase keeps us reading steadily. He points out the great influence of satire, noting that nearly every character and nearly every speech has something of the satiric outlook. The dramatist pillaged John Donne. His method of progression is curiously individual, writing from speech to speech or idea to idea, with no development from one into the other as in Shakespeare: the ideas seem put into the stream of thought from outside, "yet the very cumbrousness of this adds, in a way, to the passion and force of his scenes, as a swift stream seems swifter and wilder when its course is broken by rocks and boulders."[50] Brooke can even defend Webster's pausing for generalizations as a desire to discover the general rule your particular illustration defines, as did the Greeks with their chorus, as do Ibsen and Shaw with the former's catch phrases or symbolic background and the latter's arguing out of the moral. And of Webster's notebook technique: "'Originality' is only plagiarising from a great many. So Webster reset other people's jewels and redoubled their lustre."[51] But in many ways, Webster is like a primitive artisan, achieving a great effect here only to lose it when, say, a fable about a dogfish or salmon is lugged in.

Brooke's conclusion states perhaps the most important concept we have had, a concept of emotional unity unheeded by certain later critics:

The end of the matter is that Webster was a great writer; and the way in which one uses great writers is two-fold. There is the exhilarating way of reading their writing; and there is the essence of the whole man, or of the man's whole work, which you carry away and permanently keep with you. This essence generally presents itself more or less in the form of a view of the universe, recognisable by its emotional rather than logical content.[52]

This much is very true indeed. But we may question Brooke's later analysis of this world as a feverish nest of maggots: "Maggots are what the inhabitants of this universe most resemble. The sight of their fever is only alleviated by the permanent calm, unfriendly summits and darknesses of the background of death and doom. For that is equally a part of Webster's universe. Human beings are writhing grubs in an immense night."[53] Brooke's enthusiasm for the striking phrase here gets the better of him. A nest of maggots would not interest us. The Duchess-Antonio love scene does not strike us as the writhing of two grubs; the pathos of the Duchess in her agony of Act IV moves us beyond the power of such an insipid nest. We think of Giovanni's scenes, and of others. Brooke here has used the wrong simile, but he has used an approach that is necessary for any critic wanting a full appreciation: that of seeing Webster as a dramatist who maintains a view of the world, recognizable not by any logical rules of behavior, but by its emotional tone. While *John Webster and the Elizabethan Drama* remains in the line, for the most part, of scholarly impressionism, Brooke's idea of Webster's steady view of the universe is later explored by critics who perhaps take more learned looks, but who never surpass Brooke's vigor.

And with this book, and in certain of Brooke's poems, we see what is to come: a new interest in Jacobean drama and a new poetry partially inspired by the mood therein. Brooke's patriotic idealism ran high, but, as noted, there was a mood beginning to filter through which might have become a postwar disillusionment similar to that of Siegfried Sassoon, his slightly older contemporary, and, of course, T. S. Eliot. The hint of Webster remains in Brooke's last poetry: the young Duchess herself might have said ". . . The worst friend and enemy is but Death."

But nevertheless, even amid a slowly growing acceptance for Jacobean poetry and drama, as evidenced by the revivals of the Phoenix Society in the second and third decade of the century, William Archer stood steadfast. He remained firmly rooted in the Ibsen middle-class-realistic-well-made-play-tradition, and he would not be moved. Though he overlaps Eliot and Brooke and some of their inspired commentary on Webster, poetry, and drama, he stands firm. While Archer could be incorrigibly uninformed about the genre of Elizabethan drama, he made his points decisively and there were those who listened when he stated that Webster was a

great poet who wrote "haphazard dramatic or melodramatic romances for an eagerly receptive but semibarbarous public."[54] There
are those who still listen.

There are two more onslaughts by Archer after his first article
several years before. In writings in between, disparaging mention
was occasionally made of Webster, but a renewed frontal assault
was not made until January, 1920, in an article in *The Nineteenth
Century*, inspired by the spectacular failure of a Phoenix Society
staging of Webster's *The Duchess of Malfi* a few months previous.
(A fuller account will follow.) Thus Archer begins by noting that the
so-long-delayed reaction against the cult of the lesser Elizabethans,
initiated by Lamb and caricatured by Swinburne, is indeed "being
powerfully promoted by the activities of the Phoenix Society. . . .
the privilege of listening to *The Duchess of Malfi's* occasional
beauties of diction was felt to be dearly bought at the price of
enduring three hours of coarse and sanguinary melodrama."[55] Flail-
ing at Swinburnian "passage-worship," Archer tells us the way it
was—and other reviewers backed him up:

With the death of the duchess, the interest of the play is over; for
Antonio is admittedly a shadowy character as to whose fate we are very
indifferent; and though we are willing to see Ferdinand, the Cardinal,
and Bosola punished, we could quite well dispense with that gratification.
Webster, however, is not the man to leave any of his dramatis personae
alive if he can help it. . . . There is scarcely any room on the stage
for all the corpses; which is perhaps the reason why, in the Phoenix
revival, Ferdinand stands on his head to die, and waves his legs in
the air.[56]

Much of the article covers old ground. Why does Ferdinand delay?
Why doesn't the duchess ever give a word of thought to the
offspring of her first marriage? (One comes to wish that Webster had
taken two minutes during composition to remedy these situations,
and thereby saved much time for critics and reviewers.) Archer
closes with the hope that in the near future criticism of the Elizabethans will be taken from the hands of scholars who know nothing
of the theater and who "have not the elementary power of distinguishing between poetic and specifically dramatic merit."[57]

His final attack on Webster, coupled with a cutting analysis of
Ford, Beaumont and Fletcher, and Tourneur, came in his 1923

volume, *The Old Drama and the New,* a title indicative of bitter things to follow.

And indeed they do. To prove the superiority of modern drama he discusses five Elizabethan plays, because it is either "implicitly assumed or explicitly contended by a good many people, that all these liberties or licences ignoring time, soliloquizing, scene shifting not only facilitated but ennobled the art of the Elizabethans, and that the modern drama in renouncing them has exchanged its birthright for a mess of realistic pottage."[58] Archer has, for the most part, enlarged his *Nineteenth Century* article, and again he sights along his barrel at all logical inconsistencies. He disparages the construction of the play ("What should we say if a modern dramatist presented such a broken backed play to us?") and turns furiously onto the horrors: "Is the invention of this ghastly practical joke the dead man's hand . . . a thing to be admired, and to earn its inventor a place only a little below Sophocles and Shakespeare? I suggest any morbid-minded schoolboy could have conceived it. . . . It is a grisly monstrosity. . . . The wax works . . . are a monstrous improbability . . . the device of a dramatist in search of crude physical horrors."[59] Of Lamb's commentary that other dramatists' terrors "want dignity," he writes: "A more topsy-turvy criticism than this was never penned. Is Ferdinand's trick with a dead man's hand a dignified terror?"[60] All of these master strokes, for Archer, are the work of a calculating playwright with an eye on the box office. The horrors are coldly mechanical: "There is no warmth of imagination, no glow of extravagance about them. They are the work of a man deliberately setting out, in the coldest of cold blood, to make our flesh creep."[61] Bosola's couplets are haunting indeed, but inappropriate as any one of Donizetti. In short, a fine poet may be an inept dramatist. In a sense, Archer reflects one aspect of Brooke's study (which he had read) and his commentary on the literary man's writing for the theater. Webster emerges from this treatment as a poet who subjugated his great talent in an effort to court the semibarbaric public of the Elizabethan-Jacobean age.

Archer never realized that the age was not wholly semibarbaric, and that an Ibsen play might have been hooted off the stage of the Globe. But the time spent by Archer on castigating Webster has had its effect, even when we realize that Archer knew next to nothing about Elizabethan traditions or genres. Robert Ornstein wrote almost forty years later, in 1960: "Although it is possible now to

patronize the misguided William Archer, the specter of his criticism
still hovers over Webster's plays. For however inadequate Archer's
critical theories were, his attacks on the formlessness of Webster's
tragedies contained an irreducible kernel of aesthetic truth."[62]
There will come other, more penetrating efforts which nevertheless
will arrive at some of the same points Archer did, though by
different routes.

Four years after Archer's last outburst and in some ways almost
as an answer to it, came Frank Laurence Lucas' definitive edition
of *The Complete Works of John Webster*, which included, with
the two tragedies, *The Devil's Law Case, A Cure for a Cuckold*, and
*Appius and Virginia*; conjectural works, the *Characters, Anything
for a Quiet Life, The Fair Maid of the Inn*; and the poetic works, *A
Monumental Column, The Malcontent Induction*, and *Monuments
of Honor*.[63] We look briefly at the Lucas work here because the
introduction gave a telling answer to Archer and because as far as
critical methods are concerned, it seems to belong earlier in the third
decade than it actually is. Lucas stands outside the pale of many of
the new theories which began to permeate the scholarly atmosphere
with the arrival of Hulme and then Eliot. Lucas seems to have paid
little heed to the writings of Eliot and his followers, either in critical
analysis or in his own writing style: in many ways Lucas' romantic
phrasings take us back to Lamb, Hazlitt, and Swinburne. Thus we
should not be surprised to hear him condemn in a later (1933)
Cambridge Poetry lecture the "anemic arrogance" of "the critical
school of T. S. Eliot,"[64] nor at his occasional Swinburnian turn of
phrase: "Like some great ragged thundercloud he piles up slowly to
overshadow his world with the sinister yellow darkness that he
loves; the atmosphere grows stifling; and then comes the sudden
glare before which the situation lies revealed in all its vivid naked-
ness, with an intensity of black and white that calm daylight could
never have given."[65] But this is by no means to disparage Lucas.
The editor praises the youthful vigor of Rupert Brooke's account,
and his introductions share much of this same enthusiastic liveliness.
It is that oddity, an edition for the lay reader: ". . . my object
above all else has been . . . to get Webster enjoyed."[66]

As stated, Lucas is outside the world of Eliot. His introduction is
the work not of a New Critic, but of an historical critic; and the first
thing Lucas does is to deal with Archer's attacks. Archer's approach
is hardly the best way to look at the Elizabethans, he writes, for

it was a succession of great moments they wanted on the stage, not a well-made play. [They: the Red Bull and Phoenix audiences.] They did not at each instant look forward to what was coming or back to what had been. If a dramatist gave them great situations, ablaze with passion and poetry, it would have seemed to them a chilly sort of pedantry that peered too closely into the machinery by which these were produced. They did not want their fireworks analyzed.[67]

Archer, implies Lucas, must not be able to discern the difference between a detective story and a fairy tale. And he notes, importantly, that "*The White Devil,* well acted, can carry an audience breathless with it over all the breaks and rough places in the plot, with the irresistible onrush of a great roller surging up a rocky beach."[68] Archer is furious because we allow the Elizabethans their conventions. "But why was the privilege given them? Because they justified it by their results—above all, by their poetry."[69] Lucas, ever the historical critic and not really the aesthetic critic, thinks we must look at his tragedies "as his audience saw them—less as wholes than as a series of great situations. . . . But his work remains more than a mere chaos of dramatic fragments, and he is a highly successful playwright in his own Gothic style."[70] Webster is the master of the sudden flash and the brooding, sullen atmosphere. And among his contemporaries, "Donne and Donne alone . . . has the same wildcat way of springing straight at the throat."[71]

Lucas' discussion of his characters reflects the commentary of Brooke. It is their unexpectedness of behavior which gives them life: "They have the power, which real people possess and puppets lack, of growing familiar to us and yet at certain moments saying or doing what we did not look for from them."[72] Painted with broad brushes, the characters are yet treated occasionally with a delicacy of touch. Vittoria and Flamineo are the greatest, in that they continue, for Lucas, to exist with the reality of living people. But for all the high-spirited gaiety of the Duchess, "she becomes too much the passive martyr."[73]

Webster's greatest talent, outshining his unequal technique and uncertain psychology, is, of course, his poetry—his gift "not only for the pure poetry of word and image, but for the poetry also of personality and atmosphere; and lastly for the poetry of a most embittered and tragic view of life."[74] To criticize Webster without a personal taste for poetry "is to be like a deaf man judging Wagner; and Archer's attack was little wiser."[75] His two main qualities of imagery are his bitterness and the love of the macabre. There seems to be an undertone of personal grievance and disappointment with the world, but personal or not, he caught the mood of his time.

And finally, Lucas writes on the emphasis certain critics have put on the horrors in Webster, making him the Elizabethan Edgar Allan Poe. They have forgotten, he writes, Shakespearean slaughter and Gloucester's blinding. And of the dead man's hand: "Too many of the present generation have stumbled about in the darkness among month-old corpses on the battlefields of France to be much impressed by the falsetto uproar which this piece of 'business' occasioned in nineteenth century minds."[76]

If there is any philosophy, writes Lucas near his close, it is "the courage of despair. . . . Indeed it seems as if he felt courage to be the one vital thing in life."[77] There is little moral outlook for Lucas; Webster's world is one where there is no consolation "but the gallant splendour, the ironic laughter of a humanity that is braver and cleverer than the blind Universe which drags it down."[78] And of the fact that the good pay for their virtues in Webster's world as the evil pay for their sins: "The charge Sir William Watson brings against Webster is, in short, perfectly true—'virtue in this disordered world is merely wasted, honour bears not issue, nobleness dies unto itself.' Only it happens to be true of the real world, too."[79] And as if anticipating later criticism, Lucas adds "There is nothing mean in the view that goodness often does not pay. The meanness lies in demanding that it should."[80] The real accusation, ultimately, "for those who want to belittle Webster because he is not Shakespeare, is that, when great, he is not myriad-minded. . . . Not all the larks in the real world are caged, and there are greenwood-trees besides the yew."[81]

Of the two tragedies, we may note briefly that Lucas prefers *The White Devil* and the splendor of its heroine, and its steady progression to its catastrophe. There is a wondrous unity of tone in *The Duchess of Malfi*, a new and gentler grace, and two or three supreme scenes; but the Duchess is too passive, Antonio is not good enough for the woman he has won, and the play should have ended with Act IV: "It lives too long, when it outlives the heroine."[82] For Webster's editor, there is little point in Act V.

The John Webster, then, of the definitive edition, emerges as a writer whose greatest talent lay in the creation of two or three characters and situations, and especially "in the world which he has

made their background, in the light of poetry and the darkness of a
great despair."[83] And courage is the only virtue in a hopeless,
amoral world. Lucas writes this against the background of the
twenties, a world which for many writers was similar to Webster's.
It had already seen a poem which made partial use of Webster's
atmosphere of decay; and as for Webster's great virtues, courage
and endurance in the face of this atmosphere—Hemingway's *A
Farewell to Arms* would appear two years later, in 1929.

# 5

# ELIOT, LEAVIS, AND *SCRUTINY*

The true Shakespearean critic will be concerned to make himself, as far as possible, a contemporary of Shakespeare. . . . But more important, he will also be concerned to make Shakespeare a contemporary, to see his particular relevance for our time. His essential qualification, then, is a lively interest in the present and the immediate future of poetry, an ability to make first-hand judgments, coupled, we would add, with an understanding of the extra-literary implications of poetry—its relation to "the general situation"—*at present*. . . . we demand that the Shakespeare commentator shall at least be able to recognize critical excellence, that he shall know what the real problems are that need elucidation.

L. C. Knights' *Scrutiny* review of
Eliot's *Elizabethan Essays*
(December, 1934)

For the modern critical approach to Webster we need only substitute his name for that of Shakespeare.

For many years Webster criticism when favorable has been more of a eulogistic nature than anything else. The brilliance of his poetry has been saluted, his unity of tone occasionally celebrated, his cold-blooded horrors duly appreciated. But from the twenties onward, there is a concerted critical effort to explain why he is effective, if he is, or to give specific reasons for his failure. The writings and influence of T. S. Eliot, supplemented by F. R. Leavis' *Scrutiny* magazine, have done much to shape later evaluations. Almost all of the important later Webster criticism owes something to their doctrines.

Perhaps we first should look at the critical trend in the twenties and thirties to see again some of the reasons for a resurgence of energy in Elizabethan scholarship. During this period there were stage revivals, new and definitive Elizabethan editions, and much scholarship. It was Webster's mood, for one thing, which was sympathetic to the outlook of many thinkers in the twentieth-century wasteland which saw two world wars. Yet another reason for a certain Elizabethan renaissance was, of course, Eliot's revaluation of the literature of our past, the subjugation of the Romantics and the elevation of the Elizabethan-Jacobean dramatists and metaphysicals.

T. E. Hulme helped to begin it all in his now famous essay, "Romanticism and Classicism," written *ca.* 1913–14: "I object even to the best of the romantics. I object still more to the receptive attitude. I object to the sloppiness which doesn't consider that a poem is a poem unless it is moaning or whining about something or other. . . . The thing has got so bad now that a poem which is all dry and hard, a properly classical poem, would not be considered poetry at all."[1] In another article, he began to develop a view that from the dregs of the Renaissance until now, a Romantic state of mind has existed which shouldn't have. "It is perhaps enough to say that, taking at first the form of the 'humanities,' it has in its degeneracy taken the form of a belief in 'Progress' and the rest of it." He attacks the romantic conviction of Rousseau that man is by nature wonderful, of unlimited powers which external obstacles have probably concealed; he can say, possibly as he sees a world war rage around him, that his conviction is that "man is by nature bad or limited, and can consequently only accomplish anything of value by disciplines, ethical, heroic or political. In other words, it [Classicism] believes in Original Sin."[2] Discipline and control—these seem to be the key factors in his critical writings: "Man is an extraordinarily fixed and limited animal whose nature is absolutely constant. It is only by tradition and organization that anything decent can be got out of him."[3] And on poetic expression:

What I mean by classical verse, then, is this. That even in the most imaginary flights there is always a holding back, a reservation. The classical poet never forgets this finiteness, this limit of man. He remembers always that he is mixed up with earth. He may jump, but he always returns back; he never flies away into the circumambient gas.[4]

. . . . . .

It is essential to prove that beauty may be in small, dry things. The great aim is accurate, precise, and definite composition. . . . language has its own special nature, its own conventions and communal ideas. It is only by a concentrated effort of the mind that you can hold it fixed to your own purpose. . . . The artist I take to be the man who simply can't bear the idea of . . . "approximately." He will get the exact curve of what he sees whether it be an object or an idea in the mind.[5]

. . . . . .

. . . it is the zest with which you look at a thing which decides you to make the effort. . . . It doesn't matter an atom that the emotion produced is not of dignified vagueness, but on the contrary amusing; the point is that exactly the same activity is at work as in the highest verse. That is the avoidance of conventional language in order to get the exact curve of the thing.[6]

Finally, good (*i.e.*, classical) poetry should deal with a complexity that is, after all, organic. " . . . the parts cannot be said to be elements as each one is modified by the other's presence, and each to a certain extent is the whole."[7] This seems to be the classical vision of romantic organicism; but we come out with a cleaner, trimmer work of art.

In short, we are, says Hulme, at the end of an age, as witnessed by the artistic exhaustion of the nineteenth century. He notes prophetically, "We shall not get any new efflorescence of verse until we get a new technique, a new convention, to turn ourselves loose in."[8] And Webster's critical fate can almost be predicted from one or two of Hulme's lines: ". . . even in the most imaginary flights, there is always a holding back, a reservation. . . . the great aim is accurate, precise, and definite composition." As we read Hulme and Eliot, we remember that although Webster possesses some of the virtues Eliot and Hulme require, such as "zest" in composition and freshness of phrase, Webster is essentially a romantic writer: "I am Duchess of Malfi still," rings the famous cry.

The "new convention to turn ourselves loose in" came with T. S. Eliot. Finishing the work of Hulme and then moving forward, Eliot and his praise of the Elizabethan and Jacobean dramatists and the nondramatic metaphysical poets, and his establishment of their lofty place in the direct line of English poetry—which, for Eliot, ceased after the metaphysicals—reawakened the interests of many serious readers, and is worth a brief re-examination here. Like Hulme, Eliot saw something unfortunate happening to the English mind between George Herbert and Robert Browning. But unlike Hulme, he was specific. The famous essay in 1921 on the metaphysical poets spelled it out: explaining the methods of intellectual condensation of these poets, he writes:

This telescoping of images and multiplied associations is characteristic of the phrase of some of the dramatists of the period which Donne knew; not to mention Shakespeare, it is frequent in Middleton, Webster, and Tourneur, and is one of the sources of vitality of the language. . . .

If so shrewd a critic as Johnson failed to define metaphysical poetry by its faults, it is worthwhile to inquire whether we may not have more success by adopting the opposite method: by assuming that the poets of the seventeenth century (up to the Revolution) were the direct and normal development of the precedent age; and, without prejudicing their case by the adjective "Metaphysical," consider whether their virtue was not something permanently valuable, which subsequently disappeared, but ought not to have disappeared.[9]

The later Elizabethans and early Jacobean poets were notably men who incorporated their erudition into their sensibility—"their mode of feeling was directly and freshly altered by their reading and thought. In Chapman especially, there is a direct sensuous apprehension of thought, a recreation of thought into feeling, which is exactly what we find in Donne."[10] Then comes the widely quoted passage concerning the intellectual poet and the reflective poet, the latter group, unlike the Jacobean dramatists and poets, being unable to "feel their thought immediately as the odour of a rose. A thought to Donne was an experience, it modified his sensibility."[11] There follows the equally famous dethronement of Milton and Dryden, whose magnitude of certain effects concealed the absence of others. The language became refined; the feeling became crude. The dissociation of sensibility had set in; the main line of English poetry veered after the seventeenth century dramatists and poets.

In his 1923 "Andrew Marvell" Eliot continued to praise the Elizabethans and Jacobeans, and continued to reset thinking as to the true mainstream of English poetry: "The seventeenth century seems for more than a moment to gather up and digest into its art all the experience of the human mind which . . . the later centuries seem to have been partly engaged in repudiating."[12] This essay finds his celebration of wit (unexaggerated) opposed to magniloquence, defined as the exploitation of the possibilities of magnificence in language, an exploitation which dissociates thought from feeling. Milton's grandeur triumphed, however, and by the time we reach Collins and Gray, they and other poets "had lost their hold on human values, that firm grasp of human experience which is a formidable achievement of the Elizabethan and Jacobean poets."[13] This only supplemented Eliot's earlier remarks in his essay on Massinger. There, quoting Tourneur and Middleton, he noted that their fresh juxtaposition of words into new and sudden combinations illustrates "a very high development of the English language which we have never equalled. And, indeed, with the end of Chapman, Middleton, Webster, Tourneur, Donne, we end a period when the intellect was immediately at the tips of the senses. Sensation became word and word was sensation."[14] Massinger lacked his predecessors' art; and Massinger led forward to Milton.

The answers come easily enough when we ask ourselves what specifically attracted Eliot to Webster. Webster's freshness of phrase, his vocabulary, like Donne's at once colloquial and weird, giving new meaning to experience (the proper function of a poet, for Eliot), his irregular verse, and his view of a disintegrating world in which nearly every virtue is missing. All of these qualities in Webster left their mark on the young writer who, at thirty-four, made use of them in the universe of *The Waste Land*. But perhaps Webster's main influence comes under the general heading of a borrowed atmosphere.[15] In Webster as in Baudelaire, Eliot found earlier "unreal cities," not wholly filled with brown fogs, dull canals, murky streets, but with similar repulsive imagery and a corresponding emphasis on the sordid, the decaying, and the completely disintegrated. Ultimately, perhaps, Eliot found the same element in Webster which attracted him to William Blake. Writing in 1920 on Blake, Eliot notes in his work that elusive substance of great poetry, a "peculiar honesty,"

which, in a world too frightened to be honest, is peculiarly terrifying. It is an honesty against which the whole world conspires, because it is unpleasant. Blake's poetry has the unpleasantness of great poetry. Nothing that can be called morbid or abnormal or perverse, none of the things which exemplify the sickness of an epoch or a fashion, have this quality; only those things which, by some extraordinary labour of simplification, exhibit the essential sickness or strength of the human soul.[16]

Thus the attraction of Webster for Eliot, and, from our previous examinations, thus the general Elizabethan-Jacobean attraction for Eliot. Most of Eliot's writings on the Jacobean dramatists and metaphysical poets were actually book reviews or articles in *The*

*Criterion, The Athenaeum,* and elsewhere; reprinted later in *The Sacred Wood, Homage to John Dryden, Elizabethan Essays,* and his *Selected Essays,* they brought a revived interest in the earlier period, enabling poets of his own time to see more clearly the actual tradition which they had inherited. Eliot tried to prove that these were our greatest ancestors, whose writing appealed simultaneously to thought, feeling, and the senses; their poetry illustrates that it is quite possible to assimilate and absorb varied experiences and to reunite them in a new unity. Their poetry proves that it is possible to *think* in lyric verse; and what they thought has relevance for us today. Eliot's own verse was read, and his criticism heeded.

When we finally arrive at Eliot's specific judgment of Webster— and his actual Webster commentary is limited to four short articles plus brief mention here and there in other essays—one line stands out, and perhaps continues to influence commentators of today: Webster, he wrote in 1924, provides "an interesting example of a very great literary and dramatic genius directed toward chaos."[17] This is not a wholly new criticism, but Eliot had previously given a new emphasis to craftmanship.

We must go back to Hulme and his celebration of Organization and Discipline in men and in literature. In classical poetic flights, he wrote, there is always a holding back. Eliot took these doctrines and amplified them; we find them in his criticism of Webster, and, of course, underlying his criticism of almost everybody else. Thus we are not surprised, after reading Webster and then the following passage from Eliot, to hear that the dramatist is "directed toward chaos." In any time, in any age,

the larger part of the labour of an author is critical labour, the labour of sifting, combining, constructing, expunging, correcting, testing: this frightful toil is as much critical as creative. I maintain even that the criticism employed by a trained and skilled writer on his own work is the most vital, the highest kind of criticism; and (as I think I have said before) that some creative writers are superior to others solely because their critical faculty is superior.[18]

In the 1923 essay, "The Function of Criticism," he turns to critical methods which should complement the artist's critical labor and states opinions which become law for Leavis and the *Scrutiny* group and the American "New Critics," and which firmly renounce most of the critical methods we have seen thus far. A critic must have a highly developed sense of fact as opposed to gifts of interpretation. Who can really confirm the "interpretation"? Interpretation is only valid if it gives us facts we might have missed. Eliot offered something fairly new:

Comparison and analysis . . . are the chief tools of the critic. . . . Comparison and analysis need only the cadavers on the table; but interpretation is always producing parts of the body from its pockets, and fixing them in place. . . . Of course the multiplication of critical books and essays may create, and I have seen it create, a vicious taste for reading about works of art instead of reading the works themselves. But fact cannot corrupt taste. . . . The real corrupters are those who supply opinion or fancy; and Goethe and Coleridge are not guiltless—for what is Coleridge's *Hamlet*: is it an honest inquiry as far as the data permit, or is it an attempt to present Coleridge in an attractive costume? . . . For the kinds of critical work which we have admitted, there is the possibility of cooperative activity, with the further possibility of arriving at something outside of ourselves, which may provisionally be called truth.[19]

In these comments we have the formulation for the close view and almost the official rejection of the impressionistic methods of the nineteenth century.

For many critics, then, the rules called for a close scrutiny of the tangible object, without reference to whether a frantic day's activity had anything to do with the poem written that evening; reference to biography or the age was unimportant. Good writing holds up, whatever the age; and it holds up because of the craftsmanship of the author. There is a large emphasis, in the Eliot-Hulme writings, on the process of composition, as we have seen from Eliot's remarks on the importance of an author's critical labor. We can foresee Eliot's qualified praise of Webster and his "directed-toward-chaos" comment in other observations concerning craftsmanship: writing on Dante, for instance, he tells us that "the aim of the poet is to state a vision, and no vision can be complete which does not include the articulate formulation of life which human minds make."[20] (Is Webster's vision articulate? Is it formulated? For some, yes; for Eliot, no.) And in Eliot's most famous essay, "Tradition and the Individual Talent," we have his idea of the impersonal aspect of art: "Poetry is not a turning loose of emotion, but an escape from emotion; it is not the expression of personality, but an escape from personality."[21] And the emphasis is always on the way the writing

holds together: "For it is not the 'greatness,' the intensity, of the
emotions, the components, but the intensity of the artistic process,
the pressure, so to speak, under which the fusion takes place that
counts."[22] And as we read his account of Webster's sporadic greatness, we might remember his lines from an essay on John Ford:

The whole of Shakespeare's work is one poem, and it is the poetry of it
in this sense, not the poetry of isolated lines and passages or the poetry
of the single figures which he created, that matters most. A man might,
hypothetically, compose any number of fine passages or even of whole
poems . . . and yet not be a great poet unless we felt them to be united
by one significant, consistent, and developing personality. Shakespeare
is the one, among all his contemporaries, who fulfills these conditions;
and the nearest to him is Marlowe. Jonson and Chapman have the consistency, but a far lower degree of significant development; Middleton
and Webster take a lower place than these.[23]

And so we move to Eliot's specific criticism. We have noted
Webster's favorable influence on Eliot; but as already intimated,
Webster is not Eliot's ideal dramatist. Eliot turned to Webster
specifically on four occasions: he reviewed a 1919 production of *The
Duchess of Malfi;* he reviewed Lucas' 1927 edition; he mentions him
in his "Four Elizabethan Dramatists" essay; and he delivered a radio
talk in 1941 for the BBC's Third Programme. Of these, only the
"Four Elizabethan Dramatists" essay has been collected.

In the latter, which is subtitled "A Preface to an Unwritten Book,"
Eliot concerned himself with conventions and the fact that many
Elizabethans lacked dramatic boundaries. We see in this 1924
writing Eliot's usual concern with form and disciplined creation. He
first criticizes Lamb who, by publishing excerpts of Elizabethan
plays, set in motion the fatal idea that drama and poetry are two
separate things. (Four years earlier, Eliot had had similar harsh
words about Lamb: ". . . a form is not wholly dead until it is
known to be, and Lamb by exhuming the remains of dramatic life at
its fullest, brought a consciousness of the immense gap between
present and past."[24]) But Eliot's main interest is in answering
Archer's attacks: he tries to explain *why* the Elizabethan dramatic
faults *are* faults.

It is that the Elizabethans were artistically greedy. The Elizabethans actually admit the same criteria of realism that Archer
asserts, *but:* "The aim of the Elizabethans was to attain complete
realism without surrendering any of the advantages which as artists
they observed in unrealistic conventions."[25] They aim in too many

directions: it is essential that a work of art "should be self-consistent, that an artist should consciously or unconsciously draw a circle beyond which he does not trespass: on the one hand actual life is always the material, and on the other hand an abstraction from actual life is a necessary condition to the creation of a work of art."[26] Let the Elizabethans have their ghosts; the convention itself is perfectly all right. Never mind Archer. Only let there not be so many *varieties* of ghosts. The weakness of their drama is not their lack of realism, but is "the same weakness of that of modern drama, it is the lack of a convention."[27] In all, the "art of the Elizabethans is an impure art."[28] Closing, Eliot would like to see an examination of Webster (and here he makes the previously noted remark that he is a genius directed toward chaos), Middleton, Tourneur, and Chapman in the light of these commentaries on the need for conventions. We realize that this essay would be the starting point for Eliot's feelings on Webster—a man who practised, with occasional greatness, an art that was essentially impure. It was an art which needed boundaries to arrest the flow of spirit. We cannot help realizing, as we finish the article, that while Eliot repudiates Archer's methods of investigation, he very nearly arrives at the same conclusions as Archer himself.[29]

Eliot's review in *The Criterion* of Lucas' Webster edition was not included in any of his collections of essays, but there is no need to regret its loss. Primarily, Eliot concentrates on challenging editor Lucas' view of the Renaissance as too fanciful (like the Elizabethan's imaginative picture of Italy and Spain); he says very little about Lucas' subject. In fact, after questioning Lucas' views of the age, he closes without giving his own.

Although the edition is magnificent, he writes, the introduction is questionable. Lucas' picture of the time—men free from repressions and conformities until a darker mood set in—is "too highly coloured by Elizabethan drama: it is a literary view. On the other hand, his criticism of Webster is coloured by an imaginary and partial impression of what the Renaissance must have been like." Lucas fails to distinguish clearly between "the attitude of an age, the attitude of a group of dramatists, and the attitude of an individual. . . . the three are never quite commensurable."[30] For the most part, the essay is bad Eliot. The chief trouble with the review is that it criticizes without correcting.

In another uncollected essay, Eliot writes on seeing *The Duchess*

*of Malfi* produced in London in 1919, a disaster of which the reports
will come later. The Phoenix Society had staged the play in November of that year, with Cathleen Nesbitt as the Duchess. This staging
seems to have been most unfortunate. All the reviews blamed the
failure on the inability of Webster's plays to be produced; only Eliot
saw it as a serious indictment of the modern stage. He admits that
the result was not only dull, but ridiculous. Never was the poetry
allowed to reach the audience; Miss Nesbitt was never the Duchess,
only herself creating a part: "We require only that she transmit the
lines, but to transmit lines is beyond the self-control of the modern
actor, and so she did what the modern actor does: she 'interpreted'
them. She had to throw in a little titter, a feminine gesture or
two . . . and she became not the Duchess, but something like the
correspondent in a drama of divorce."[31]

We may observe that Eliot, in defending the general fifth act
assassinations, makes a remark which is true in theory: they are "a
form of Exit. They no more indicate a strong appetite for blood than
the Nuntius and Confidente indicate a strong interest in the servant
class."[32] But, we might note, it takes a soul of high seriousness not
to be amused at the collapse of bodies in front of us during a staging
of the play.

Finally, Eliot arrives at his chief intent in his review, a biting
criticism of the current scene: "We want the enjoyment of spoken
poetry across the stage, the design of a scene, of costume . . .
something very fine taking place before a number of people. No
modern poet is capable of writing it, and there is not the smallest
likelihood that the modern actor, with his interpretative gifts, would
allow the poetry to reach the audience even if a poet wrote it and a
producer accepted it."[33] Shakespeare survives because his drama is
better constructed; even then the poetry is tolerated because over-
looked. Eliot, in the tradition of discipline, wants a new breed of
actor. One kind alone cannot perform properly in the large variety
of stage plays which exists. A performance by the Phoenix of an old
classic is bad archaeology. And he makes a plea for an actor's breed
(which we realize does not exist and never will): ". . . we have seen
every Hamlet but Shakespeare's. . . . There is no such thing as the
interpretation of poetry; poetry can only be transmitted; in consequence, the ideal actor for a poetic drama is the actor with no
personal vanity. . . . the training that any contemporary actor has
received is apt to make him devote more attention to himself than to

such a person as John Webster."[34] Poetry on the stage is dead, he laments, and has been for two hundred years. Perhaps thinking of what he was to write in years to come, he calls for a writer concerned with a dominant tone, an intense effect, one unworried over entrances and exits. Meanwhile, he says, it is a good idea to revive Webster and his company, because it also revives our dissatisfaction with the conditions under which they are produced. In short, the failure of this revival is not Webster's failure, but the producer's and actors'. But what Eliot seems to want, we must add, seems impossible. To be sure, we now have classical repertory groups and various "specialized actors," but, though he denies it elsewhere,[35] Eliot seems to want an actor to be a vanilla-flavored mannequin. The truth remains that we hear an interpretation any time we hear a reading.

The only occasion on which Eliot dealt at length with Webster was a BBC radio broadcast. The talk was later reprinted in *The Listener* for December 18, 1941, during the tumult of the first days of the Second World War. Addressed to the reading public at large, it is clear and concise.

Eliot's general view in 1941, at least, is that Webster ranks with Marlowe and Shakespeare in the sense that each was representative of one of the traditional three stages of artistic progression. Marlowe's work is exemplary of the rise of the drama, Shakespeare of course represents the perfection of the art, and Webster is symbolic of that drama in its decline.

Later Eliot holds up *The Duchess of Malfi* as Webster's greatest play. He takes a cue from Lucas' introduction about the audience's desire for the Big Scene, and never-mind-the-logic: "Plays are written to be seen and heard: very few of the audience of *The Duchess of Malfy* would see it again and again, or would read it afterwards."[36] And he arrives at this familiar appraisal: "I therefore ask you to look at *The Duchess of Malfy* and to remember it, first of all, by certain scenes."[37] And we realize that we are back in familiar territory: there follows the traditional praise of the marriage scene, the eavesdropping-by-Ferdinand scene, the torture scene, which is ranked next in power to the Lear storm scene. And then:

But if there is this important difference between the work of Webster and that of Shakespeare—the difference between the truth which can be expressed in great scenes and the greater truth which can only be expressed in a whole play, there is also a great difference between Webster and most of his contemporaries. Beaumont and Fletcher could also write single impressive scenes, but there is this difference, that there is throughout a consistency of tone, if not of plot and character, which indicates, I believe, a profounder moral and artistic seriousness.[38]

Webster's consistency of tone results partly from his great gift of language and style, a natural, overflowing gift reminiscent of Donne.[39] As he closes, Eliot begins to touch on moral aspects involved, but a touch is all we get. He writes of the twinges of "spiritual terror" we find in *The Duchess of Malfi,* and points out that it is not accurate to say that even though in the decline, "his work shows a *moral* decadence. In a world without meaning there can still be horror, but not tragedy. Webster's drama is tragic, and belongs to a world in which right and wrong, the soul and its destiny, are still the most important things."[40]

Eliot's call for a new view of English poetry—a renewed appreciation for those Elizabethans and Jacobeans able to fuse together thought and feeling—and his own exploitation of many of the same writers in his poetry had a lasting effect. Further, it was generally agreed that modern poets would have to follow their earlier English forebears and shape new poetic instruments in the face of their own new world: "The poet must become more and more comprehensive, more allusive, more direct, in order to force, to dislocate if necessary, language into meaning."[41] In all the activity Jacobean drama prospered, as did Webster, in several favorable articles during the time.[42] But Eliot, after his general praise, had made some specific qualifications, and partially out of these qualifications came two attacks by the writers of *Scrutiny* with reverberations which are still being heard.

Frank Raymond Leavis' first editorial in 1932 for a new magazine, *Scrutiny,* made some strong pronouncements, the first of many years of similarly vigorous assertions, concerning the relationship between literary criticism and morality:

The general dissolution of standards is a commonplace. . . . Those who are aware of the situation will be concerned to cultivate awareness and will be actively concerned for standards. A review is necessary that combines criticism of literature with criticism of extra-literary standards. We take it as axiomatic that concern for standards of living implies concern for standards in the arts. . . . it is only a small minority for whom the arts are something more than a luxury product, who believe, in fact, that they are "the storehouse of recorded values" and, in consequence, that there is a necessary relationship between the quality of the individual's response to art and his general fitness for a humane existence.[43]

With Leavis and his *Scrutiny* group, we have a line of thought inherited from Coleridge and Arnold: a moral criterion is involved in the exercise of critical talent; a moral dimension in the critic's work is necessary. Thus criticism will be a matter of affirmations, judgments, exclusions: neutrality or eclecticism has no place in *Scrutiny*. For criticism is the most serious of businesses. Leavis wrote in the introduction for a *Scrutiny* collection in 1934:

> Literary criticism is concerned with more than literature, just as the "contemporary sensibility" is more than a matter of literary taste. A serious interest in literature cannot be merely literary; indeed, not only must the seriousness involve, it is likely to derive from, a preoccupation of—which must be a preoccupation with—the problems of social equity and order and of cultural health. . . .
> Criticism . . . is at one and the same time a discipline of sensibility and a labour of intelligence. The Scrutiny critics believe that the way to forward true appreciation of literature is to examine and discuss it, and that what the belletrist's fear of intelligence and analysis protects is not taste or sensibility. . . .
> In fact, the more serious one's interest in literature . . . the more insistent will one be on purity of approach and rigour of critical method—on the discipline that insures possession of the datum and relevance (that is, force) in the use of it.[44]

Much of the view is inspired by Eliot, who maintained in various essays that we should consider poetry as poetry and not as another thing, and that most important was the consideration of the relation of poetry to the life of its time and to other times, *i.e.*, now.[45] But while Eliot proposed, in "Tradition and the Individual Talent," to halt on the frontiers of metaphysics and mysticism, he did not do so; after the twenties he explored both. The task of the close, vigorous examination was left to Leavis and his group, who added a sharper sense of the moral outlook to Eliot's doctrines of discipline and self-criticism in composition.

Thus in Leavis' *The Great Tradition* (1948) we have the literary values that are central to English tradition set down primarily as moral values, made literary through the author's sensibility which is

in close touch with important human issues and with the writer's
most serious interests. Self-knowledge, self-control—such terms run
throughout his discussion of George Eliot and of "form": "Is there
any great novelist whose preoccupation with 'form' is not a matter of
his responsibility towards a rich human interest, or a complexity of
interests profoundly realized?—a responsibility involving of its very
nature, imaginative sympathy, moral discrimination and judgment
of relative human value?"[46] The impulse to artistic creation reaches
satisfying results for Leavis only when it is the correlative of ethical
preoccupations; a great work is ultimately a pattern woven of just
such preoccupations. Leavis writes in *The Great Tradition* of
"writers who are significant in terms of human awareness they
promote; awareness of the possibilities of life."[47] When a writer is
successful, for Leavis, a vitality is produced from an intense moral
seriousness, controlled at every step by a self-disciplined critical
talent.

In his writings on poets and poetry, we have many of the same
ideas, always emanating from the same nucleus: the self-discipline
of the poet. In *Revaluations,* a 1936 collection of essays in which
Leavis fulfilled Eliot's plea for a new view of the past by examining
many earlier writers, Leavis, writing on methods, condemns Shelley
for excessive use of language as gesture, or artistic insincerity.
Remarking on Shelley's views on the power of inspiration which
causes the imagination to well up and spill over on to the page, he
challenges the idea that inspiration "is not something to be tested,
clarified, defined and developed in composition."[48] He writes of a
poetic impulse being nurtured in the inner life of the poet; the
creative process, if it issues in satisfying poetry, will *be* a testing, a
clarifying, a defining, a developing. In his 1932 *New Bearings in
English Poetry,* he writes on what the poet can do, through careful,
precise expression: "He is a poet because his interest in his experience is not separable from his interest in words; because, that is, of
his habit of seeking by the evocative use of words to sharpen his
awareness of his ways of feeling, so making these communicable.
And poetry can communicate the actual quality of experience with a
subtlety and precision unapproachable by any other means."[49]
Later he celebrates the arrival of Eliot, and specifically the "Portrait
of A Lady" for its strictness, precision, and its "formal verse
medium" which "makes possible a concentration and a directness,
and audacities of transition and psychological notation."[50] Else-

where Leavis furthers Eliot's doctrines of the objective correlative, the damning presence of emotion for its own sake, and the worthiness of concrete realization, sensuous particularity, and lyrical wit.

The belief in such ideas, supported by Leavis' view of the necessity of a moral framework in great art, resulted in *Scrutiny's* being hailed (quite often in the United States) and condemned. For the *Scrutiny* writers, a great work of literature came to be one in which a genuine moral vision was communicated through a concrete rendering of life. Every detail in a literary work had to spring from the depths of the writer's moral being, and nothing less than a work of art was acceptable: if the work was merely good entertainment, it should be thrown out. The magazine reflected a Matthew Arnold remark to the effect that the good is the enemy of the best. The *Scrutiny* critics' lack of restraint in criticism when the work failed to meet their standards was refreshing or appalling, depending on whose side one was on. Leavis in *Mass Civilization and Minority Culture* alienated many by his celebration of a tiny minority culture dedicated to the preservation of the Good and in which only he and a handful of others seemingly were included. The basic problem is that whereas we don't mind hearing someone say "I like this," or "I don't like this," we do object to hearing someone say dogmatically, "This is good," or "This is bad." *Scrutiny* did the latter, and vigorously.

Thus came one sample reaction, from J. B. Priestley, in a fiery letter to the *New Statesman* in 1956: Leavis is not really a literary critic at all, wrote the irate Priestley, but is

sort of a Calvinist theologian of contemporary culture. To be an author, in his view, is to invite damnation, for only a few, D. H. Lawrence, himself, and a favourite pupil or two—will be saved. . . . The very title of his critical journal, *Scrutiny*, suggests that in it authors will have to undergo some kind of customs and passport examination, that the editors and his contributors will be there with narrowed gaze, tight lips, and service revolvers.[51]

Priestley condemns Leavis' absolutist criticism, that something is or is not literature, and complains that generally the bad critic "never seems to be addressing ordinary sensible readers, men and women of the world, as the great critics always did, but only an elect few, a shadowy elite, for whom alone Literature exists."[52] Such is the nature of adverse British *Scrutiny* reaction. In the United States, however, *Scrutiny* and its emphasis on the close reading of a work complemented the practices of the New Critics, who likewise were alarmed at the dissociation of sensibility, and a loss of order and integrity in the modern consciousness.

It may come as anticlimactic when we realize that F. R. Leavis has not written at all on the subject of John Webster. But members of his group have, and their dismissal of Webster is based on many of the Leavisite grounds which we have just noted. They underlie and permeate the writings of W. A. Edwards and Ian Jack, and in fact one gets the impression that their leader was watching over their shoulders during composition. Edwards' attack came in the thirties, after Eliot's attention and Lucas' highly praised edition; Jack's outburst followed in the late forties when there had been more interest created by stage revivals of the twin tragedies. Although published widely apart, the articles seem each to reflect an important aspect of Leavis' theories: Edwards castigates Webster primarily for a lack of self-discipline and a propensity for extraneous matter, while Jack criticizes the lack of a moral vision in the Webster plays. Put them together and the result is the F. R. Leavis approach.

Edwards' article appeared in 1933 in the *Revaluations* series, where essays were exactly that. Famous writers of the past were freshly discussed, and more often than not, found wanting. Edwards first admits that Archer was wrong in his approach, and should have taken Knight's point of view in *The Wheel of Fire:* each play of Shakespeare is to be taken as a dramatic poem, an expanded metaphor. Thus we can forget Webster's inconsistencies of plot. But we cannot forget that Webster is of the Overbury circle and is a character writer. To the ruination of the whole, Webster fails to practice any critical self-discipline and constantly injects characters and sententious maxims when there is no artistic need for such. Flamineo, for instance, is like Polonius, "unloading his store of maxims without bothering to find out whether they are needed. It is not that his pregnant observations lack point, so much as they are somehow not entirely relevant at the moment."[53] Hamlet's, he adds, are. Webster could not fit in his commonplace writings dramatically: Bosola is as guilty as Flamineo as he "swoops down" on an old woman "to unload his notes on cosmetics."[54] The style of the conceited character writer will not do in dramatic writing:

For dramatic writing such a style of writing is too formal, too far from speech idiom. We need only contrast the character of the Cardinal's whore with Ulysses' reaction towards Cressida. . . . We are left thinking of the Cardinal's last epigram and trying vainly to recollect the others. At the end of his speech we lack any clear conception of the whore, and are conscious only of an admiration for the Cardinal's talent as a wit.[55]

The numerous aphorisms are discreet components, never modifying each other. Webster rarely succeeds in writing a successful passage of verse, still less a whole scene.

As far as plotting is concerned, Edwards reminds Lucas that it is not necessarily true that the audience wanted a succession of great scenes. The public had a good grammar school education; the public cheered *Volpone* and *The Alchemist* and listened to difficult sermons. (We wonder, however, if it was the same public.) Edwards feels that Webster simply had a taste for melodrama.

Webster exhausts the stock resources of the tragedy of blood; and Edwards admits no comprehensive vision of life, except some unity of morbid, sinister tone common to his time. "Webster has value for us as a writer who gives powerful expression to a predominant mood of his age."[56] But, he adds, does it reflect a general mood of the age, or just the conventional urbane and precious satire of the character writers rather than the terrible passages in *King Lear*?

Webster the sensationalist tries to shock and thrill us to the end, but nothing can overwhelm the monotony of the tragedies. We aren't really interested in his rotten court, partly because we have no measure of its lack of greatness: we have no Prince Hamlet to stand as a moral yardstick for everyone else. In a criticism later answered by Travis Bogard in 1955, Edwards sees no development of character, only static souls who are creatures of the moment, acting only from animal impulse and believing only in snatching what comes and then dying gamely. Perhaps these subhuman figures are satiric, but Webster seems to believe what Flamineo and Bosola say about dying gamely in a mist of error. (Edwards does not elaborate on this.) Lucas, and others, says Edwards, believe this to be tragedy, and feel that Webster gave supreme utterance to the disillusionment of the time. "One can only ask them in conclusion to reread their Swift, their Jonson, and their Shakespeare and with these touchstones of excellence consider Webster's contributions again."[57]

Ian Jack, writing in *Scrutiny* on "The Case of John Webster" many years later, emphasizes not so much the lack of critical

intelligence in Webster as the absence of a steady moral vision; and
for *Scrutiny*, this finding puts a writer in the second rank. Jack
writes that in Webster, we have the Elizabethan picture of a unified
world falling into ruins, not allowing any comprehensive moral
statement: "Great tragedy can be written only by a man who has
achieved—at least for the period of composition—a profound and
balanced insight into life. Webster—and his plays are our evidence
—did not achieve such an insight."[58] The "integrity of life" passage
and other moral sententia do not add up to anything important:
". . . this background of moral doctrine has nothing to do with the
action of the plays: so far from growing out of the action, it has all
the marks of having been superimposed by the poet in a cooler, less
creative mood than that in which the Duchess and Flamineo had
their birth. There is no correspondence between the axioms and the
life represented in the drama. This dissociation is the fundamental
flaw in Webster."[59] No philosophy of life kindled Webster's imagination as did certain aspects of Hell or Chaos. There is no imaginative coherence. There is, writes Jack, the often-noted unity of mist,
but one mood isolated and out of focus cannot be a basis for a
profound tragic vision. Jack makes the questionable statement that
Webster restricted his genius to the revenge tradition, not the Shakespearean morality tradition; and the revenge tradition is severely
limited. Rupert Brooke had, in 1916, made a good answer to this:
the boundaries of the revenge play are wide.

Jack disparages Webster's use of Machiavellianism and Stoicism
in place of the doctrine of Degree: "The strident courage which
Flamineo shows in dying . . . manifests Webster's peculiarly limited and deformed notion of ethics. We find in Webster only the
virtue of Hell: the courage of despair. . . . Denied insight into any
virtue other than Stoical courage, Webster tries to erect unflinch-
ingly perseverance in evil into the sum of moral goodness."[60]
Vittoria is dishonorable—let's admit it, he writes. But Webster, with
artistic insincerity, makes her look honorable. Without a profound
hold on any system of moral values, Webster can write wonderful
dissembling verse which seems to proclaim her honesty.

Things are futile in the world of Webster: "We do not for a
moment believe that when the Duke and Cardinal are dead the
state of Amalfi will return to a condition of health and normality . . .
we can form no other notion of another world which will be
revealed when the rottenness of Amalfi has . . . been purged

away."[61] Finally, Jack closes with strong words. The dramatist, he attests, is mainly interested in sensation, interested only in making our flesh creep:

There is, in fact, something a trifle ridiculous about Webster. . . . An eruption of real humour—of the Shakespearean sort—would knock Webster's waxworks into a cocked hat. . . .
Webster . . . is a decadent . . . incapable of realizing the whole of life in the form in which it revealed itself to the Elizabethans. By concentrating exclusively on the narrow aspect of life revealed in one mood, he threw the relation of the whole out of harmony.[62]

Though it is not a *Scrutiny* article, we might note the account of Webster in the widely read 1956 paperback series *The Pelican Guide to English Literature*. It reflects the stern *Scrutiny* evaluation through its editor, ex-*Scrutiny* writer Boris Ford. L. G. Salingar's chapter "Tourneur and the Tragedy of Revenge" takes up where Jack leaves off. A good word on Webster is not to be found:

His paraphernalia of revenge and torture are neither purely sensational nor emblems of poetic justice, but are presented with an effort at naturalism, and with the aim of exciting nervous horror and foreboding. . . . Webster is sophisticated, but his sophistication belongs to decadence. The poet's solemnity and his groping for a new basis for tragedy only serve to expose his inner bewilderment and his lack of any deep sense of communion with his public. . . . His dialogue swings between maxims too sententious for the occasion and outbursts bordering on hysteria. . . . seeming changes of mind merely give a colouring of dramatic irony, while the characters continue as before; this theatrical sleight-of-hand links his methods of construction with Fletcher.[63]

We should mention one more *Scrutiny* article, "The Tragedy of Blood," by James Smith, which appeared in 1939. It is a difficult article, laboriously written, but it is a rather hesitant defense of Webster. It is mistitled; Smith's chief interest is to show, by much quotation, that the lack of values in *The White Devil* point indirectly to a positive. Trying to answer Edwards, Smith looks at the first scene: "Antonelli and Gasparo rebuke Lodovico for his brutish lack of prudence; he them, for their diabolic cunning. And thus, by something it would not be improper to call construction, standards are introduced into the picture of a world of evil; though as yet there is no one in it who illustrates them by his actions or his words."[64] Smith writes that we see evil working out its own destruction, evil that is presented to us from within—not its effects on a virtuous person. There is confusion, pointless activity, until, and Smith goes a bit far: "in the mind of the spectator alone there is awakened the notion of order; he desires vehemently to see it transferred to the stage and so his attention is held until the close of the fifth act. With the arrival of a new ruler, a new generation, the whole evil world is destroyed."[65] But this world is destroyed only to rise again, writes Ian Jack in his later article. Smith's effort remains in the background in comparison with the two vigorous *Scrutiny* critics who find fault with Webster. One problem Smith faces is that of a laborious style of writing which is interspersed with numerous quotations; and his constant appeal to the mind of the theater audience to serve as a standard for order is a questionable approach. An audience can only become involved to a certain extent; it cannot help write the play.

To return finally to F. R. Leavis: his guiding principles result in the condemnatory articles in *Scrutiny* and influence still other writers to come. One might surmise that Leavis' own thoughts on Webster were similar to those expressed in his writing on Swift, particularly if one bears in mind the writings of Leavis' group on Webster. Leavis' account of Swift, a *Scrutiny* article published later in *The Common Pursuit*, finds this later satirist essentially a negative writer, just as Edwards and Jack found Webster:

> . . . even in the *Argument*, where Swift's ironic intensity undoubtedly directs itself to the defence of something that he is intensely concerned to defend, the effect is essentially negative. The positive itself appears only negatively—a kind of skeletal presence, rigid enough, but without life or body. . . . The intensity is purely destructive. . . .
> A great writer—yes; that account still imposes itself as fitting, though his greatness is no matter of moral grandeur or human centrality; our sense of it is merely as a sense of great force. And this force, as we feel it, is conditioned by frustration and constriction; the channels of life have been blocked and perverted.[66]

Swift, writes Leavis, makes no affirmation, except in the energy of his creation; he cannot provide a norm or guide. Nor, adds the *Scrutiny* group, can Swift's forerunner, John Webster.

The years preceding the publication of Muriel Bradbrook's *Themes and Conventions of Elizabethan Tragedy* (1935) and Una

Ellis-Fermor's *The Jacobean Drama* (1936) were full of Elizabethan scholarly treatises besides those already mentioned, but most of them had little worth. Felix Schelling's 1925 *Elizabethan Playwrights* added little to Webster study, being the usual impressionistic survey of the tragedies: Webster was great here, bad there; his method was that of a master mosaic. E. W. Hendy pointed out in 1928[67] that Webster knew his wildlife, particularly birds. Hendy seems to have spent much time counting references to such; he notes 250 passages about birds, beasts, and insects. Elizabeth Holmes' *Aspects of Elizabethan Imagery* (1929) was one good close look at the imagery during the time. Webster's variety and sharpness of imagery is similar to Donne's, she notes, though Webster makes use of little figures to say big things: "Fate's a spaniel, we cannot beat him from us," and so on. Unlike Donne, Webster does not often use in his images theology, philosophy, and music, which for Donne often represent a life of order. Instead, we have imagery based on science, witchcraft, poison, artillery, diseases, secrets of law, properties of plants, and the deformed and deadly in nature. Creatures lower than man in the natural scale are made to share the human atmosphere. J. A. Bastiaenen's *The Moral Tone of Jacobean and Caroline Drama* (1930) reads like Canon Charles Kingsley and his righteous outrage reincarnated; Walter Pritchard Eaton's work of the same year was not much better. *The Drama in English* carried on the Archer-Ibsen tradition, as Eaton looks at the English drama from the point of view of the modern stage craftsman. He points out that if *The Duchess of Malfi* were revived, its most tragic moments would be greeted with derisive laughter (which did happen) or the silence of blank astonishment: "Masterpieces are not so greeted, for masterpieces endure beyond the age and taste which breed them."[68] And we have the usual Archer-inspired criticisms: "It used to be a common practice in schoolboy initiations to stuff a kid glove with wet sand and place it in a blinded neophyte's palm, telling him he was holding the hand of a corpse. . . . Webster's scene is just about on this level of 'tragedy.' "[69] We need not quote further from Eaton; suffice it to say that Webster entered the 1930's with a hoot of derision. Eaton's criticism lacks the intellectual background of W. A. Edwards, which followed soon; but possibly Eaton's average-reader approach reached a wider audience.

Then came Muriel Bradbrook's *Themes and Conventions of Elizabethan Tragedy*, published in 1935, followed a year later by

Una Ellis-Fermor's *The Jacobean Drama.* For several years it appeared that these two scholars had had the final, definitive say about the Jacobean age.

The work of Miss Bradbrook is an excellent piece of historical criticism and provided another answer to realistically minded critics who strove to see the plays of the Elizabethans as straightforward, naturalistic, psychological documents. Her effort was to "attempt to discover how an Elizabethan would approach a tragedy by Chapman, Tourneur or Middleton";[70] in so doing she turned her attention to a body of conventions constituting stage traditions. A convention she defines as "an agreement between writers and readers, whereby the artist is allowed to limit and simplify his material in order to secure greater concentration through a control of the distribution of emphasis."[71] And the essential structure of the drama of Shakespeare's time "lies not in the narrative or the characters but in the words."[72] It is the poetic use of words which creates the only unity in Elizabethan tragedy, for the "last thing which occurred to the Elizabethan was to put two and two together. . . ."[73] Conventions, she writes, "imply a limitation of interests, and the Elizabethans achieved the unification of their plays by leaving out the interconnections between the different kinds of material."[74] There follow in the book demonstrations of Elizabethan conventions of presentations, action, and speech, plus examinations of what the Elizabethans read and wrote. Then comes a section on the conventions of particular dramatists; and her assessment of Webster at times follows the Eliot-Leavis-Edwards treatment.

Webster was too literary, she writes. Reflecting the Eliot-Leavis theory of the inspired whole, she writes that Webster "was concerned with perfection of detail rather than general design: this is reflected in his structure as well as the texture of his verse. For example, Webster uses the ghost for a momentary effect of terror or pathos, and does not relate it to the other supernatural suggestions of the play."[75] (One thinks immediately of Eliot in his essay "Four Elizabethan Dramatists" decrying in particular the too fanciful use of ghosts.) Writing on *The White Devil,* she notes that his characters, like Tourneur's Vindice, have double natures (another convention), "but instead of alternating, the two halves are blurred and run together. This also makes for naturalism. As a result, there is no pattern of characters, nor is there any structure of themes as in Tourneur's plays."[76] Years later, *Scrutiny's* Ian Jack would reflect her objection to Vittoria: in defending her life, Vittoria's speech is so well done "that the language contains no trace of dissimulation (as the publicity of Iago can be felt behind his speeches). . . . Her splendid bluff rings true; too true for dramatic effectiveness."[77] Ultimately, beauty and glamour are mixed with lust and selfishness. In either case Vittoria remains a splendid figure piece rather than a natural character in spite of the realism of individual scenes. The other characters such as Brachiano reflect a certain ambiguity also. A character is heroic here, monstrous there: "This blurring of contradictory aspects is different from their juxtaposition, and is clearly a sign of decadence. It suggests A King and No King or Love's Sacrifice."[78]

Miss Bradbrook's conclusions on The White Devil are well worth considering: Webster has written too much naturalism into what basically is a nonrealistic presentation: "The difficulty of The White Devil is that the feelings are meant to be naturalistic, but the characters are not. The impression of the parts conflicts with the impression of the whole."[79] Only the dominant sardonic tone holds the play together.

The Duchess of Malfi has a similar shaky unity, with the action hovering in an ambiguous manner between the natural and the supernatural, though it remains a more successful presentation. In an excellent character analysis of the Duchess—the most interesting one we have yet been given—Miss Bradbrook shows a certain growth on the part of the Duchess, who has actually gone against the church (we must look at her action through Elizabethan eyes) and tradition by her secret marriage to one less great than she. (Our attention is called to the remarks of the pilgrims in III, iv.) It is a growth toward an awakening of responsibility. She never acknowledges that her brothers have the right to judge her; but she does acknowledge a need for a corrected judgment. Here lies the interest of the prison scenes: instead of being sadistic exhibitions, they are symbolic of the Duchess' purgatory. A close analysis of the scenes is given, with the emphasis always on the way the Elizabethan saw it. The young widow is purged from "I am Duchess of Malfi still" to "I have so much obedience in my blood/ I wish it in their veins to do them good." At length she comes to her knees.

We must assume that the Duchess' marriage was wrong, although in law the Duchess was innocent; by social standards she was at first reckless and intemperate; by ethical and religious standards she was an instinctive creature awakened by suffering to maturity. Hers was original sin, not personal sin; like King Lear's uncontrolled greed for affection and rage of frustrations. What happened to the Duchess was as little deserved as what happened to Lear: neither of them get common justice; by the end of the play neither of them desire it.[80]

But unfortunately there are serious incompatibilities in the emotional structure of the play, and they are of the type which Eliot hinted at in the twenties and Edwards in *Scrutiny* had spelled out in 1933:

He was capable of extraordinary power over the single phrase, yet again and again he produces one which is irrelevant to the feeling of the scene as a whole, or to the character, or to the reader's feelings towards the characters. The felicitous phrase is there for its own sake; or at most, the touching sentiment, the poignant feeling is there for its own sake, without any regard to the structure of the feelings as a whole.[81]

Tourneur's verse is more coherent, thanks to the disastrous pitfalls of Webster's notebook method which makes one speech unconnected with another. Although the homogeneity of the two tragedies is remarkable, there is a latent danger in the Webster style: "a unity which is only a unity of tone and temper is likely to be precarious and unstable, since it is founded upon eclecticism, and dependent upon continuity of mood alone."[82] And, when we remember the dictates of Leavis and Eliot, eclecticism has no place either in criticism or in the original creation of the work of art itself.

Miss Bradbrook reflects Edwards specifically in her criticism and Eliot more generally in her historical appraisal: Eliot wrote in 1924 of the lack of stable conventions in the Elizabethan drama; Miss Bradbrook shows us how, in *The White Devil*, Webster confuses realistic feelings with conventional, symbolic characters and symbolic scenes. Webster should have kept within the bounds of a single convention: there is a blurring, some artistic sloppiness. Such errors are not tolerated in the line of criticism which Professor Bradbrook reflects.

Like Muriel Bradbrook, Una Ellis-Fermor does not actually write from deep within the Eliot-Leavis tradition; she too utilizes an historical approach but nevertheless reflects some of their serious concern for the perfection of the whole. She sees Webster as grafting on to his drama a moral system which is extraneous, insincere, and meaningless.

Again like Miss Bradbrook, Professor Ellis-Fermor notes the conventions of prologue, soliloquy, rhetoric, and their use throughout the whole span of Elizabethan drama; but she concentrates on the approach which takes the Jacobean drama as representing and arising from a general questioning, pessimistic state of mind which in turn arose out of the political uncertainties of the day. And she sees little hope in the Jacobeans. Unlike Miss Bradbrook's view of the "progression to greatness" of the Duchess, her view is that Webster, like his colleagues, only momentarily allowed himself hope: the Duchess' confident piety "is obliterated and washed over by subsequent event as though the dramatist himself renounced it, except as a will-o'-the-wisp of thought of no permanence or stability."[83]

Her method of viewing the plays returns us again to the G. Wilson Knight approach (first set out in *The Wheel of Fire*, 1930), of the play as extended metaphor. She urges us to see the drama "as a two-dimensional map of moods and personalities in their relation to each other rather than as a single dimensional line of progression from event to event,"[84] and compares its structure to paintings and symphonies. She writes that the drama offers two types of experience: "One type . . . is primarily concerned with the subject matter as a chronological record of event and proceeding from this we arrive at an aspect of form described most naturally in terms of plot, story, and the causal connection of event. The other experience is spatial instead of temporal and it regards the play as a grouping of moods, characters, forms of diction or prosody and looks for form in the interrelation of these."[85] The second of these experiences growing out of Webster drama reflects the moods, characters, diction of negation, in which men and women are brought to the shattering, revealing moment of death—to see only nothing. The critic feels that of the dramatists, Webster most clearly perceived the chaos and conflict in which the tragic thought of his generation was caught, "and, while unable to climb out of the 'deep pit of darkness,' yet discerned for a moment through the eyes of one of his characters the 'stars' that 'shine still.' "[86] But this seems a vision of no matter as we read Professor Elis-Fermor's account of Webster's chief characters. No answer comes to them at the point of death: "Their looks are cast back over life, not forward into the 'long silence' or the 'mist.' All that Flamineo can tell . . . is thus negative. 'We cease to dye by dying. . . .' " The Duchess is the only character "who sees, or thinks she sees" beyond this mist; but she passes from the play and the "final comment is given to Bosola, the Machiavellian." Webster "brings his people, by the most careful preparation, to the position in which, if ever, a man should see absolute reality— and before them is only a mist. . . . This negation, the quality of nothingness, this empty, boundless, indefinible grey mist is the final horror, the symbol of ignorance, of the infinite empty space in which man hovers, the material and the spiritual world both in different terms unreal."[87] His purpose, she feels, is to create "a picture of the world in which his characters move; a world created of their own thoughts."[88] In order to do this, Webster has eliminated all obstacles such as logic or continuity: his true plot is not the event, but the progress of minds toward deeper and deeper self-knowledge. We might wonder at this last observation, for Miss Ellis-Fermor spends much of her time in showing us how no answers are provided in any self-examination.

It is, in all, a gray world, with many satiric thrusts, but a world without hope. His moral system is superimposed, and meaningless. While she does not exactly condemn Webster for a non-functional apparatus, as Leavis might, she notes that it just doesn't work:

From the sententiae of the play we perceive that Webster has built up for himself a moral system which does not correspond wholly with his instinctive affections . . . nor with the profounder and hardly less instinctive doubts that troubled his spirit. . . . In spite of 'choric figures' comments on life, death, and fate . . . it is the characters Webster loves, not the moralists through whom he preaches, that possess our minds. . . . And so the accompanying moral commentary, though pithy, clear, and often deeply impressive is seen to be not so much a different medium of Webster's thought, but actually the vehicle for a group of ideas quite different from his instinctive love of nobility and of courage, even if it be Satanic.[89]

Both of these feminine critics of the thirties share certain beliefs with the *Scrutiny* writers and Eliot. One important concept of Webster, held by many today, takes shape for us in their work: it is the essentially non-moral Webster (in the sense that his world lacks the moral unity of Shakespeare's universe where the Good essentially prevails) who was powerful but often artistically sloppy. Bradbrook's is the Webster who could create a tragic figure of a young widow who is purged to greatness; but he is also the Webster of confused dramatic conventions, who tries to fuse together naturalism and symbolism and further adds the extraneous line of no real significance. Ellis-Fermor's is a satiric Webster who creates a compelling world of gray negation where there is nothing but a mist and, unfortunately, a moral system perfunctorily tacked on which does not correspond with his instinctive affections.

Some of the points raised by these important chapters were restated forcefully a decade later by Moody E. Prior in *The Language of Tragedy* (1947): ". . . whereas Webster possessed more than any other seventeenth century writer of tragedy except Shakespeare a gift for intense and figurative language and skill in adapting this language to dramatic dialogue, he failed, unlike Shakespeare, to avoid the more obvious theatrical evasions and violations of logical consequences to which the conventions and current devices of this drama so readily lent themselves, and against which Jonson protested."[90] *The Duchess of Malfi* has an ordered design, Prior notes, through the unifying imagery of animals, birds, and the like; but it was Webster's limitation to fall back on "the easy shorthand of theatrical effectiveness" to get him over difficulties in technical problems. In *The Duchess of Malfi*, the commonplace devices are like "beads on a string. . . . the probabilities in this play are not given direction by the implications of a moral system and hence the appearance of these maxims is misleading."[91]

We return finally to the words of Leavis, his commendation of "writers who are significant in terms of human awareness they promote, awareness of the possibilities of life," and his notation that the critic should "take it as axiomatic that concern for standards of living implies concern for standards in the arts."[92] Then again we recall those of Eliot: "The larger part of the labour of an author is critical labour, the labour of sifting, combining, constructing . . . this frightful toil is as much critical as creative."[93]

# 6

# THE GRAY WORLD OF WEBSTER

Two major views of Webster the writer with little hope and a tenuous moral vision are those of Clifford Leech and Robert Ornstein, writers who generally maintain the theses of Eliot and Miss Ellis-Fermor that there is a difficulty in composition and that moral focus is dim or nonexistent. And Gunnar Boklund in a major study of *The Duchess of Malfi* admits the importance of the theme of integrity of life, but also sees an amoral world of shadows where virtue may not live long.

Clifford Leech gives the life of the dramatist in his brief, well-written book *John Webster* (1951) and then deals with the tragedies. His overall theme harks back to Eliot on craftsmanship and the "genius directed toward chaos," in whose world is seen the gray negation discussed by Miss Ellis-Fermor. There is, for Leech, no total design, no moral vision present: writing of *The Duchess of Malfi*, for instance, Leech states that Webster "has excelled in the moving exploration of the human mind, yet his play is blurred in its total meaning. It is a collection of brilliant scenes, whose statements do not ultimately cohere."[1] (We may note some modifications of these views in his 1963 study of *The Duchess*, to be considered later.) Never has the world been golden in Webster, as perhaps the sun shone in Shakespeare before Lear divided his kingdom. And never will the world become so: ". . . we cannot believe that Giovanni should inherit his father's dukedom, or that the surviving son of Antonio and the Duchess of Malfi should be established in his mother's right."[2] We do not learn or profit by the fates of the

124

characters; there is no road but the gallows-road. And, Leech adds, because of his ultimate incoherence, ". . . we can, I think, assume that Webster did not fully realize the significance of his plays."[3] The critic refers to Webster's preface to *The White Devil*: did he really wish to be read by *Philaster's* light?

Writing of *The White Devil*, Leech calls our attention to Webster's device of not always making Vittoria so resolute, as in her quailing under Cornelia's curse. Thus we are more likely to believe in her bravery of spirit if she is, after all, prey to fear. (But we are tempted to note that Vittoria's defiance is so great that we hardly notice her few moments of terror.) Flamineo is the great character of the play, writes Leech, almost a tragic figure in spite of his pandering. The best comments are from him; he stands outside himself like Iago, reacting to the evolution of circumstance. Although in their madness Cornelia and Brachiano seem to become spokesmen for a misty otherworld, and in spite of the ending with Giovanni and the ambassadors, "there is little suggestion in this play that the evil figures exist within a framework of good. After death there is only a mist."[4] *The White Devil's* lesson is, if anything, that if what comes after life is uncertain, "there is a terrible certainty in the recognition of evil. That is the poetry of Vittoria and Flamineo, and their power to stare it in the face gives them something of nobility."[5] As for the conclusions to both plays, they "with their half-promise of a quieter time to come are only incidental in the play's effects."[6]

*The Duchess of Malfi* he finds blurred in total meaning, as we have noted already. Act V is an anticlimax, as so many critics have told us. It is for Leech an overlong recession from the climax; there is no more tension, no more doubt. Contradictory statements abound. And did Webster fully sympathize with his Duchess? Leech, like Miss Bradbrook, goes back and looks at the state of the times and Webster's own character of "A Virtuous Widow." On the surface at least, the Duchess is a warning to the rash and wanton. Like Lear she violates "degree." For Leech, "There is grandeur in her egoism, but its implications are essentially anarchic."[7] Yet Webster sees her as innocent with part of his mind: witness the pilgrim's commentary in Act III, iv. And nothing matters in the torture scenes but for the Duchess to remain herself, although "the starres shine still" is the "completest assertion in Jacobean drama of man's impotence, of the remoteness, the impersonality of the cosmic powers."[8] (The madmen, for Leech, represent the final dissolution of an apparently ordered world.) The last act, following upon this great scene, is forgotten. We remember only "the young Duchess, kneeling down to die."[9]

But a blurred vision is maintained. Not only are we unsure of whether the Duchess is guilty or innocent, but the character of Ferdinand is not completely successful: "he cannot carry Act V, and Webster's play ends in tedium."[10] Leech is the first critic to psychoanalyze Ferdinand: there is no motive for his guardianship of the Duchess but an incestuous passion, which Webster may not himself have realized. (See the modern staging below: John Gielgud followed this idea in his portrayal.) Nevertheless, Ferdinand lacks a quality of vision, he lacks awareness and dignity. And Bosola "never comments on Ferdinand's attitude toward the Duchess and he is the chorus. When the character is amorphous, insufficiently thought out, it cannot effectively act as the medium through which the dramatist's vision of the universe is conveyed to us. And in *The Duchess of Malfi* Ferdinand's part in the action constitutes him a major character."[11]

Both plays are too full of sentential remarks, though Webster excels "in the sudden flash, in the intuitive but often unsustained perception. . . . When he deliberately aimed at the impressive, he achieved only the ponderous."[12] Webster, writes Leech, may not have fully realized what he was writing or understood it, but, he adds, not all dramatists fully understand their creations. His greatest failure is not merely in inconsistent characterization, but in the want of a central vision. Leech closes with a plea for staging of the plays, for by them "we come closer to that vision of suffering humanity which Webster experienced in fits and starts. And when the fit was on him, his intuitions were sure and deep."[13] We come away from Leech's account, well written and sometimes lyrical in expression, realizing that it derives perhaps from one line of Eliot's criticism: "The whole of Shakespeare's work is one poem, and it is the poetry of it in this sense, not the poetry of isolated lines and passages or the poetry of the single figures which he created, that matters most."[14]

Robert Ornstein in his *The Moral Vision of Jacobean Tragedy* (1960) views the Jacobean drama not unlike Professors Ellis-Fermor and Leech. Ornstein too sees a grim Webster of little underlying moral purpose, save for the Duchess' effect on the men around her in Acts IV and V. He notes:

The moralist teaches men how to avoid catastrophe; Webster is concerned only with how to accept it. The moralist explains the justice of men's fall; Webster does not reassure us that measure for measure is the law of existence. Armed with the doctrine of free will the moralist cannot believe in fatality; but in the hideous mist of error that enshrouds Webster's characters no man can be called master of his fate and no choice is clear until circumstances force men's decisions.[15]

Professor Ornstein's important book carries on the ideas of Miss Ellis-Fermor in relating tragedy to the confused age in which the Jacobeans lived; the dramatists were caught between old and new ways of determining the realities upon which moral values rest. His book is a partial answer to those critics who find Christian philosophy embedded in the tragedies of Shakespeare and some Jacobeans: one thinks of G. Wilson Knight's *"Measure for Measure and the Gospels"* as an early example. Ornstein writes:

Jacobean tragedy is Christian in the sense that its moral values derive primarily from a Christian ethical tradition or from Classical ethics made compatable with Christianity. But that tragedy is Christian in the more significant sense that it is concerned with man's salvation or with his obedience to divine law is far more dubious. Like Elizabethan sonneteers, who often use religious terms to heighten the expression of feeling in their love poems, Jacobean tragedians frequently use religious ideas and images to heighten the emotional, moral, and spiritual drama of their plays.[16]

And in his conclusion, he states that there is, when we examine Jacobean tragedy in its fullness, little reassurance. There is some restoration of order and decency, to be sure,

yet how often are the forces of good ineffectual in Jacobean tragedy and how very much will the decent man accept before he endangers his security by taking sides or before he obeys his nobler instincts. It is not until the Duchess is dead that Antonio and Bosola decide to change their lives. . . . We are often aware that what has been restored is not commensurate with what has been destroyed. . . . The myth and ritual critics tell us that the tragic hero is sacrificed for the good of the community or the state and that the sacrificial pattern purges pity and fear. I wonder, though, whether we feel any differently about Hamlet's death because Fortinbras, a military adventurer, ascends to the throne of Denmark.[17]

His treatment of Webster is somewhat sketchy, and we feel the need of a central, unifying vision as some critics feel the similar need in Webster. Ornstein, having earlier made the comment that in the interpretation of great dramatic art "the appeal to convention can become like the Renaissance appeal to authority—merely a substitute for critical thinking,"[18] questions Lucas' excusing Webster's spottiness with the idea of the audience's demand for a succession of great moments. "The plotting of *The White Devil* is no more episodic than *Lear*; it seems more episodic because *The White Devil* lacks the moral emphasis and focus which unifies the sprawling structure of Shakespeare's play."[19] Like others before him, Professor Ornstein sees the moral aphorisms as tacked on, "a bit like annotations by another hand—Christian glosses, as it were, on a pagan epic of courage and consuming passion. They do not suddenly crystallize a moral judgment embodied in Webster's portrayal of character, nor do they capture the essential significance of the lives on which they comment so weightily."[20] There are few Jacobean tragedies, he adds, "in which innocence and guilt seem as irrelevant as in *The White Devil*. . . . Morally sensitive characters like Isabella and Marcello are weak and ineffectual, too easily silenced, murdered in dumb show or by a casual sword thrust."[21] Borrowing from Leech, Ornstein notes also that there is no previous norm of aristocratic values. There is no suggestion that the world was ever less corrupt. Virtue does exist, but "it is impotent and ultimately meaningless—swept away into the same mist that enshrouds the fates of assassins and adulterers."[22] The power of the play, writes Ornstein, comes from the dramatization of the isolated criminal will shattering moral restrictions, the great moments of agony and duress that lay bare the soul. When the grand design of *The White Devil* should be finally elucidated, "we see nothing more than a series of exterminations that temporarily rid Giovanni's court of vermin."[23]

*The Duchess of Malfi* he finds to be a more mature play, "not so much the expression of a personal nihilistic disgust with life as a relatively detached study of the moral cowardice that robs life of meaning."[24] The Duchess does achieve a spiritual victory, although in Webster's world innocence still crumbles before the onslaught of Machiavellian violence. The Duchess herself is the greatest character in the play, and there is "a beauty in her death that shakes the cynical nihilism which is Bosola's defence against conscience. . . .

Caught in the trap that Fortune set for her she ceases to be Fortune's slave."[25] But there is no great moral system involved, though he admits a movement away from the lack of moral discriminations in *The White Devil*. Some form of moral awareness comes to all the characters around the Duchess, and they do indeed awaken to their contemptuousness. But for Antonio and Bosola, self-knowledge ultimately warps their later actions. But the piety of the Duchess seems only an "intuition of a realm of values" obscured by corruption; Bosola in Act V comments "only the courage to be greatly good in a world which offers a hundred crooked subterfuges and which demands the sham, not the reality of virtue."[26] But in a world of predominant evil, Ornstein emphasizes, the actions of the Duchess nevertheless reaffirm the dignity of man. She is triumphant over adversity.

The critic concludes that if Webster had had more of Shakespeare's tolerance, he might have escaped the gloomy pit of his tragedies. But the virtues he admired "flowered only in the darkness of mortal agony. He lived in such imaginative communion with death that perhaps he could not respond to the beauty of spring without also remembering the mocking fragrance and beauty of a decked hearse."[27] And finally, to appreciate the Jacobeans, one needs to be something of a Stoic: "The hope that all will be well is only an illusion in tragedy. Its great affirmations are qualitative, not quantitative. . . . To accept the affirmations of tragedy we must have the courage to cherish beauty as it is being destroyed and to rejoice in the fulfillment of human greatness no matter how indifferent to man's fulfillment or annihilation is the universe."[28]

A book difficult to put in any critical category is Travis Bogard's *The Tragic Satire of John Webster* (1955) because of his highly individual approach. Nevertheless, he belongs more in the Leech-Ornstein critical line because of his emphasis on the satiric in Webster as opposed to any emphasis on his basic morality. Reminiscent of their appraisals is Bogard's commentary on Bosola:

Only in the end, when the Duchess is dead, does his integrity reassert itself. But it is then too late for redemption.

He fares no worse than the other characters, for in Webster's world there is no justice, no law, either of God or man, to mete out punishment for evil and reward for good. . . . Evil and good are dragged down together in death, just as they are meshed together in life. The only triumph comes when, even in the moment of defeat, an individual is

roused to assert his own integrity of life. . . . In Webster's world characters are significant not because of their morality but because of their
struggle.[29]

Essentially, Bogard attempts to show Webster's indebtedness not
so much to Shakespeare as to the satiric and tragic method of
Chapman and Marston; and more important, he tries to illustrate how
Webster made the satiric voice co-equal with the tragic. Oddly
enough, he writes, Webster achieves pure tragedy only when a
satiric counterpoint is introduced to the tragic plan: Bogard states
that in Webster's great tragedies "a vision of man as he might be is
held in a steady focus with the view of man as he is."[30] Perseverance in integrity of life—the only positive—is not harmed by the
prevailing satiric tone: "In integrity and the struggle to preserve it,
there has been an affirmation despite the end, despite evil, despite
the knowledge that the world is moribund and rotten—a fit subject
for cruel, satirical analysis."[31]

The sententious statements of Webster serve him as agents of the
satire and represent his own point of view by pointing up the
significance of a speech or scene. For Bogard—and not for many
others—the *sententia* are made to serve the purpose of characterization at the same time that they are subtly defining the action. Cornelia's outbursts, the choral commentary of Bosola and Flamineo,
are all in character and effective. Meanwhile, along with the satiric
thrusts, Webster tried in numerous didactic passages to explain and
offer remedy for the suffering of men, but was unable to do so. He
could not see life other than as a moral chaos, and "remained unable
to discover an acceptable system for the evaluation of good and
evil."[32] And Webster remains a strange satirist, for whom no
philosophy is possible because of man's mortality. Bogard asserts
that Webster could not solve his problems or compromise with
them:

Webster tries to present the ugliness beneath the artificial glory. Every
character of importance, every situation, the noblest ethical statement in
both tragedies is attacked by Webster's relentless analysis. His entire
energy is directed toward teaching man "wherein he is imperfect." Yet
this was done without any clear hope of making man perfect, for perfection was meaningless, "a bare name, and no essential thing."[33]

We think here of Leavis on Swift.

And thus for Bogard, Webster can only celebrate the capacity of

individuals to struggle to maintain integrity. It is no matter if Canon
Kingsley and others berate Webster for lack of "that development of
human souls for good or evil that is Shakespeare's especial power."
Writes Bogard, "Not development but stubborn consistency to self is
the distinguishing element of Webster's tragic action."[34] Although
Shakespearean tragedy is individual, Websterian tragedy is social,
with individuals serving as normative examples of Webster's conception of life. A character is only important in his relationship with his
fellow man. And integrity of life is the only virtue. Thus the
characters

are in the end what they were at the outset. The naturally evil men and
women remain evil; the good remain good. The more heroic are completely, even stubbornly consistent. It is a matter of pride with them that
misfortune does not change them. Their entire struggle . . . is to keep
themselves as they are, essentially. . . . It is important, therefore, that
the great individuals of Webster's tragedies do not change. If they did,
the one positive value in the world, the only measure of man, would
prove chimerical. . . . Inner struggle and development have no place
in the Websterian view of life. . . . no regeneration through suffering
is possible.[35]

At length, after a close study, Bogard concludes that the ultimate
tragedy in Webster's world is the presence of evil and decay which
drags all mankind to death, not any one person. And the "function
of satire is to reveal man's common mortality and his involvement in
evil; the tragic story is the story of a few who find courage to defy
such revelation."[36]

Bogard's account is mostly his own, as stated earlier. Some of his
ideas go back to Lucas' introduction, and traces of Leech appear
from time to time. We may note two things about the idea of tragic
satire: first, it is never quite clear how the hope of tragedy and the
despair of satire can be reconciled. Second, Bogard writes as a critic
in the study, too often divorcing the imagery of the poetry from the
dramatic action on the stage. Nevertheless, such comments as those
on the lack of development in the characters (although we recall the
effective Bradbrook approach to the Duchess) are extremely persua-
sive.

Other articles add to this general approach to Webster criticism.
B. J. Layman wrote in the September, 1959, *PMLA* a closely argued
analysis of Vittoria and Flamineo's relationship. In his inter-

pretation of the play, Layman tries to show us the truth of
Flamineo's last lines "Shee hath no faults, who hath the art to hide
them" (V, vi, 247); his thesis is that Vittoria actually achieves
nobility by an ability to assume a Yeatsian mask of virtue and goodness, and that she balances the outright evil of Flamineo. Out of this
odd equilibrium comes only a portion of moral truth, and nothing in
any way kin to a moral vision. Webster has in fact tried "to sunder
us from familiar and conventional moral themes and attitudes."[37]
Layman's is an effort to explore the deception of Webster and to
answer Ian Jack's charge that Webster simply makes Vittoria behave
as if she were honorable, the effort of an insincere artist. Yet, though
we are impressed with Layman's intellectuality, his basic tenet that
a sinful individual can become noble by pretending to do so is
difficult to accept. His account bears some relationship to Bogard's
belief that Webster himself was unable to discover a system for the
evaluation of good and evil, and that we are left with a world of
moral ambiguity.

J. R. Mulryne, in his 1960 article on Webster's two tragedies in
*Jacobean Theatre*, writes on the great and breathless blank verse
which overrides the metric pattern to tremendous effect; but he can
find no sense of order in *The White Devil*, and though he finds a
moral norm in *The Duchess of Malfi*, he notes the absence of the self-
critical faculty. In *The White Devil*, for instance, we have no simple
moral viewpoint: the murders of Camillo and Isabella take place in
dumb-show, distancing the events from our sympathy; they are
"insulated from our pity."[38] Mulryne sees *The White Devil* as a
world of "moral and emotional anarchy." He emphasizes Webster's
humor: "An elusive but unmistakable current of humor is made to
play about almost every scene and incident; it sets at a distance the
anarchy the play embodies and yet in some ways intensifies it, for it
is utterly corrosive of any value that would seem about to stem the
tide of anarchy and give us a resting place for our sympathy."[39]
Webster's mocking intelligence continually modifies the great and
passionate events of *The White Devil;* and when Giovanni comes
and we hear of future order, we don't believe it.

His commentary on *The Duchess of Malfi* is familiar. Although he
finds it more satisfying than the earlier play and full of events which
bring forth our sympathy more than any other Jacobean play
outside Shakespeare, he notes an absence of self-critical intelligence,
manifested in a "general tendency to relax the dramatic movement

for the insertion of material that does not support the forwarding of the central dramatic interest."[40] However, the play survives, but only by virtue of the superb control of tone and atmosphere. As for a lack of motive on Ferdinand's part, it is "the very absence of a real motive in the oppressors that helps to make the Duchess' tragedy so unnerving."[41] If anything, adds Mulryne, it is an incestuous passion which grips Ferdinand. While *The Duchess of Malfi* challenges, exalts, and disturbs us less than its predecessor, it carries with it greater depths of emotion and even coherence. Indeed, part of this coherence comes from an ease of statement in the play, not found in *The White Devil*. This fluency itself comes from an identifiable moral viewpoint which serves as a yardstick by which the characters may be judged. For Mulryne, the moral norm appears chiefly in terms of sexual constancy and honesty. Throughout the play we are never in doubt as to the evaluation of any of the characters' actions. Further, Mulryne sees the Duchess-Antonio relationship as the play's central situation.

We should add to this criticism mention of J. R. Brown's introduction to his 1960 Revels edition of *The White Devil*. He sees the play as a concatenation of impressionistic renderings of isolated moments, a histrionic anthology of extreme situations. The play is, as we have heard more than once before, rich in its parts, but "a gothic aggregation rather than a steady exposition and development towards a single consumation."[42] Characterization is impressionistic, or momentarily perceived, with only Flamineo most consistently presented. The basis for Webster's dramatic vision is found in the play's title and its connotation of appearance versus actuality. We rarely know when a character's speech is reliable, and "our response becomes subtle and intricate, and also insecure."[43] There is, in a sense, a moral norm extant: "Man lives in a net: if he sins . . . some retribution must follow; he cannot deceive without bearing the consequence. Man's judgement is within, perhaps unknown to others, perhaps unrecognized as such by himself."[44] Men's actions influence themselves, and one evil deed may hurt others. But at the end, there is no guarantee of any moral readjustment in this confusing world. Is there any hopeful promise in the words of Giovanni? "There is no answer; the play leaves us with a sense of insecurity. The predicament which Webster presented is continual."[45]

Having studied the sources for *The White Devil* in 1957, Gunnar Boklund enlarged his approach for his study of the companion tragedy; the result was *The Duchess of Malfi: Sources, Themes, Characters* (1962). It is an interesting and thorough study which finds Webster a sophisticated writer, not a decadent dealing in horror for horror's sake, and a man independent, in certain areas, of his sources.

Much of the book is concerned with Webster's sources: Boklund surveys the important ones, Painter, Sidney's *Arcadia*, Cinthio's *novella Oronte*, Bandello's account of the *Duchess*, Grimestone's translation of Goulart, and Guicciardini's *Storia d'Italia*. He finds Webster creating largely the tremendous villainy of the Aragonian brothers, the honesty of Antonio, and the random operation of fortune. He finds the interpretation of Ferdinand as a victim of incestuous passion improbable, in that the tenor of the supposedly decisive passages is almost the same as in Painter. Ferdinand for Boklund is an "abstraction, an epitome of brutal, uncontrolled violence."[46] Indeed, Webster's method is to demonstrate the simple and static properties of several of the main figures in various situations.

Among his notes on the characters we have Boklund's observation that there is an ambiguity about moral concepts which the Duchess and Antonio are supposed to follow. He sees the Duchess as a headstrong woman overwhelmed by passion, one who loves not wisely but too well. Webster is interested in the distinction between nature and custom. Antonio, he feels, has been cut down from sources to mere human size, and has become a moderately virtuous, weak commoner who is caught among circumstances over which the average man has no control. The Duchess herself has also been reduced to woman. They become, at the hands of the evil symbolic power of the Cardinal and Ferdinand, the people that things are done to.

Bosola remains an enigma, writes Boklund. He is an expert rationalizer finally brought out of himself by the Duchess. "It is in Bosola's reflections that the contrast between seeming and being is most searchingly considered. He sees through appearances, the sham and pretense of social life, and so does his adversary and counterpart the Duchess."[47] In both their efforts to be the things they are not—to uphold appearances—they are tied together in the logic of Webster's dramatic thought.

The horrors of Act IV are considered in detail, and Professor Boklund can account for the artistic integrity and thematic appropriateness of each. That these interesting explanations ever occur to anyone while Act IV churns along in front of him is questionable. Boklund's hardest task—he admits this himself—is to deal with the device of the madmen. Their compelling reason for existence, he writes, is to suggest powerfully the ultimate disorder to which Ferdinand would reduce his sister. Their relevance is increased by Ferdinand himself going mad.

Not too unlike other conclusions is the ultimate meaning of the play for Boklund:

It is important to realize the pattern is not a moral one. Good and evil alike suffer from . . . frustration of plans. . . . Not only does providence lack a tool in *The Duchess of Malfi*, it does not operate, even in the form of nemesis. What governs the events is nothing but chance, independent of good and evil, physics and metaphysics, and symbolized most appropriately in the figure of a madman. Webster's use of ironic reversals is thus part of a larger scheme: plot and theme combine and cooperate to produce a final effect of unrelieved futility, foreshadowed several times in the past by Bosola's bitter denunciations of the world. . . . In a final analysis of *The Duchess of Malfi* the theme of futility, as developed in the last act, is obviously of central significance.[48]

But Boklund carefully notes that "with far less ambiguity than in *The White Devil* moral integrity is accepted as the true guiding principle of man's life; its representatives even seem to be on the way toward establishing a duchy of virtuous living where evil triumphed before."[49]

In his concluding chapter, an examination of the play as a Jacobean tragedy, Professor Boklund restates some of his previous points on the abstract nature of the characters: the Cardinal, for example, leaves behind "a definite impression both of the destructive power of evil within society and the self-destructive power of evil within the human mind. . . ."[50] Although Antonio should have received greater attention, he is essential in the conflict. But Boklund, like many others, calls him a perfunctory character. As for the other creations,

What more than anything else contributes to the impressions of recognizable human beings that his characters convey is his habit of suddenly concentrating attention on a particular process within a particular character's mind and his genius of finding the right words for it. . . . Suggestive abstraction, the application of touches of psychological insight and sudden poetic expressiveness—these are the means by which Webster creates his characters.[51]

He turns again to the violence, noting that everything outrageous can be defended on thematic grounds. But he considers the risky business of staging Act V and admits a desire that Webster had used a little less horror; the results would have been equally as effective. Finally, at the close of the play when

the theme of *integer vitae* is again sounded and its hopeful representative introduced, this dark mood cannot be dispelled. The amoral world is depicted as repellent in its rottenness, its safety and glory no more than illusions, and the moral alternative is stated unmistakably, firmly and attractively as Webster's sense of realism permits, but even the moral individual will live in the general "shadowe or deepe pit of darknesse." And he may not live long. . . . The conclusion of the play demonstrates, ironically, but unmistakably how restricted is the power of virtue and how problematic the transformation of evil. It may occasionally be defeated through self destruction, as indicated by Ferdinand's madness, but otherwise only through the workings of chance, which rather than any force that might be called divine seems to govern the world of the play.[52]

The year following the publication of Boklund's work brought Clifford Leech's brief re-examination of *The Duchess of Malfi* (1963) for the *Studies in English Literature* series, analyses aimed at the English sixth former and university student with the emphasis on various works as literary art in today's world.

In his aforementioned 1951 volume, Leech was generally concerned with total meaning. In this later study his view is close and specific. There seem to be certain modifications of earlier views, primarily in his acceptance of certain inconsistencies noted in 1951. Also, from Leech's notes in 1963, we cannot help feeling that Webster *did* realize the significance of this play, though in 1951 Leech had presumed the contrary. Although Leech had written earlier that Act V is soon forgotten following the previous and terrifying scenes, he maintains now that the intention of Act V is "surely to suggest the presence of the dead Duchess haunting those who have lived along with her. She is mentioned in every scene; her murder is the immediate cause of every detail of the action here; Ferdinand dies invoking her."[53] He still does not admit the total success of this act, but he does recognize that even the echo device is effective on the stage.

In other areas, Leech has not changed his mind. Bosola, he writes, is a grotesque kind of pander, who will bring brother and sister together in torment. He is not much as moral force: he goes to Milan "for revenge at least as much as for justice. We cannot see him as the voice of righteousness. He is petty beside the dead woman, even beside the mad Ferdinand, who knows more fully what horror is (though he does not probe it)."[54] As an instrument of justice, he "is pitifully imperfect, while he has shown address as tormentor and executioner."[55] Leech holds to his view of Ferdinand as incestuous lover. The peculiar intensity stems from the fact that Ferdinand himself is unaware of the reasons behind his persecution.[56] Indeed the whole story, for Leech, is one of human ignorance: Bosola is confused; the Duchess loves Antonio and shows no glimpse of his shortcomings; Antonio wrongly suspects Cariola of treachery, and so goes the story. They are, most certainly, "in a mist."

He considers the planning and composition of the play, and sees each act representing a phase in the story. Thus after an effect of constriction in the early acts, the new locality of Loretto moves us into the unknown, and in Act V we are confronted with the mystery of Milan. The fables serve for a distancing effect, something like a Greek chorus.

Finally, he considers Webster's tragic vision. It is concerned with suffering rather than action, freely incorporating physical violence. Indeed, the tortures are a ritualized black mass. The tragedy would not be effective if the victim were a pathetic sufferer. And this is not the case here. The Duchess is a human being with qualities of strength, sensuality, greed, humor, courage, foolishness:

These make her a person we can know. . . . She curses, she comes near to a loss of control . . . she clings to an assertion of her identity and rank. . . . These things strengthen our sense of her humanity, our sense of her achievement in learning a fit way to die. If *The Duchess of Malfi* gives us knowledge of the dreadfulness of suffering, the strange modes of expression and of fugitive escape that are led to when men are in its grasp, it gives us also a knowledge that is equipollent and encouraging.[57]

Yet only a year following these words of an encouraging knowledge arising from the Duchess' fortune came another article criticizing Webster's "blurred vision" (to use Leech's term in 1951). Jane Marie Luecke considered *The Duchess of Malfi* in "Comic and Satiric Confusion in a Tragedy" for *Studies in English Literature* in 1964. In spite of Professor Bogard's thesis, she feels that the latent confusion in the play arises "from an injudicious mixing of, and a failure to integrate, the comic and satiric elements. These elements are so pronounced as to weaken, if not destroy, the tragic effect."[58] She believes that for the first few acts, the play could pass as a tragi-comedy. The protagonist she finds a woman, not a duchess, seeking to close herself in social actions rather than find herself in a conflict of wills or circumstances. The Cardinal is hardly tragic. And al-though Ferdinand is more complex, his madness is fit for tragi-comedy; he never really comes alive. His is the rage of a madman, not the torment of a man caught in a fatal passion. Julia is the bored whore of comedy. And Bosola is a great problem: he is a divided malcontent, speaking first as impersonal observer and satirist and then as someone personally involved. "He is then no longer a satirist, he is a figure of tragedy. . . . 'A hero from one genre is always a failure in another.' "[59] Yet the play is not a failure when we see it whole, as "one cosmic frustration. . . . we are tempted to conclude that perhaps the very confusion we have descried in the play creates its own particular catharsis."[60] However, she adds, "Webster over-shot his mark, and in attempting to give universal magnitude to characters and situations which are at best limited he causes his audience to stop just short of being taken in by his cynicism. Consequently, the catharsis for those who have read with their hearts (the object of tragedy) is at best that of cosmic satire rather than of tragedy—frustration, the same frustration that results from hearing about martyrs with mistaken causes."[61]

Thus we close for the present a long line of modern Webster criticism, the line which includes writers who may or may not celebrate various characteristics of Webster, but who often agree that Webster is vague in total meaning and that for all the great lines, great scenes, and great tonal unity, there is a lack of thematic unity. The tragedies leave us in a morally ambiguous world. The good as well as the evil characters exist only to be snuffed out; and it makes no difference whether one has led the life of Cornelia or of Brachiano.

# 7

# THE MORAL VISION

George Chapman, saluting Sir Thomas Howard in his dedication to *The Revenge of Bussy D'Ambois*, writes of "material instruction, elegant and sententious excitation to virtue, and deflection from her contrary, being the soul, limbs, and limits of an authentical tragedy."[1] We turn to an Elizabethan critic of Sidney's *Arcadia*, John Hoskins, and learn further that "he that will truly set down a man in a figured story must first learn truly to set down an humour, a passion, a virtue, a vice, and therein keeping decent proportion add but names and knit together the accidents and encounters."[2] Because of such commentary, particularly the Chapman statement, our last group of critics has seen new meaning in Webster's lines: "for mine own part I have ever truly cherish'd my good opinion of other men's worthy labours, especially of that full and heightened style of Master Chapman . . . wishing what I write may be read by their light. . . ."[3]

F. P. Wilson writes in his brief but important *Elizabethan and Jacobean,* "The dramatists, alike with the poets and prose writers, assumed a Christian universe. Their plays are worked out for the most part in terms of this world, but the beliefs and moral values of the Christian religion are not challenged."[4] Travis Bogard's belief that Webster could find no system for the evaluation of good and evil has, for these writers, nothing to substantiate it historically. Wilson's is, after all, an historical approach, prefaced by such works as Willard Farnham's *The Medieval Heritage of Elizabethan*

*Tragedy* (1936), Howard Baker's *Induction to Tragedy* (1936), and Theodore Spencer's *Death and Elizabethan Tragedy* (1936). These studies emphasized the close relation between Elizabethan tragedy and medieval life, with its emphasis on the Moral Way. Elizabethan tragedy, these writers showed, is in many ways but the culmination of a continuing dramatic tradition stemming from the mysteries and moralities of the Middle Ages. E. M. W. Tillyard's *The Elizabethan World Picture* (1943) gave us the world as seen by the thinkers of the day, with their firm belief in the words of the tenth homily: "Almighty God hath created and appointed all things in heaven, earth, and waters in a most excellent and perfect order." This was Shakespeare's world; he has rewritten the tenth homily in Ulysses' speech on order. More recently, writers continued such an approach in their studies of Shakespeare as an artist writing within a Christian milieu: S. L. Bethell's *Shakespeare and the Popular Dramatic Tradition* (1944); John F. Danby's *Shakespeare's Doctrine of Nature* (1949); Paul N. Siegel's *Shakespearean Tragedy and the Elizabethan Compromise* (1957); H. S. Wilson's *On the Design of Shakespearean Tragedy* (1957); and Irving Ribner's *Patterns in Shakespearian Tragedy* (1960)—all give support to F. P. Wilson's belief that "Shakespearean tragedy is as powerful in its expression of good as in its expression of evil."[5]

Wilson's approach to the Jacobean age is an important one, leading to several accounts of Shakespearean tragedy and new evaluations of Webster and the other Jacobeans. His main thesis is that there is no break between the Elizabethan and Jacobean tradition of belief and that "the beliefs and moral values of the Christian belief are not challenged."[6] If Jacobean tragedy makes little reference to heaven, there remains a Christian framework: this was a church-going, sermon-reading age. The dramatists, writes Wilson, are not much interested in dogma; they are more concerned with the problem of evil and suffering, the pull of this world and how it can be reconciled with the aspirations of the next, and man's behavior at the supreme moment of life—at death. But all of this exploration takes place against a background of a Christian universe under divine ordinance.

In his section on drama he emphasizes its symbolic function and here notes Hoskins' comment on the *Arcadia*. "Few dramatists," he adds, "perhaps only Webster and Middleton, share some of Shakespeare's power of expressing a play's moral intention in and through

characters that can be mistaken for creatures of flesh and blood."[7]
He further notes that to expect

in Elizabethan or Jacobean drama in general a realistic representation
of human character comparable to what is found in some fifteenth- and
sixteenth-century paintings is to expect what is not there and seriously
to misinterpret what is there. In Marlowe there is a strong infusion of
the morality play. Greedy-for-power, Insolence, Greed, Pride, are some
of his characters. In Jonson, Marston, and Tourneur, also, the characters
are humors or moral qualities and any convention is considered justifiable
if it subserves the moral idea. . . . The moral attitudes are patent and
rigid from the start. . . . It is the rarest thing outside Shakespeare to
find the gradual modification of character by character or experience.
There remains in Jacobean as in Elizabethan drama a strong infusion
of the morality play.[8]

His comment on Webster is fairly brief; his chief contribution is
explaining Bosola's function as Bellman. In 1605 a rich Londoner
gave money for the delivery of a speech outside the dungeon of
condemned Newgate prisoners the night before the execution and
for another speech during the stop by the church wall made by the
cart carrying the prisoners to Tyburn. The melancholy words were
accompanied by a tolling handbell; and thus Wilson's main point:
the Jacobeans inherited "from the later Middle Ages a preoccupation with death which seems to us abnormal. Their lives were
guarded about with symbols of dissolution; the death's head and the
*memento mori* were still in vogue."[9] He praises Webster's power of
concentrated speech (although Middleton's plainness of speech gets
the profoundest tragic effects outside of Shakespeare, he adds).
Wilson closes the chapter with the note that Webster, Tourneur, and
Middleton come nearest to Shakespeare "in seriousness of purpose,
in moral imagination, and in the gift of compression by which a line
becomes taut with meaning and the disturbance of the rhythm is as
much a work of the imagination as the word and the image. . . ."[10]

Thus for Wilson, the greatest Jacobean dramatists were the
moralists of their time, sharing an ethical vision which gave form to
their plays. Their characters were symbols; and only through great
poetic illusion do Shakespeare, Webster, and Middleton convince us
that their characters are real. Actually, the characters are specific
symbols used to project universal truths, in the best of the medieval
traditions. These principles Wilson set down; and a few years later
Lord David Cecil applied them more thoroughly to John Webster.

Cecil's account of Webster as moralist came in his *Poets and Storytellers*, which appeared in 1949, the same year in which Ian Jack's *Scrutiny* article attacked Webster as a formless dramatist incapable of moral unity. No one, wrote Cecil, has truly grasped the nature of Webster's achievement. "With Shakespeare, he stands apart from the other Elizabethans as an author who, while accepting the dramatic conventions of the time, turns them to a different and higher purpose."[11] He rises above his fellows in intellectual and spiritual insights:

He uses the Elizabethan freedom to express a vision of the conflict of spiritual forces, that, in his view, lie behind the appearances of life as we see it. This is what gives his work unity and significance. . . . Each play presents us with an act of sin and its consequences. . . . His theology is Calvinistic. The world as seen by him, is of its nature incurably corrupt. To be involved in it is to be inescapably involved in evil: all its apparent beauties are a snare and a delusion.[12]

Webster, he writes, is strictly a child of the Reformation, of a Christian society. For him, the cause of human tragedy is the deliberate sinning of free men, men who lay up their treasures not in heaven, but on the glories of church and state. (We remember the line "Let my son fly the courts of princes.")

There are only the very good and the very bad in Webster, and it is the bad character who is active and dynamic. The good characters—Isabella, Marcello, Cornelia, Antonio, and the Duchess—are passive: "They cannot identify themselves with the activities of the sin-tainted world. . . . Helpless victims, they are swept into the turmoil set up by the furious energy of the wicked."[13] A pessimistic attitude? Not at all, if we can accept Cecil's view. In a sense, he explains, Webster does believe in the ultimate victory of virtue:

The good are only defeated on the material plane. Morally they triumph. No amount of suffering corrupts them or breaks their courage: on the contrary, their virtue shines even brighter for the blood-stained darkness that gathers about them. Furthermore, though they may be destroyed, so also—and far more dreadfully—are their enemies. God is not mocked, the evil doer is caught in the net he has woven for others. And he realizes why. . . . Before they die the villains are always forced to recognize the supremacy of that Divine Law, against which they have offended. . . . Always at the end of Webster's plays the Divine Law is vindicated. The final scene of each presents a new and virtuous generation entering to re-establish that moral order which has been destroyed by the acts of sin which have caused the tragedy.[14]

Webster's tragic vision, then, is the world as a fallen place where suffering outweighs happiness, and evil is the controlling force. "Yet it is also a place where the moral law cannot be thwarted indefinitely. So that finally evil destroys itself, justice is vindicated."[15]

Then Cecil studies examples of these principles in the two tragedies. Flamineo, for instance, the intellectual sinner, dies with a defiant mocking courage—"but it masks an absolute despair. Though no longer capable of appreciating the value of good, he yet realizes that evil doing is also profitless."[16] And Cecil praises the much berated Act V of The Duchess of Malfi. To be sure, the Duchess, our chief object of sympathy, is dead. But the main theme, "as always with Webster, is the act of sin and its consequences. Till these consequences are followed out to their final conclusion, the dramatist's intention is not made plain. Moreover, the central figure, as far as that action is concerned, is the man who murders her, the man who has elected, against the promptings of his better self, to be the devil's agent in the drama."[17] And of course, Bosola's strain of good leads to repentance.

Not only does Webster have a moral vision, according to Cecil, but he is a "stern moral teacher whose plays are carefully designed to enforce the philosophy of human conduct in which he believes."[18]

Following F. P. Wilson, Cecil notes the heavy symbolism of Webster, for it is as symbols that many of Webster's horrors must be seen. To incarnate his spiritual drama with the fullest intensity, he must use symbols. The Duchess of Malfi torture scene, then, becomes a symbolic hell on earth. The villains do not need motives: symbolically, they are corrupted by original sin. The madmen, the severed hand, and other devices become symbolic incarnations of spiritual terror.

Thus Cecil depicts a Calvinistic Webster. We might only note that other critics have already made an answer to some of his propositions: particularly we might not share Cecil's confidence about virtue triumphant. We almost tend to overlook this fact of the quiet ascendancy of Good in the passionate, sweeping action carried on by the villains. The bad ones of Webster are indeed active and dynamic—and more interesting than the good souls, as villains usually are.

We might mention in passing R. J. Kaufmann's brief review of J. R. Brown's 1960 edition of The White Devil in the Revels Plays series. As noted earlier, Brown sees the play as an anthology of extreme situations. Kaufmann, without elaborating, disagrees: "Surely, above all things Webster created a poetical context, a strange moral atmosphere which compels us to see the characters (however isolated they periodically may be through pride and fear) as strongly related and mutually qualifying each other."[19] He maintains further that *The White Devil* achieves formal integration by being a "family tragedy," along with such different plays as *King Lear, The Revenger's Tragedy,* and *Women Beware Women.*

In *Jacobean Tragedy: The Quest for Moral Order,* Irving Ribner finds the greatest Jacobean tragedians seeking "in their various ways to discover some meaning in human suffering, some kind of affirmation which can make life possible in a world which seems to give reason only for despair."[20] This quest, he adds, has been the traditional mission of tragedy as an art form. And specifically, Webster's plays "are an agonized search for moral order in the uncertain and chaotic world of Jacobean scepticism by a dramatist who can no longer accept without question the postulates of order and degree so dear to the Elizabethans."[21] In *The White Devil,* Webster creates a poetic impression of the contradictory world he sees, "but he can find in his story no pattern to relate good and evil and provide a basis for morality."[22] But out of Vittoria's preservation of her integrity of life, Webster finds one positive value, the implications of which are explored in *The Duchess of Malfi:*

If death may reveal an inherent nobility in human life, such nobility is real, and it may be the basis of a moral order. In *The Duchess of Malfi* we see a new morality emerging in the final act out of evils more chilling in their horror than those of the earlier play. This search for moral order links Webster to Shakespeare in the highest range of tragedy, and to fully perceive Webster's achievement we must see his later play as the exploration of a value postulated in the earlier one and as the final resolution of the problem with which both plays are concerned.[23]

And as F. P. Wilson had noted several years earlier, Webster's plays "have an ethical and an allegorical dimension. They are symbolic works, and if their poetry is great it is because of its perfection as the instrument by which the artist reveals a vision of man's relation to the forces of evil in the world and affords a basis for renewed acceptance of life which is tragic reconciliation."[24]

*The Duchess of Malfi,* states Ribner, shows the social consequences which Vittoria's integrity may have when embodied in a virtuous woman, and its power to afford a basis for morality. "In his next play," he writes, "Webster goes to show the power of a pride in life to destroy some of the world's evils and thus to justify the fact of human existence in a world seemingly without other value."[25] The moral statement of the play is not in the many axioms of Delio and other virtuous characters, but in the whole impression of the drama: "*The Duchess* is a unified work, with mood, action, characterization and poetry all carefully shaped together as an assertion of the inherent dignity of man."[26] And the much-maligned fifth act becomes for Ribner "of crucial importance, for its function is to exhibit the effect upon the debased world of the human spirit's triumph in spite of the body's destruction."[27] The nobility of the human spirit enables man to survive and triumph in spite of the world we find in *The Duchess of Malfi*. The characters are not to be taken as real people. As Wilson had observed earlier, they are imaginative symbols, particularly the figure of Bosola, who plays several symbolic roles, primarily that of tutor to the Duchess in the awakening of her greatness in the torture scene. His line "look you, the stars shine still" (IV, i, 120) stands for Ribner as an assertion of the permanence of nature: "While the stars shine there is certainty, for we cannot doubt the reality of the universe and of an illuminating beauty which persists in spite of all."[28] The stars for this critic become a symbol of hope. In the final act Bosola becomes the agent in which the spirit of the Duchess lives, and it is this spirit which comes to dominate the world of the Aragonian brothers. Bosola carries her values into the final act, "becoming an instrument of justice which affirms a moral order."[29]

Ultimately, the lesson of the play, as Ribner sees it, is a lesson in nobility, nobility which encompasses love, humanity, and regeneration. In her famous lines of self-assertion, "I am Duchess of Malfi still" (IV, ii, 139), the Duchess "affirms the permanence of the spirit which is the really vital part of man. . . . This is Webster's answer to the pain of living and the fragility of the human condition."[30] We must accept, Webster is saying, the tragedies of life without complaint, and we must come to death with courage. This is the final moral statement of the play, "to which all the parts of *The Duchess of Malfi* were carefully designed to give poetic expression,"[31] and which unifies and illuminates the entire drama.

Alexander W. Allison is in essential agreement with Professor Ribner's thesis regarding *The Duchess of Malfi*. Writing in the

Spring, 1964, issue of *Studies in English Literature,* he considers
"Ethical Themes in *The Duchess of Malfi,*" and finds Webster pretty
much as Swinburne did: morally noble. "In Webster's overtly moral-
istic work, the relationship of the agents to one another and the
patterns of similarity and difference between them are devoted
chiefly to illustrating human potentialities for good and evil."[32]

The article is largely a character study of the main roles. Allison
considers the major design in which good and evil may enter into a
diversity of relationships with human psychic traits. The Duchess,
for example, is like Ferdinand in temperament but not in character.
Ferdinand shares her self-will and erotic bent; indeed, her flaw, as
tragic protagonist, "is a temperamental excess of which one token is
her eroticism."[33] Her tragic failing is reflected, on a lower level, in
Ferdinand's frenzy. Webster places Bosola and Antonio "in the wide
area between his heroine and her antagonists, so that he may have,
finally, an evenly graduated scale—a calculus of human ethical
potentiality."[34] And Allison forms a scale: the Cardinal is on the
lowest ring; Ferdinand is the next to lowest, since he is compulsive
rather than deliberate, daemonic rather than diabolical. In the
middle is the ambivalent Bosola and the loyal, ineffective Antonio.
The Duchess, of course, represents the one positive virtue. As she is
stripped of earthly goods, she comes to rely the more fully on herself
and on God. Allison sees Act IV as an existential confrontation:
though possessed by human failings, the Duchess represents the
good person who, as evil closes in, comprehends her world fully.

And it is a world of powerful and oppressive evil, Allison notes.
Yet,

. . . The play as a whole subsumes all such promptings toward cynicism
and despair and makes an affirmation in their despite. For the last act
states that evil, however strong, can sustain itself only by preying upon
virtue and hence contains within itself the seed of its own destruction.
It follows that the principle of virtue has an autonomy and permanence
which evil lacks: some moral agency must exist which is beyond the
power of change and decay after all.[35]

T. B. Tomlinson's account of Webster in *A Study of Elizabethan
and Jacobean Tragedy* (1964) might be considered here, if with
reservation as to this categorizing. Tomlinson appears to think
Webster a definite moralist who nevertheless arrives late on the
scene in *The Duchess of Malfi;* for this critic *The White Devil* has

little moral focus. The forces of good are outnumbered in *The White Devil*, and, more importantly, the forces of evil have all the best lines. There is, in spite of Travis Bogard's explanations, too much of a division between the satiric and the tragic for Tomlinson, and the result is that "Webster presents us with admiration and horror fatally unrelated to each other."[36]

Tomlinson's book is an interesting one, if not always convincing. He relegates Webster, Marlowe, Chapman, Ford, Kyd, and Beaumont and Fletcher to secondary positions, and places Tourneur and Middleton with Shakespeare as among the Chosen. His chief thesis seems to be that it is vitality, energy, and even vulgarity which impart the tragic force, with the hero and his environment closely related. The world against which he struggles paradoxically nourishes and supports him. (Bradley, of course, would have the hero isolated.) *The Duchess of Malfi* is on the brink of decadence, but not quite over. (When the drama loses its energy, tragedy declines.)

In Tomlinson's opinion, Webster pulls *The Duchess of Malfi* together in the fourth act with massive concentration and "by a sudden and comparatively crude moral awakening . . . which defies anyone to say that this is not a unified work!"[37] There is, at the last minute, an intense moral effort.

The first three acts offer brittle fragments of experience, if they do present a possible sense of expectancy about what is to come. But generally there is much frenzied activity which perhaps leaves the door open for a later focusing agent. The door opens in Act IV:

The point of Ferdinand's instability, Bosola's gloating over corruption, the Cardinal's venality, is now seen to be that Webster is asking, or to put it more accurately, has at last got round to asking, what of the person who, surrounded by all this, *has* some individuality, integrity, wholeness? . . . Part of Webster's real point, obscured in the beginning of the play, is now becoming clear. . . . What is, after all, the status and nature of "innocence" in a guilty or disorganized or stupid world?[38]

And now the writing tightens, with the dominant, repeated image of the Duchess imprisoned in horrors growing upon the reader as a single experience. He transposes the Racinian idea of "the figure or personalized image, asserting itself against the engulfing chaos, failing to struggle free, indeed on the contrary deriving (as a total image rather than merely as a person or character) great force and power from the twisting violence of the 'background' (Ferdinand, Bosola, the madmen, etc.)."[39]

Rather than seeing the Duchess as an heroic figure, Tomlinson finds instead a sort of collectivized imagery: "We see the total situation as a dominant image in which the figure of the Duchess, posing in familiar attitudes, is both tainted (or twisted) by the bitterness of Bosola and at the same time borne up, heightened in significance by a kind of sympathy with the violence she opposes."[40] And as she curses, Tomlinson cannot see her fully as a lonely representative of mankind: she is infected in this torture scene by the chaos she represents. The madmen challenge the Duchess to escape being, in a sense, one of them: "so all-embracing and inevitable is the corruption with which she is surrounded that in a sense she belongs to the brother's world—certainly to no other—and some of the mud must stick."[41]

Act V depends upon the dominating and organizing impact of the preceding act; it does relapse into the impressionism of the opening scenes, but this time there is direction and purpose. The characters, particularly the Cardinal, come alive; and Tomlinson senses a pity for all on the part of Webster. The world is truly a mist of error, but

All of them recognize failure, weakness, extinction, and recognize it, if anything, with clearer sight than Bosola himself originally did. There is less fantasy now. When the Duchess died, many questions were left open. In a sense they still are: What is after all her particular status and worth in this kind of situation? But in the case of the other three, some termination, some finality is there. Within the often fascinating Jacobean irony, there is with each of them a recognition of the rightness and accuracy of the way the action of the play has finally developed. . . . In terms of the emptiness that is awaiting people like the Cardinal, the play here achieves a pretty clear-sighted statement of the emptiness of Webster's world in its entirety. The irony and clarity of the verse raise the whole thing above the pessimism that has been lying in wait for Webster all through Act V (if we believe Eliot, all through the play) . . . .

The case for The Duchess of Malfi, then, is simply that, centering as it does on the "prison" image of Act IV, it succeeds in presenting a new and particular attitude to living, a fresh statement of the familiar Elizabethan problem of clarity in chaos, vitality in destruction. Moreover, Webster's success comes because of, not despite, the decadence and disintegration that threaten him at every turn. . . . The result is an image of impressive greatness, but greatness defined partly in terms of anarchy and violence.[42]

Finally, we may take note of the excellent edition in 1964 by John Russell Brown of *The Duchess of Malfi* in the Revels Plays series. In his introduction to the tragedy Brown makes an effort to explain the principle of unity which binds up the play, a unity that is based not so much on a "moral vision" but on a "perceptive concern" for the characters and society we see in *The Duchess of Malfi*. His notes are included here, since he does find Webster "concerned" with the ethics involved, though Brown is a considerable distance from the views of the other critics in this chapter. And his work indicates a new turn in Webster criticism as we reach the mid-sixties.

Considering first the structure, Brown notes that the characters have been made to reflect upon each other: the aggressive Julia, for instance, with the Cardinal and Delio in Act II, and with Bosola in Act V, invites comparison between herself and the Duchess who woos and loves in private. She is "an ingenious reflection and elaboration of central concerns in the tragedy."[43] The structure is bolstered by contrasts: one brother is ruled by passion, the other by intelligence; two ordinary men succeed at court, Antonio by virtue, Bosola by corruption. And Antonio later comes to find that the "quest of greatness" is a child's game with a bubble, while Bosola urges worthy minds to suffer "for what is just." Whole scenes, Brown says, "are linked together behind the dialogue, as in a diagram,"[44] the first presence chamber scene with the Duchess at ease with her court, and the second, when she is alone and has to rush from the stage. Brown records many such scenes and follows other critics in noting the verbal accentuation which further ties the play together. Finally, in his comment on language, Brown makes an attempt to justify the sententious couplets which abound and often annoy: ". . . in performance they prove their worth in strengthening, by momentarily simplifying, the composition: they are necessary 'fixes,' or 'holds.' Nor are they isolated moments, but related to a tendency towards sententious speech in almost all the characters."[45]

Brown's chief contribution is his consideration of the principle of unity in Webster's view of the men and actions in this tragedy:

First, an "atmosphere," developing in the course of the tragedy. . . . Around 1920 this was Webster's chief appeal. . . . Since then critics have searched vigorously for a unified "moral vision," and have divided opinion; and this division points to the play's other unity. So does the play's style and structure. It is a unity of empirical, responsible, skeptical, unsurprised, and deeply perceptive concern for the characters and society portrayed. . . . Webster was interested in pretence and self-deceit, changes and reversals of roles, as modern writers are. . . . He did not question moral laws methodically like Donne . . . but he was skeptical of particular examples: regretfully his duchess contrasts man's restrictions to the freedom of "birds that live in the fields."[46]

His originality is found "in the moments of gentleness and clear thought which he gave to his giddy world, or in his sense of reality which made him place the last moments of his duchess . . . in the fourth act,"[47] knowing the importance of the last act, but also knowing that it would be painful and inept to try to put her death elsewhere.

Brown at length pays tribute to the large and sweeping effect of the play in performance, noting the crowded court scenes of the first three acts which alternate with the private scenes. Act IV brings the prison, which provides a steady dramatic focus. Act V is a mixture of stealth and swiftness. In a tragedy of confusion, hesitation, and contradictions, "The simple eloquence of the shape of the action is especially impressive. . . . And briefly, in the last silent homage to the son of the duchess, there is a hint that men may, perhaps, wish for some renewal and order."[48]

8

# WEBSTER AND
# THE MODERN STAGE

Clifford Leech has noted that one difficulty in making a judgment of John Webster is that his plays are not yet securely in the theatrical repertory:

> We may see an occasional performance if we are lucky and seize our chances, but we need more than that if we are to have a reasonably full confidence in our own judgment. Those of us who rank *The Duchess of Malfi* as major tragedy . . . need to test this against the effects of diverse performances. . . . When Great Britain and the United States develop an appropriate sense of a dramatic repertory . . . we shall know more surely than we do now where some of our dramatists surely belong.[1]

J. R. Mulryne, however, has pointed out that today Webster's tragedies are produced more often than are those of any other of Shakespeare's contemporaries;[2] and a survey of modern professional stagings (and the recollection of nineteenth-century efforts) shows that they are often produced with results that might indeed discourage future repertory companies. Ian Jack has stated flatly that "there is something a trifle ridiculous"[3] about the playwright, and a review of the critical reaction to some twentieth-century productions of Webster would seem to furnish proof: impressive sums have been lost in professional efforts; and audiences have tittered through the years at the most tragic scenes. In fact, a comprehensive survey of *The White Devil* and *The Duchess of Malfi* in the modern professional theater seems to indicate that where Webster belongs is not on the stage, but in the study. However, two postwar productions in

151

London of the two dramas achieved some success, and in 1960 a production of *The Duchess* was hailed by one English critic as "intense and powerful";[4] so perhaps there is some hope that Webster will gain through intelligent staging in the theater the prestige he enjoys in the study. But intelligent, sensitive productions of Webster are generally rare in the modern theater, perhaps because we as audiences lack the proper historical imagination. Yet we may wonder if these several failures are all our fault.

The first London staging of *The Duchess of Malfi* in nearly thirty years came on November 24, 1919, through the auspices of the Phoenix Society, an organization devoted to the re-establishment of classic authors on the English stage. The *London Times* reported the next day that the difficulty of reviving a Jacobean tragedy in a skeptical age is that "just when the author . . . wants to make your flesh creep he is more likely to provoke you with laughter. There was certainly some tittering yesterday afternoon towards the close of *The Duchess of Malfi*, when Bosola killed Antonio and then the Cardinal and then Duke Ferdinand, but not until after Ferdinand had run him through the body, so that there were four corpses on the floor in a heap."[5] The writer admits that no one smiled at the Duchess' tortures. Oddly, one violent death is tragic; four, comic. Although some of the personages were interesting for the *Times* critic (he liked William Rea's sense of isolation in Bosola), it seems to have been impossible to achieve the frame of mind which accepted Burbage and Betterton: " . . . *The Duchess of Malfi* is no longer a live classic, but a curio for connoisseurs." The *Athenaeum* found fault with the actors; the *Spectator*'s critic censured Webster the dramatist: we forget how *The Duchess of Malfi* will look "when the play is acted and we must listen at immense length to an impartial rendering of the whole naive, fantastic jumble of blood and rhetoric."[6] J. K. Prothero in the *New Witness* saw some order in the chaos, and evaluated the production as at least good melodrama with good heroes and bad villains; and W. J. Turner in the London *Mercury* condemned the tittering audience which lacked historical imagination. Turner, the only real (if hesitant) defender of the production, like even Ferdinand, who died standing on his head. The reactions of T. S. Eliot and William Archer have been noted previously. Only Eliot saw the afternoon as an indictment of the modern stage; Archer, of course, was repelled by Webster's inability to write like Ibsen.

The 1919 production, suffering from various acting styles and insufficient knowledge of the art of speaking blank verse, passed into memory as a disastrous experience. We might note that an amateur production at Cambridge of *The White Devil* one year later did find the general approval of E. M. Forster in the *New Statesman:* the actors "at their worst . . . were impassive, and at their best they were very fine indeed."[7] (The group, the well-known Marlowe Dramatic Society, four years later staged *The Duchess of Malfi* to another appreciative review in the same journal. The accounts indicate that the actors primarily stood and recited verse.)

In October, 1925, the Renaissance Theatre ventured a professional production of *The White Devil,* with a cast headed by Cedric Hardwicke and Viola Tree. The producers took no heed of the Phoenix Society's experience with *The Duchess of Malfi,* made the same mistakes, and generally received the same notices. James Agate in the Sunday *Times* criticized Webster: " . . . evil by becoming normal has ceased to be extravagant, and goodness no longer is." And, questionably, he notes that "it is difficult to see in Vittoria Corombona anything but the 'vamp' of the American film." The play had its moments, but any catharsis was impossible.[8] F. L. Lucas, then at work on his edition of Webster, reviewed the play for the *New Statesman;* and according to his report, the trouble was with the actors. Brachiano was too short, Camillo too handsome. The fatal error was a lack of dignity about the whole enterprise: the actors' movements amounted to "a flapping and a flopping," and, Lucas notes parenthetically, "Who can hope to speak passionate verse lying on the floor?"[9] The cutting was atrocious; there was no murder of Camillo and Isabella, and thus no reason existed for Vittoria's trial. The London *Mercury,* usually kind to classic revivals, found "a wild and mangled Webster,"[10] and the *Nation* stated that "the 'art of the theatre' is one thing: the 'literary play' is another; and they appear to be mutually destructive."[11] And so went the tenor of the reviews. The characters for most critics never approached reality; speeches here and there were good; but no dramatic unity ensued.

The 1919 production of *The Duchess of Malfi* seems to have killed it professionally for sixteen years. But in January, 1935, at the Embassy Theatre, Joyce Bland portrayed the Duchess and Roy Graham played a blond, effeminate Bosola in a production that held on for two weeks in spite of lukewarm to cold reviews. The production was generally tame: the masque of madmen was a ballet, of sorts; and amber lighting deemphasized the horrors. The *Times* stated that the actors lacked Elizabethan ferocity, that "something that belongs ineradicably to our milder age comes between them and Webster."[12] James Agate, however, in a later summation for the Sunday *Times,* thought it "a whale of a play," and to a certain degree, paraphrased Lucas' introduction to the collected works. Look at the scenes, he instructed, not the plot. Though he had reservations about the actors (granting that the part of the Duchess "starts off by being a good one and then somehow isn't"), "never once did I have to murmur 'Renaissance'."[13] But his was the one positive tribute. The *New Statesman* raised an issue which is central to the staging of Webster:

Can modern players . . . hope to compass the full-bloodied fury of Webster, or even Ford? This charnel house atmosphere to a modern audience is dangerously quaint, and when the number of bodies on the stage exceeds two, the titters begin, titters which not even Webster's packed bitterness can silence. Blame the audience or blame the players, the result is the same, a slackening of dramatic tension which assuredly is there, a sensation of good humored curiosity rather than the emotional exaltation which is so fine a poet's due.[14]

But the London *Mercury* blamed Webster for some of the problems: "A play goer has not the reader's untrammeled mind. . . . unless he is impressed with the reality of the representation he needs poetry more majestic . . . than any Webster commands."[15] Ivor Brown in the *Observer* summed up most of the reaction when he noted that "Monday night's audience ended rather with superior smiles than with emotional surrender."[16]

*The White Devil* made a fleeting appearance two months later in March, 1935. The New Phoenix Society staged it as an example of what would be coming if support were given. The *Times* critic thought it a good beginning, but lamented the plot's "crude devices, its childish solemnity with daggers and pistols and knavish tricks."[17] Most of the critics complained of a lack of unity in the production, a criticism voiced by many of the stage critics of the twenties and thirties. Reflecting many of Webster's academic critics, the reporters often note the excellence of a particular scene here and there, but the lack of any real coalescence in the whole. The *Observer* summed up for the critics of the 1935 *White Devil:* the "nods, becks, and wreathed smiles" of the audience proved that "three hundred years" is a long time for catharsis that is less than immortal to retain its power."[18]

It was something of a historic occasion when in January of 1938 *The Duchess of Malfi* was televised in a BBC studio. The production, for the reviewer in the *Listener,* proved enjoyable only when Esme Percy as Bosola was speaking the Websterian verse. Otherwise, the production suffered from cuts and (understandably) fluffing of lines. It was, for the one available critic, "a melodrama of almost unbelievable crudity."[19] (We may gather that the director played for the horror: among the shots was a long closeup of two sinister Negroes strangling the Duchess.)

Finally, in April of 1945, a production of Webster was acclaimed. Staged at the Haymarket Theatre, George Rylands' production of *The Duchess of Malfi* featured John Gielgud as Ferdinand, Peggy Ashcroft as the Duchess, and Cecil Trouncer as Bosola. Everything went right for this production: the actors were seemingly superb, with Gielgud giving his famous incestuous portrayal of Ferdinand; the cuts were reasonable; and tragically enough, the time was right. England was emerging from the grimmest conflict in her history, and perhaps the commanders at Buchenwald and Warsaw proved the possibility of creations like the Cardinal and Ferdinand. In an accidental but telling stroke, the London *Times* ran its review directly underneath five terrible pictures of German concentration camp atrocities.[20]

The *Times* reviewer called it the "most resolute" of attempts to reanimate a classic "which time has tamed."[21] Although the audience could not discard its "thwarting modernity" it "followed all that happened on stage with a respectful curiosity which rose at times to emotional sympathy." The tortures, he notes, were more decorative than horrible. The *Spectator,* in praising Gielgud's portrayal of Ferdinand as a victim of incestual passion, felt that his performance fully proved "that long before psychoanalysts and other semiscientific jargon of the psychologists a gifted writer could delve quite as far into human character as a Freud or any other quasi medical specialist."[22] (The *Times* preferred Trouncer's Bosola, a "murderer of fortune prematurely aged in the galleys.") The critical reservations took the usual form in criticism of *The Duchess:* the superfluity of the last act. J. C. Trewin in *Punch,* after admitting that Webster had held the stage superbly, called Act V "a mopping up operation."[23] Kenneth Tynan wrote of the shaky structure of the play which fortunately was bound up by Trouncer's portrayal of Bosola.[24]

The production was a success, and ran for several weeks at the Haymarket. For a while, at least, Webster was reinstated.

The success of *The Duchess of Malfi* led to the second Webster triumph in recent years; this time *The White Devil* gained honors through Michael Benthall's production in March, 1947, which featured Margaret Rawlings in the title role and Robert Helpmann as Flamineo. The costumes were lavish; the basic set was spare, with dark, gold-veined ducal pillars serving as a backdrop to a production which emphasized violence and death over psychological subtlety. As an example of the former, Flamineo met a gruesome death through four knife-wielding henchmen. (And there the play ended. No Giovanni appeared to serve, as he does for some critics, as a symbol of restoration of order.) The next morning the *Times* warned its readers to forget Shakespearean subtleties of character development and to enjoy the conscience-less characters, the vividness of the "strokes of horror which they practice on each other" and "the vigor of the language."[25] Stephen Potter noted in the *New Statesman* that everything seemed "credibly horrible" and was "presented with something of Webster's own exultation."[26] Kenneth Tynan found the staging "infinitely terrifying."[27] But Eric Keown of *Punch* was "frequently deafened, for there is too much shouting." Admitting that the production should be seen ("and will certainly be heard"), the critic in concluding made a most significant observation: "The interesting thing about this so-called tragedy is that it is our senses only which are touched by it and not our hearts."[28]

The Benthall *White Devil* survived several other critical reservations and went on to play for four months, becoming a resounding triumph for Webster on the modern stage.

America does not yet seem ready for Webster in the professional theater. There was a successful showing off-Broadway of *The White Devil* in 1955, which was staged for one night only; two years later *The Duchess of Malfi* played for two weeks at the same theater as something of a bloody curioso. And an earlier effort in 1946 to bring *The Duchess* to Broadway and duplicate its 1945 London success resulted in disaster. W. H. Auden adapted the play (giving to the Cardinal Ferdinand's lines about inheriting the Duchess' treasure!), and George Rylands, director of the London production, attempted to duplicate his previous staging. Elizabeth Bergner played the Duchess, Donald Eccles the Cardinal, and John Carradine Ferdinand. As Bosola, the Auden-Rylands production cast the Negro actor Canada Lee in white makeup, an oddity in casting that probably symbolized the entire blighted production.

The metropolitan critics had a field day in inventing harsh and witty attacks. The next morning New Yorkers read that *The Duchess of Malfi* was a slow, long, unimportant curio and that by 11:20 P.M. everyone was dead; that it was dull and silly; that it was far better off in the library where it belonged; and that it was one of the longest evenings ever spent on Broadway.[29] Atkinson in the *Times* felt that Auden's revision, which kept the Duchess in the obvious forefront of the play throughout, resulted in, of all things, a genteel horror play; and Morehouse of the *Sun* summed up everything succinctly: the play was a "gory old melodrama . . . slow-footed and ponderous in its march to the killings."

The play did not last. Though some may question the capacities of literary appreciation among some of the tabloid reviewers, we find the same dissatisfaction among the reviewers for the more literate journals. The production became, for a while, a legendary failure.

Webster was not redeemed on the American professional stage until 1955 at the Phoenix Theater, and the success of *The White Devil*'s staging was brief. The off-Broadway Phoenix was in its first year, and a regular feature was one-performance stagings of little-performed plays, sandwiched in between the regular bill. Thus in March, during a run of *The Master Builder*, came Jack Landau's production of *The White Devil*. It was done in modern dress, without scenery (two steps, two half curtains, and some spotlights), and played for the violence and movement of its script. Atkinson called it "one of the biggest shows of the year," delighted in the unstopping of mounting terror, and concluded—rather mysteriously —that the actors gave the ancient melodrama "a good shaking up. It's a lot of fun."[30] Hewes in the *Saturday Review* found it stimulating, though "a far cry" from the 1947 London staging, and made one of the standard criticisms of Webster-on-the-stage: as Flamineo, Fritz Weaver "tended to become ludicrous in the final blood bath."[31]

The only comments from any modern director on Webster are those of Jack Landau, the able director of the 1955 production.

Writing in *Theatre Arts* several months later, Landau stressed the dramatic violence of certain scenes—as do so many reviewers of Webster. It is rare that the stage critic sees the unity which the critics in the study—such as Cecil, Bogard, Ribner—so often call to our attention. For Landau, "the real interest is not Webster's implied moral tone but the dramatic conception of particular scenes. The play is a mine of electric situations, and the great problem in producing it is how to contain so many of them in one evening. . . . The literary value of *The White Devil* is very great, and from an academic point of view, the play is very penetrating. . . . But it was written for the stage, and that's where its greatest impact is. . . . It is a nightmare world like any gangster world."[32]

Landau's production never appeared again, in spite of two or three efforts to find a stage for an extended run. (Ten years later, Landau again directed *The White Devil*. See n38 below.)

Two years later Landau staged a poorly cut version of *The Duchess of Malfi* at the Phoenix in something approximating Edwardian dress, though Bosola and other henchmen were garbed as Mussolini secret police. The tenor of the next morning's reviews was that here was a fairly well-staged curiosity for viewers interested in Grand Guignol theater. Walter Kerr of the *Herald Tribune* had "a wonderful time," since blood "runs right over the footlights, spreads slowly up the aisle and spills well out into Second Avenue."[33] The Duchess' kissing the dead man's hand was nothing, he reports, for "Webster hasn't begun to drool yet." Hooded figures soon appeared from the orchestra pit with ropes and strangled Cariola upstage, the Duchess downstage. The actors played it all straight, Kerr writes, and the usual tittering did not occur—until "Corpse Number Nine doubled up." Richard Watts in the *Post* called it "one of the most absurd melodramas that was ever written in earnest," but finally noted that as a "carnival of ogres on parade, the *Duchess of Malfi* still has its curious interest." John McClain of the *Journal American* wrote that "the bodies are stacked up like cordwood when the final curtain descends. . . . If it's blood you want, you'll get it by the barrel at the Phoenix." John Chapman in his brief *Daily News* review recalled the 1946 production as "windy and boresome" and found this production little better. *Time*'s review a week later summed up the general reaction ". . . where this production succeeds most—as Grand Guignol—it stands forth least in stature."[34]

As of this writing, the most recent effort to produce Webster professionally was in London in December, 1960. The Stratford-on-Avon company began a winter stay at the Aldwych Theatre with *The Duchess of Malfi,* followed by *Twelfth Night.* This was the first professional London staging of *The Duchess* in fifteen years; and it was, depending on which critic one read, a "resolute handling" or a "well-dressed bore."

Donald McWhinnie's production featured Peggy Ashcroft in her second portrayal of the Duchess, Eric Porter as Ferdinand, and Max Adrian as the Cardinal. The five act structure was ignored, and there was no presence-chamber. Two critics found it stimulating, and nearly all the reviewers found something good somewhere. The *Times* felt the staging to be very fine, a "resolute handling" of the drama. Resolution, the critic adds, is needed "to conceal a slackening of poetic tension after the somewhat too early death of the heroine." The reviewer notes that the actors held the audience fascinated "before the fatal stabbings and poisonings multiply themselves with comic regularity. . . ."[35] H. A. L. Craig in the *New Statesman* hailed the production as marking the possible beginning of a true National Theatre; he saw in McWhinnie's production "a metaphysical melodrama" in which man does not go out "like a drugged beast. Webster has something absolute to say."[36] This in spite of the strange cutting of Bosola's last lines.

Craig makes an enigmatic note of the abuse put upon the producers for beginning the season with Webster. On this side of the Atlantic we can only observe that all the reviews were not of Craig's tenor. Eric Keown in *Punch* enjoyed the first half of the play very much, with its "rare patches of the poetry." But Webster's unfortunate way with final endings leads Keown to this accounting: "Peggy Ashcroft (the Duchess) and Cariola (her maid) die standing up, Derek Godfrey (Antonio) sitting down, Eric Porter (Ferdinand) and Max Adrian (the Cardinal) are already grounded and have only to collapse a little way, while it is left to Patrick Wymark (Bosola) to make a really thunderous Lyceum fall from the vertical. This total massacre is distinguished by a wealth of varied rattling, sobbing, and penetential groans."[37]

Alan Brien in the *Spectator* did not fault the play on grounds of improbability: ". . . in dramatic poetry, or poetic drama, anything can happen as long as the play remains congruous within itself. The trouble with *The Duchess of Malfi* is that it is written in quotations." Not finding any sense of metaphor, Brien objects to what he calls

Webster's overcolored "copywriter's prose," with images which "crumble at analysis." The poet's much praised psychology "consists entirely in loading each character with one dominant passion which goes endlessly churning on whatever is happening on the rest of the stage. . . . Webster is treated with an awed admiration which is seldom accorded to Shakespeare. The result is a well-acted, well-directed, well-dressed bore."[38]

# CONCLUSION

We are left in the mid-twentieth century with a John Webster whose fame is far less tenuous than it was in 1660, 1760, or 1860. In England, in 1960, one could go to London's Aldwych Theatre and see Dame Peggy Ashcroft as the Duchess of Malfi. In America, by 1960, one could go to a corner drug store and find on the book racks a paperback copy of *The Duchess of Malfi* in a "General Reader's Edition."[1] There has been an excellent recent novel which is a retelling of the Duchess' story;[2] and of course hundreds of undergraduates meet Webster yearly in their journey through *The Waste Land.* Webster's reputation is secure, and one doubts that, in the future, any shade of Canon Kingsley, or William Watson, or William Archer will rise to seriously challenge that reputation.

But the critics, as we have seen, are still in disagreement concerning the limits of that reputation; and too often in the theater, audiences laugh in the wrong places.

For a final effort in understanding these reactions, let us return to a statement by Eliot:

The whole of Shakespeare's work is one poem, and it is the poetry of it in this sense, not the poetry of isolated lines and passages or the poetry of the single figures which he created, that matters most. A man might, hypothetically, compose any number of fine passages or even of whole poems . . . and yet not be a great poet unless we felt them to be united by one significant, consistent, and developing personality.[3]

Is Webster a "great poet" by Eliot's definition? The author thinks the answer is in the affirmative, but this positive reply is followed by a number of serious qualifications.

161

Webster does realize a tragic vision, a fact that the *Scrutiny* group missed by looking too closely at parts rather than wholes. We can, I think, see a "consistent, developing personality" in the two famous tragedies. There is first the Webster of *The White Devil* who seizes upon the one positive virtue, integrity of life, in a crumbling world far different from the ordered world of Shakespeare and Hooker. Webster's world in *The White Devil* lacks standards; indeed, as more than one critic has pointed out, there is no Hamlet to serve as a moral yardstick for everyone else, and we have no measure of this court's lack of greatness. Only when Vittoria, an evil courtesan, is roused to assert her integrity of life is there triumph. But though we admire her—and after all, she *has* been faithful to Brachiano—we have to condemn her. However, in his next play Webster develops this theme of human worth and replaces his evil heroine with the Duchess of Malfi, an agent for good. As Professor Ribner has shown us, and as one or two earlier critics had mentioned briefly, her tenacious clinging to that same virtue has the power to work for the forces of good, as we see a rejuvenated Bosola in Act V, acting as a living symbol of justice; and Webster would have us believe that a new moral order may ensue, based not on any set system of Christian belief, but on the dignity of man. Tragedy, as a form, as John Mason Brown reminds us, "has always been, and remains, a kind of religion in its own right. It has sought to impose a pattern on the patternless; to create an independent logic by relating cause and effect where actual living is most frequently illogical; and to wring ecstasy from misdeeds and tribulations."[4]

This is what Websterian tragedy endeavors to do, in its world of Jacobean disillusionment and uncertainty. Furthermore, there is indeed a consistent, developing personality behind his two greatest plays, just as we can find similar significant development in a Shakespeare, a Yeats, an Eliot.

But in Webster's development toward the larger ethic demonstrated in *The Duchess of Malfi*, there is trouble along the way, a trouble in craftsmanship. Many critics seem to indulge Webster his faults, excusing him on the grounds of the ultimate success of his unity of tone—and, for a few acute observers, his unity of tone *and* thought. But for all the conceptions of play-as-poem, a basic deficiency in execution prevents the inclusion of Webster in the company of just such writers as Shakespeare, Yeats, and Eliot.

"The larger part of the labour of an author," wrote Eliot, "is critical labour, the labour of sifting, combining, constructing, expunging, correcting, testing. . . ."[5] And while we remember Henry Fitzjeffrey's sardonic portrait of the slow-moving "Crabbed Websterio," and though we have the playwright's own words in *The White Devil* preface as to his pace in composition, implying a critical lingering over details, I think that when we look at his plays afresh, we find the lack of a self-critical faculty. The very fact that through the years Webster can be all things to all men—moral, immoral, a great poet, a fake, gripping an audience one moment, making it laugh when it should not the next—implies a hand that might have been steadier in its grip on the quill. For a writer who does indeed take such meticulous care in so many places—note for instance his consistent imagery, his lines and even his scenes which play off against each other (*i.e.*, the Duchess-Antonio love scene, as opposed to the Julia-Bosola confrontation)—his passion for all-inclusiveness is so great that it mars the whole.

It is not that Ferdinand needs a definite motive for revenge. It is not that the Duchess had a previous son; and it is not that the horrors are too sickening. It is simply that there is often too much of everything. For dramas with important symbolic dimensions, his plays are amazingly realistic. As realistic dramas, they are poetically symbolic. Although Webster intended for us to note how the Duchess' spirit lives on in Act V in the reawakening of Bosola and his acts of justice, what has gone before is almost, for the moment, too much to forget. In the study, as we take our time in quiet perusal, we might agree—and several critics do—with Edmund Gosse that in the utter darkness at the close of *The White Devil* "we can for a moment before the curtain falls glance at the young Giovanni, virtuous and brave, rising like the morning star, to herald peace and good will to men."[6] But in the mighty sweep and passion of the evil that has gone before, are we, especially in the theater, really so convinced? Lord David Cecil feels that "the good are only defeated on the spiritual plane. Morally they triumph. No amount of suffering corrupts them or breaks their courage: on the contrary, their virtue shines even brighter for the blood-stained darkness that gathers about them. . . . always at the end of Webster's plays the Divine Law is vindicated."[7] How reassured do we really feel? The Duchess' spirit triumphs indeed, as Webster so intended. But hope for the future? His villains have been drawn so vigorously, that some in the theater and in the study have come away in the mood of

Edna St. Vincent Millay in her comments on the false promises of
Spring:

> To what purpose, April, do you return again?
> Beauty is not enough.
> You can no longer quiet me with the redness
> Of little leaves opening stickily.
> I know what I know.[8]

We know what we know about the world of Vittoria Corombona,
and remain unconvinced by Cecil's view of Webster as Calvinist.

Webster goes in too many directions, and taxes us, even though
we grant him the irrelevance due an Elizabethan artist as we wait to
perceive the design of the whole. In *The White Devil*, for instance:
while we cannot agree with Leech that Webster is blurred in his
total meaning, there is some blurring of characters. One is never
quite sure whether Flamineo is a Malcontent, tool villain, or Machi-
avel, nor whether Brachiano is a hero or villain: he is a "noble
youth" in Francisco's eyes in V, ii, 79. There is a mixture of the
realistic and the symbolic: we are taken by the realism of the
language of hatred and lust involved in the play; but the sources of
these emotions are figures of symbolic proportions, and blurred
proportions at that. Again, on a more physical level of action, note
the rapid changes of attitudes in Brachiano and Monticelso, and the
absurd business in the last scene in which Flamineo feigns death,
tricking Vittoria and Zanche. Cries he, arising:

FLAMINEO:        I am not wounded:
> The pistols hold no bullets: 'twas a plot
> To prove your kindness to me; and I live
> To punish your ingratitude.
>                                                    V, vi, 149–52

Granted, in the paradoxical title of the play we have a clue to the
thematic idea of appearance *versus* reality inherent in the play, and
an important theme it is; but in handling it, Webster sometimes
suggests other than he intended: the arrival of Beaumont and
Fletcher.

When we turn to *The Duchess of Malfi*, we find a more mature
play, and as noted, a working out of the thought which had ended
in a philosophical impasse in the previous play: through the influence of the Duchess' great spirit of nobility, Bosola is able to shake

his cynical nihilism and cleanse the world of its evil. Those who echo throughout the nineteenth century George Saintsbury's belief that "the fifth act is a kind of gratuitous appendix of horrors stuck on without art or reason"[9] are short-sighted. However, though the purpose is good, Webster stumbles in the execution. Perhaps in the quiet of the study we can overlook the flaws of Act V; but can we in the theater when we see it before us?

In looking more closely at Act V, we may note first that to one modern critic, it is undeniable that "Webster intended Bosola as a major tragic protagonist,"[10] and for him (and others), he is. Even if we can convince ourselves (and it is difficult) that Bosola has the daring, the courage which brings on a climactic struggle with moral law, the structure of the quite-necessary Act V is shoddy, and damages—though not fatally—Webster's good intentions. The fourth act ends with Bosola's bitter soliloquy of remorse, and his resolve to take positive action. But instead of concentrating on Bosola, Webster begins Act V with a scene between Delio and Antonio. (And what a listless figure Antonio is. He displays an important reconciliatory spirit in Act V, as critics have told us; but Antonio simply does not interest us vitally. He is pallid.) The Delio-Antonio conversation is followed by further chat between Delio and the Marquis. Bosola does not make another appearance until many lines later in scene two, and then must stand by for almost ninety lines while Ferdinand takes the stage. And after his moving, thrilling resolve in IV, ii, Bosola gets only one bad line to say before others break in again: "Mercy upon me, what a fatal judgment hath fall'n upon this Ferdinand!" When finally he is left alone with the Cardinal, he gets nine lines to the Cardinal's thirty-four. In the ensuing encounter with Julia, he plays a completely passive role. Assuredly, this is a low-level counterpart to the Duchess-Antonio wooing scene; but for a tragic protagonist, Bosola hardly dominates. And again he goes offstage for the Julia-Cardinal book-kissing scene, which is tremendously theatrical, but structurally in error, a judgment based not simply on twentieth-century standards (Archer's method) but in terms of Webster's intentions. Bosola finally gets another soliloquy at the end of scene two, in which he reminds us of his mission which we may have forgotten about by now. He must say this after a young girl has died a spectacular death on the stage before him and the audience, and while she is still lying there. But as soon as he gets his speech out, we are confronted not with any of his actions, but with the ineffective echo scene, followed by the Cardinal and his absurd instructions to the servants. This incorporation of the "boy-who-cried-wolf" theme is another stroke reflecting the theatrical trickery of Beaumont and Fletcher.

In short, again Webster gives us a bit too much of everything. The tensions slackens in Act V, there is no doubt about it. At length—and there is the problem, "at length"—Bosola has his revenge. And though Eliot insists we should take the stabbings of the last scene only as a special form of exit, theater audiences, as we have seen, have tended to laugh since 1850. But there are multiple deaths in the final scenes of *Hamlet* and of *Lear*—and no one laughs. Shakespeare manages to avoid the effect of wholesale slaughter by prefacing each scene with a duel, thus preparing us for what follows by the fury of the sword play. We are ready for it; we accept it. With Webster there are sudden stabbings, with each victim given a set speech[11] before his death. In the study, we may be arrested; in the theater, we may—in spite of ourselves—be amused. We may leave the plays of Shakespeare and Jonson with future theater directors with little fear; but with Webster's plays goes the admonition, "Handle with Care." As stated, for symbolic plays—and F. P. Wilson seems quite correct—they are amazingly realistic, so realistic that the modern theater audience cannot always accept Webster's reversions to convention or symbolism.

Yet Webster's dominant theme—the nobility of human worth—eventually comes back to us, while the memory of a heap of corpses fades after we leave the theater. (Admittedly, the 1919 production climaxed by Ferdinand's clownish death took, perhaps, some time to pass from the memory.) We finally forget the problems of execution of craftsmanship which we may have noticed at the time, and are left with the unified, tragic vision of John Webster. We are left, after all the irrelevant sententia and absurdity of action, with a writer who triumphs, nevertheless, over his shortcomings, and who realizes a coherent vision of a world in which good and evil go down to grim defeat together, but a world in which one must remain virtuous and labor actively for what appears to be justice. And as we have seen, for some critics justice will prevail in the future world of Rome and Amalfi. However, we may not be particularly reassured by the appearance of Giovanni and Antonio's son. The forces of darkness are great.

What is reassuring is that Webster has a different answer to
Hamlet's question "For who would bear the whips and scorns of
time. . . ." The answer is not that the fear of something after death,
the undiscovered country, keeps us from suicide. The answer is
implicit in the death of a young woman, who, beset with hell, could
cry "I am Duchess of Malfi still."

Oddly enough, between *Scrutiny* attacks on Webster's lack of
moral focus, F. R. Leavis was writing on the importance of writers
"who are significant in terms of human awareness they promote;
awareness of the possibilities of life."[12] Webster's significance lies
directly along those lines. For we learn from Webster that there is a
heroic quality in the virtuous man's ability to survive and endure,
just as we learn much the same lesson three centuries later from
Hemingway, Faulkner, and the diary of Anne Frank.

Out of the drama of the twentieth century comes a statement
reflecting in many ways the thought of one who lived in a similarly
troubled era. Just before the final curtain in Maxwell Anderson's
*Winterset*, we hear these words:

> On this star,
> in this hard star-adventure, knowing not
> what the fires mean to right and left, nor whether
> a meaning was intended or presumed,
> man can stand up, and look out blind, and say:
> in all these turning lights I find no clue,
> only a masterless night, and in my blood
> no certain answer, yet is my mind my own,
> yet is my heart a cry toward something dim
> in distance, which is higher than I am
> and makes me emperor of the endless dark
> even in seeking![13]

Perhaps a vague statement; perhaps, for some, a sentimental one.
But it is one of affirmation during chaos, and in many ways, it is
John Webster's.

# NOTES

NOTES TO INTRODUCTION

1 We could note that of the moderns, Tennessee Williams often provokes similar reaction; we might also point out his Websterian technique: his passion for the perverse, darker sides of human nature, and his interest in creating feminine roles of major importance.
2 Henry Fitzjeffrey, "Certain Elegies done by Sundry Excellent Wits," reprinted in F. L. Lucas (ed.), *The Complete Works of John Webster* (London, 1927), I, 55.
3 Samuel Sheppard, *Epigrams Theological, Philosophical, and Romantic*, 1651, reprinted in Lucas (ed.), *The Works of John Webster*, I, 101. We may note here that there will be few references to any plays but *The Duchess of Malfi* and *The White Devil*. Webster wrote other plays; but it is on these two tragedies alone that his reputation rests. Rarely does any critic refer, for example, to *The Devil's Law Case*. Further, the critics surveyed herein are those whose work is available in English. The restriction excludes little of importance, although modern bibliographies often include Gabriel Baldini, *John Webster e il linguaggio della tragedia* (Rome, 1953).
4 Lewis Theobald, preface to *The Fatal Secret*, in Henry W. Wells (ed.), *Three Centuries of English Drama*. Readex Microprint Series (New York, 1952).
5 William Hazlitt, *The Literature of the Age of Elizabeth* (London, 1901), 96.
6 Charles Kingsley, writing in 1856. Reprinted in his *Plays and Puritans* (London, 1885), 48.
7 David Cecil, *Poets and Storytellers* (London, 1949), 29.
8 Ian Jack, "The Case of John Webster," *Scrutiny*, XVI (March, 1949), 43.

NOTES TO CHAPTER 1

1 Thomas Heywood, *The Hierarchy of the Blessed Angels*, partially quoted in Lucas (ed.), *The Complete Works of John Webster*, I, 52.
2 Webster, preface to Munday's *Palmerin of England*, in Lucas (ed.), *The Complete Works of John Webster*, III, 6. All citations of Webster will

be taken from the Lucas edition and will hereafter be cited by volume
and page number in that work.

3  Lucas (ed.), *Works of Webster*, I, 107.
4  *Ibid.*
5  Lucas (ed.), *Works of Webster*, II, 34.
6  *Ibid.*, 35.
7  *Ibid.* We may note that Middleton and Rowley wrote no other commendatory verse.
8  Lucas (ed.), *Works of Webster*, I, 14.
9  *Ibid.*, 107.
10 C. H. Hereford and Percy Simpson (eds.), *Ben Jonson* (Oxford, 1932), IV, 92.
11 Lucas (ed.), *Works of Webster*, I, 107.
12 *Ibid.*, 4, 6.
13 G. E. Bentley, *Shakespeare and Jonson* (Chicago, 1945), 288.
14 Quoted in G. E. Bentley, *The Jacobean and Caroline Stage* (Oxford, 1956), V, 1244. See also John I. Parry, "A Seventeenth Century Gallery of Poets," *Journal of English and Germanic Philology*, XVIII (1920), 270–77. There is another allusion to Webster and the "Malfy Duchess" in a comic poem by William Heminge concerning the loss of a finger suffered by Heminge's friend Thomas Randolph. Parry conjectures the date as around 1632. The only value of the poem is its roster of poets.
15 Lucas (ed.), *Worns if Webster*, I, 101.
16 Quoted in Hyder E. Rollins, "Samuel Sheppard and his Praise of Poets," *Studies in Philology*, XXIV (April, 1927), 554.
17 G. E. Bentley, "John Cotgrave's *English Treasury of Wit and Language* and the Elizabethan Drama," *Studies in Philology*, XL (April, 1943), 192.
18 We may note that Webster was not overly popular with the anthologists. According to Bentley, *The Jacobean and Caroline Stage*, V, 1244, Howes, continuing Stow's *Annals of England* in 1615 merely lists his name with twenty six other writers; Samuel Holland in his 1656 *Wit and Fancy in a Maze* also puts him in a list of better poets of the Jacobean era.
19 Lucas (ed.), *Works of Webster*, III, 29.
20 Montague Summers (ed.), *Roscius Anglicanus* (London, 1928), 25.
21 Lucas (ed.), *Works of Webster*, I, 7. "As it is now acted at the Duke's Theatre."
22 Summers (ed.), *Roscius Anglicanus*, 9.
23 Samuel Pepys, *The Diary of Samuel Pepys*, ed. by H. B. Wheatley (London, 1928), II, 107, 109.
24 *Ibid.*, 327.
25 *Ibid.*, VI, 45.
26 *Ibid.*, VIII, 155.
27 Edward Phillips, *Theatrum Poetarium* (London, 1675), 116–17.
28 Gerard Langbaine, *An Account of the English Dramatick Poets* (London, 1691), 508–10.
29 James Wright, *Country Conversations* (London, 1694), 54–55, quotes briefly from *The Duchess of Malfi*, marking the last mention in this century.
30 Herbert Weisinger, "The Seventeenth Century Reputation of the Elizabethans," *Modern Language Quarterly*, VI (March, 1945), 13–21, quotes various later tributes to certain specific Elizabethans (Webster is not named) and statements of appreciation for what many other critics at the end of the century were calling their "irregular" methods of composition.

31   Allardyce Nicoll, *A History of Restoration Drama, 1660–1700* (Cambridge, 1928), 120.

32   H. F. Scott-Thomas, "Tate and the Seventeenth Century," *Journal of English Literary History*, I (1934), 256.

33   John Genest, *The English Stage* (Bath, 1832), II, 374.

34   Emmett Avery (ed.), *The London Stage, 1700–1729* (Carbondale, 1960), II, cxiv. Professor Avery's volume authenticates Genest in the dating of this performance. The text, in the form of the fourth quarto, was published in 1708, and indicates cuts and stage directions. Missing was the pilgrim scene (III, iv), the Reputation and Salmon fables, and the lines in III, iii, referring to the son of the first marriage. Some of the vocabulary is modernized, and some cleaning up has been done: "lecher" becomes "lover," etc.

35   Genest, *The English Stage*, X, 152.

36   All quotations from Tate's version are from the microfilmed *Injured Love* in Wells (ed.), *Three Centuries of English Drama*. See also a comparative study of the two plays in Hazelton Spencer, "Nahum Tate and *The White Devil*," *Journal of English Literary History*, I (1934), 235–49.

37   Richard F. Jones, *Lewis Theobald* (New York, 1919), 291.

38   Genest, *The English Stage*, III, 393. Genest notes that there were four performances, but Arthur H. Scouten in *The London Stage, 1729–1747* (Carbondale, 1961), III, 285, lists only two. One performance on April 5, was "advertised but dismissed."

39   Quotations from Theobald's adaptation are also from *The Fatal Secret* microcard in Wells (ed.), *Three Centuries of English Drama*.

40   Anonymous letter to the *Grubstreet Journal*, April 25, 1733, reprinted in *The Gentleman's Magazine* (1733), 194.

41   David Erskine Baker, *Biographia Dramatica, or a companion to the playhouse* (London, 1764), I, 739.

42   Earl Wasserman, "The Scholarly Origin of the Elizabethan Revival," *Journal of English Literary History*, IV (September, 1937), 215.

43   *Preface to Shakespeare, Works*, eds. Whitwell Elwin and W. J. Courthope (London, 1886), X, 473. We might also note Dr. Johnson's later observation (1765) that "The unities of time and place are not essential to a just drama, that though they may sometimes conduce to pleasure, they are always to be sacrificed to the nobler beauties of variety and construction." For Johnson, the "greatest graces of a play" are to copy nature and instruct life." Samuel Johnson, "Preface to Shakespeare," in Scott Elledge (ed.), *Eighteenth Century Essays* (Ithaca, 1961), II, 661–62.

44   Thomas Warton, "Observations on The Fairy Queen," in Elledge (ed.), *Eighteenth Century Essays*, II, 772.

45   *Ibid.*, 771. Even in the preceding century John Dryden had defended Shakespearean tragedy against Thomas Rymer's criticism that the dramas were far too irregular. Dryden agreed, but argued that they nevertheless showed genius, and "Genius alone is a greater Virtue (if I may so call it) than all other qualifications put together." John Dryden, "Letters Upon Several Occasions" (1696), in John Munro (ed.), *The Shakespeare Allusion Book* (London, 1932), II, 86. See also Weisinger, "The Seventeenth Century Reputation of the Elizabethans," for further earlier appreciation of the "careless" methods of Shakespeare, Jonson, and Beaumont and Fletcher.

46   From H. A. Needham (ed.), *Taste and Criticism in The Eighteenth Century* (London, 1952), 146.

47 Another valuable article on early scholarship is Robert D. Williams, "Antiquarian Interest in Elizabethan Drama Before Lamb," *PMLA*, LIII (June, 1938), 434–44, which notes the work of many of these early editors.

48 Oliver Goldsmith, "An Inquiry into The Present State of Polite Learning in Europe," in Peter Cunningham (ed.), *The Works of Oliver Goldsmith* (4 vols.; London, 1854), 67–68. Goldsmith's criticism does reflect an unfortunate situation: the strict Licensing Act of 1736 undoubtedly drove many potential playwrights into other more rewarding fields.

NOTES TO CHAPTER 2

1 Quoted in Edith J. Morley (ed.), *Letters on Chivalry and Romance* (London, 1911), 71–72.

2 Travis Bogard, *The Tragic Satire of John Webster* (Los Angeles, 1955), xi.

3 Charles Dibdin, *History of the Stage* (London, 1800), III, 272.

4 Quoted in E. V. Lucas (ed.), *The Works of Charles and Mary Lamb* (London, 1904), IV, 250.

5 George Saintsbury, *History of Criticism* (New York, 1906–1908), III, 240.

6 William Watson, *Excursions in Criticism* (London, 1893), 19.

7 Lucas (ed.), *The Works of Charles and Mary Lamb*, IV, 178.

8 *Ibid.*, 160.

9 Longinus, *On the Sublime*, ed. by W. Rhys Roberts (Cambridge, 1907), 55.

10 *Ibid.*, 65.

11 Percy B. Shelley, "A Defence of Poetry," in John Shawcross (ed.), *Shelley's Literary and Philosophical Criticism* (London, 1909), 153.

12 Lucas, *The Works of Charles and Mary Lamb*, IV, 190; *ibid.*, 179.

13 Dykes Campbell, reviewer, quoted in Lucas (ed.), *The Works of Charles and Mary Lamb*, IV, 600.

14 H. M., "The Duchess of Malfi," *Blackwood's Magazine*, III (March, 1818), 656.

15 *Ibid.*, 657–58.

16 H. M., "The White Devil," *Blackwood's Magazine*, III (August, 1818), 556.

17 *Ibid.*, 561.

18 *Ibid.*, 562.

19 *Ibid.* This same "admiration" is evoked by Beatrice in *The Cenci*, Shelley's drama written in 1819, the year of Hazlitt's lectures. Shelley, an admirer of the Elizabethan drama, likewise pictures a guilty woman at a trial who holds the sympathy of the audience through her courage. See E. S. Bates, *A Study of Shelley's The Cenci* (New York, 1908).

20 "The Elizabethan Dramatists," *The European Magazine*, LXXVIII (1820), 301.

21 *Ibid.*, 302.

22 *Ibid.*

23 *Ibid.*, 420.

24 *Ibid.*, 422.

25 *Ibid.*, 424.

26 P. P. Howe (ed.), *The Complete Works of William Hazlitt* (21 vols.; London, 1933), V, 175; *ibid.*, VI, 301–302; *ibid.*, VIII, 31.

27 Hazlitt, *The Literature of The Age of Elizabeth*, 7, 10.

28 *Ibid.*, 96.

29 *Ibid.*

30 *Ibid.*, 102.

31  "John Webster," *Retrospective Review,* VII (1823), 88.
32  *Ibid.,* 89.
33  *Ibid.,* 90.
34  *Ibid.,* 113.
35  *Ibid.,* 119.
36  "Article IX," *The Edinburgh Review,* XXXVIII (February, 1823), 197.
37  *Ibid.*
38  Alexander Dyce (ed.), *The Works of John Webster* (London, 1830), vii.
39  *Ibid.,* viii.
40  *Ibid.,* xii–xiii.
41  Notice from the London *Literary Gazette,* April 17, 1830, p. 255.
42  Letter from Sir Walter Scott to Alexander Dyce, March 31, 1831, in H. J. C. Grierson (ed.), *Letters of Sir Walter Scott* (London, 1937), XII, 1.
43  J. M., "The Early English Drama," *The Gentlemen's Magazine,* CII (May, 1833), 416–17.
44  *Ibid.,* 417.
45  *Ibid.*
46  Nathan Drake, *Shakespeare and His Times* (London, 1838), 607.
47  Henry Hallam, *Introduction to the Literature of Europe* (London, 1839), III, 619.
48  *Ibid.,* 615.
49  *Ibid.*
50  *Ibid.,* 620.
51  Review of George Darley's edition of Beaumont and Fletcher, in *The Edinburgh Review,* LXXIII (April, 1841), 220.
52  Robert Chambers, *Cyclopedia of English Literature* (London, 1844), 211.
53  Thomas B. Shaw, *Outlines of English Literature* (New York, 1847), 130.
54  E. R. Watson, *Sheridan to Robertson* (Cambridge, 1926), 217.
55  Review from the London *Literary Gazette,* November 23, 1850, p. 890.
56  Review from the *Illustrated London News,* November 23, 1850, p. 409.
57  *Ibid.*
58  Review from the weekly *Athenaeum,* November 23, 1850, p. 1226.
59  *Ibid.*
60  *Ibid.*
61  George Henry Lewes, "The Old and Modern Dramatists" from *The Leader* for August 3, 1850, quoted in William Archer and Robert W. Lowe (eds.), *Dramatic Essays* (London, 1896), 101.
62  *Ibid.,* 104.
63  Review by George Henry Lewes in *The Leader* for November 30, 1850. Quoted in Archer and Lowe (eds.), *Dramatic Essays,* 120.
64  *Ibid.,* 121.
65  *Ibid.*
66  *Ibid.*
67  Edwin Whipple, *Essays and Reviews* (New York, 1853), II, 44.

NOTES TO CHAPTER 3

1  The article by Charles Kingsley in the *North British Review,* XXV (May, 1856), is reprinted in Kingsley, *Plays and Puritans,* 13.
2  *Ibid.,* 18.
3  *Ibid.,* 48.
4  *Ibid.,* 49.
5  *Ibid.,* 51.
6  *Ibid.,* 51–52.

7   *Ibid.*, 25–26.
8   "The English Drama during the Reigns of Elizabeth and James," *Cornhill Magazine*, II (1865), 604–605.
9   Charles Knight, *Pictorial Shakespeare* (2nd ed.; New York, 1867), VIII, 516.
10  H. A. Taine, *History of English Literature*, trans. by Henri Van Laune (Edinburgh, 1871), I, 252.
11  Austin Allibone, *A Critical Dictionary of English Literature and British and American Writers* (Philadelphia, 1872), III, 2625.
12  Thomas Campbell, *Cyclopedia of English Poetry* (Philadelphia, 1874), 49.
13  A. W. Ward, *History of English Dramatic Literature* (London, 1875), I, 514.
14  *Ibid.*, II, 67.
15  *Ibid.*, 35.
16  *Ibid.*, 248.
17  *Ibid.*, 255.
18  *Ibid.*, 256.
19  *Ibid.*, 257.
20  *Ibid.*, 260.
21  *Ibid.*, 261.
22  Algernon Charles Swinburne, "John Webster," *Nineteenth Century*, XIX (June, 1886), 861–62.
23  *Ibid.*, 869.
24  *Ibid.*, 871.
25  *Ibid.*, 875.
26  *Ibid.*, 880.
27  *Ibid.*, 879.
28  Algernon Charles Swinburne, *Studies in Prose and Poetry* (London, 1894), 51.
29  Review from the *Times Literary Supplement*, September 24, 1908, p. 305.
30  George Saintsbury, *History of Elizabethan Literature* (London, 1887), 275, 278.
31  J. A. Symonds (ed.), *Webster and Tourneur* (New York, 1888), ix.
32  *Ibid.*, xii.
33  *Ibid.*, xx.
34  *Ibid.*, xxi–xxii.
35  William Minton, *Characteristics of English Poets* (Boston, 1889), 355.
36  *Ibid.*
37  *Ibid.*, 356.
38  Edmund C. Stedman, *The Nature and Elements of Poetry* (New York, 1892), 249.
39  Arthur Dillon, "*The Duchess of Malfi*—A Note," *Library Review*, I (October, 1892), 520.
40  Review from the *Illustrated London News*, April 13, 1868, p. 319. George C. D. Odell in *Annals of the New York Stage*, VII (New York, 1931) records performances of Horne's version at the Broadway Theatre, April 5–10, 1858. The cast was headed by Mr. and Mrs. Wilmarth Waller as Ferdinand and the Duchess. Although publicity made great use of quotations from Lamb and Hazlitt, the engagement was not profitable. The theater itself closed the first of May. J. R. Brown, in his edition of *The Duchess* (London, 1964), notes that Mrs. Waller played the title role on tour in 1876, with the publicity stating that she creates a "profound sen-

sation" in the role, and is the only woman in America to portray "this grand and difficult character."

41　Review in the London *Times*, October 22, 1892, p. 6.
42　Review from the *Graphic*, October 29, 1892, p. 522.
43　Review from the *Nation*, November 10, 1892, p. 348.
44　*Ibid*.
45　*Ibid*.
46　*Ibid*., 348–49.
47　*Ibid*., 349.
48　Review from the *Athenaeum*, October 29, 1892, p. 600.
49　*Ibid*.
50　*Ibid*.
51　*Ibid*.
52　Clement Scott, review for the *Illustrated London News*, October 29, 1892, p. 539.
53　Review from the *Academy*, reprinted in Francis Wedmore, *On Books and Arts* (London, 1899), 126.
54　*Ibid*., 125.
55　*Ibid*., 124.
56　*Ibid*., 125.
57　James Mason Brown, *The Modern Theatre in Revolt* (New York, 1929), 18.
58　The term "the well-made play" or "well-knit play" usually connotes a drama with virtues of compactness, firmly drawn characterization, and crispness of style. One thinks of any play—and the term eventually comes to exclude Ibsen and the social drama in general—which can be outlined succinctly into exposition, development, climax, and denouement.
59　William Archer, "Webster, Lamb, and Swinburne," *The New Review*, VIII (January, 1893), 97.
60　*Ibid*., 100.
61　*Ibid*., 102.
62　*Ibid*., 104.
63　*Ibid*.
64　*Ibid*., 106.
65　*Ibid*.
66　Watson, *Excursions in Criticism*, 13.
67　*Ibid*., 18.
68　*Ibid*.
69　George Bernard Shaw, *Our Theatre in the Nineties* (London, 1932), I, 130–31; *ibid*., III, 317.
70　James Russell Lowell, *The Old English Dramatists* (New York, 1893), 59.
71　*Ibid*., 61.
72　*Ibid*., 72.
73　*Ibid*., 76–77.
74　Edmund Gosse, *The Jacobean Poets* (New York, 1894), 166.
75　*Ibid*., 168.
76　*Ibid*., 169.
77　*Ibid*., 168.
78　*Ibid*., 169.
79　*Ibid*., 170.
80　*Ibid*., 173.
81　Edmund Gosse, *Seventeenth Century Studies* (London, 1883), 50.

82  *Ibid.*, 53.
83  *Ibid.*, 56.
84  *Ibid.*, 58.
85  *Ibid.*, 63, 67.
86  *Ibid.*, 79.
87  *Ibid.*, 119.
88  Edmund Gosse, *Short History of Modern English Literature* (New York, 1897).
89  Frederick Carpenter, *Metaphor and Simile in the Minor Elizabethan Drama* (Chicago, 1895), 77.
90  John Corbin, *The Elizabethan Hamlet* (London, 1895), 60.
91  Edwin Whipple, *The Literature of the Age of Elizabeth* (Boston, 1895), 141, 145.
92  Sidney Lee, "John Webster," *Dictionary of National Biography*, LX, 1032.
93  *Ibid.*, 1035.
94  *Ibid.*
95  Grace Cook, "English Tragedy in the Reign of King James I," *Wellesley Magazine*, VIII (February, 1899), 233–34.
96  *Ibid.*, 234.
97  *Ibid.*, 235.
98  *Ibid.*, 236.
99  *Ibid.*, 242–43.

NOTES TO CHAPTER 4

1  Edmund Wilson, "Notes at the End of a War," *The New Yorker* (June 2, 1945), 47.
2  W. W. Greg, "Webster's *White Devil*: An Essay in Formal Criticism" *Modern Language Quarterly*, III (December, 1900), 113.
3  *Ibid.*, 118, 120.
4  Clayton Hamilton, "*The Duchess of Malfi* Considered as a Tragedy of Blood," *Sewanee Review*, IX (1901), 410.
5  *Ibid.*, 416.
6  J. E. Morris, "John Webster," *Fortnightly Review*, LXXVII (June, 1902), 1065.
7  *Ibid.*, 1068.
8  *Ibid.*, 1069. He is using an earlier line here from J. A. Symonds.
9  *Ibid.* T. S. Eliot was to rephrase this poetically in his "Whispers of Immortality" eighteen years later:

> Webster was much possessed by death
> And saw the skull beneath the skin;
> And breastless creatures under ground
> Leaned backward with a lipless grin. . . .
> *Collected Poems 1909–1935* (London, 1936), 53.

10  Morris, "John Webster," 1070–71.
11  *Ibid.*, 1071.
12  *Ibid.*
13  *Ibid.*, 1078.
14  David Patrick (ed.), *Chambers' Cyclopedia of English Literature* (Philadelphia, 1902), 427.

15  *Ibid.*
16  *Ibid.*
17  Thomas Seccombe and J. W. Allen, *The Age of Shakespeare* (London, 1903), 184.
18  *Ibid.*, 187.
19  W. J. Courthope, *History of English Poetry* (London, 1895–1910), IV, 261.
20  *Ibid.*, 262–63.
21  *Ibid.*, 266.
22  Barrett Wendell, *The Temper of the Seventeenth Century in England* (London, 1904), 87–88.
23  *Ibid.*, 85.
24  E. E. Stoll, *John Webster* (Boston, 1905), 152.
25  *Ibid.*, 128.
26  *Ibid.*, 209.
27  Herbert Grierson, *The First Half of the Seventeenth Century* (New York, 1906), 118.
28  *Ibid.*, 119.
29  *Ibid.*, 115–16.
30  Martin W. Sampson (ed.), *The White Devil and The Duchess of Malfi* (Boston, 1906), xii, xvi.
31  *Ibid.*, xxii.
32  *Ibid.*, xxix.
33  J. Le Gay Brereton, *Elizabethan Drama* (Sydney, Australia, 1909), 84.
34  C. E. Vaughan, "Tourneur and Webster," in A. W. Ward and A. R. Waller (eds.), *Cambridge History of English Literature* (London, 1910), VI, 202.
35  *Ibid.*, 200–201.
36  *Ibid.*, 204.
37  *Ibid.*, 205.
38  *Ibid.*, 210.
39  C. V. Boyer, *The Villain as Hero in Elizabethan Tragedy* (New York, 1914), 153.
40  *Ibid.*, 159.
41  *Ibid.*, 161.
42  *Ibid.*, 164.
43  *Ibid.*
44  Rubert Brooke, *John Webster and the Elizabethan Drama* (New York, 1916), 87.
45  *Ibid.*, 88.
46  *Ibid.*, 97–98.
47  *Ibid.*, 99.
48  *Ibid.*, 107.
49  *Ibid.*, 108.
50  *Ibid.*, 129.
51  *Ibid.*, 152.
52  *Ibid.*, 161.
53  *Ibid.*, 162.
54  William Archer, *The Old Drama and the New* (Boston, 1923), 29.
55  William Archer, "John Webster," *The Nineteenth Century*, LXXXVII (Jan., 1920), 126.
56  *Ibid.*, 131.
57  *Ibid.*, 132.

58 Archer, *The Old Drama and the New*, 50.
59 *Ibid.*, 57.
60 *Ibid.*, 59.
61 *Ibid.*, 61.
62 Robert Ornstein, *The Moral Vision of Jacobean Tragedy* (Madison, 1960), 128.
63 Frank L. Lucas (ed.) *The Complete Works of John Webster* (London, 1927).
64 Quoted by H. A. Mason in his "F. R. Leavis and *Scrutiny*," *The Critic*, I (Autumn, 1947), 23.
65 Lucas (ed.), *Works of Webster*, vii.
66 *Ibid.*, 17.
67 *Ibid.*, 20.
68 *Ibid.*
69 *Ibid.*, 21.
70 *Ibid.*
71 *Ibid.*, 27.
72 *Ibid.*
73 *Ibid.*, 28.
74 *Ibid.*, 29.
75 *Ibid.*, 33–34.
76 *Ibid.*, 39.
77 *Ibid.*, 39–40.
78 *Ibid.*, 41. Lucas had not read C. V. Boyer.
79 *Ibid.*
80 *Ibid.*
81 *Ibid.*, II, 34.
82 *Ibid.*, I, 40.

NOTES TO CHAPTER 5

1 T. E. Hulme, "Romanticism and Classicism," in Herbert Read (ed.), *Speculations* (New York, 1924), 126.
2 T. E. Hulme, "A Notebook by T. E. H.," *The New Age* (December 2, 1915), 112. Eliot wrote in 1934:

> . . . with this disappearance of the idea of Original Sin, with the disappearance of the idea of intense moral struggle, the human beings presented to us both in poetry and in prose fiction today . . . tend to become less and less real. It is in fact in moments of moral and spiritual struggle depending on spiritual sanctions . . . that men and women come nearest to being real.
>
> *After Strange Gods* (London, 1934), 42.

3 Hulme, "Romanticism and Classicism," in Read (ed.), *Speculations*, 116.
4 *Ibid.*, 120.
5 *Ibid.*, 131–32.
6 *Ibid.*, 136–37.
7 *Ibid.*, 138.
8 *Ibid.*, 122.
9 T. S. Eliot, *Selected Essays* (New York, 1932), 243, 245.
10 *Ibid.*, 246.
11 *Ibid.*, 247.
12 *Ibid.*, 252.
13 *Ibid.*, 256.

14 *Ibid.*, 129.
15 In *The Waste Land,* Eliot on three occasions borrows specifically from Webster: line 74, "Oh keep the Dog far hence, that's friend to men/Or with his nails he'll dig it up again!" is from *The White Devil,* V, iv, 17–98; Webster had used "wolf," and "foe to men." Line 118, "The wind under the door" comes from *The Devil's Law Case,* III, ii, 162; and we may note that the repetitions around the word "nothing" (11, 119–24) probably come from *The White Devil,* V, vi, 203–205: "Nothing, of nothing: . . . I remember nothing." Line 408, concerning the "beneficent spider" draping memories, comes from *The White Devil,* V, vi, 157–59: ". . . they'll remarry/Ere the worm pierce your winding sheet, ere the spider/Make a thin curtain for your epitaphs." It is interesting that both Eliot and Webster were flagrant borrowers. Indeed, for Eliot, a unified sensibility depends in part on the way a poet borrows: "Immature poets imitate; mature poets steal; bad poets deface what they take, and good poets make it into something better, or at least something different." Eliot, *Selected Essays,* 182. See also R. W. Dent, *John Webster's Borrowing* (Berkeley, 1960).
16 Eliot, *Selected Essays,* 275.
17 Eliot, "Four Elizabethan Dramatists," *Selected Essays,* 98.
18 Eliot, "The Function of Criticism," *Selected Essays,* 18.
19 *Ibid.*, 20–21.
20 T. S. Eliot, *The Sacred Wood* (New York, 1928), 170.
21 Eliot, *Selected Essays,* 10.
22 *Ibid.*, 8.
23 *Ibid.*, 179.
24 Eliot, "The Possibility of a Poetic Drama," *The Sacred Wood,* 6.
25 Eliot, *Selected Essays,* 97. A convention he defines as any form or rhythm imposed on the world of action.
26 *Ibid.*, 93.
27 *Ibid.*
28 *Ibid.*, 96. This charge was refuted by Inga-Stina Ekeblad many years later in a closely argued article "The 'Impure Art' of John Webster," *Review of English Studies,* IX (August, 1958), 253–67. She rejects the view that Webster uses conventional dramatic material or devices for show value when his poetry fails. Instead, she maintains that convention and realism can be fused and looks closely at the Duchess' death scene, her point being that the madmen's masque is part of a larger masque developed on the framework of realistic dramatic representation. She considers masques and anti-masques, and finds it thematically appropriate that in the center of the play we have an anti-masque, acting as an ideograph of disunity and incoherence. It is a visual and aural image of what the action of the play has led to, from the happiness and unity of the wooing scene: the Duchess' marriage, leading to her murder, is like a marriage masque turned into a masque of death, replete with "gifts" of coffin, cords, and bells. The *charivari* anti-masque of the madmen and Bosola's masque of death are thus two halves of one metaphor, mocking the Duchess and her remarriage.
29 Eliot, as has been often noted, had a disturbing habit of playing down his earlier pronouncements. Writing later in the 1956 introduction to a paperback reprinting of certain of his Elizabethan essays, he notes the exclusion of this essay and two others which "on re-examination embarrassed me by their callowness, and by a faculty of unqualified assertion

which verges, here and there, on impudence." T. S. Eliot, *Essays on Elizabethan Drama* (New York, 1956), ii.

30    T. S. Eliot, "Mr. Lucas' Webster," *The Criterion*, VII (June, 1928), 157.

31    T. S. Eliot, "*The Duchess of Malfi* at The Lyric: and Poetic Drama," *Art and Letters*, III (Winter, 1920), 37.

32    *Ibid.*, 38.

33    *Ibid.*

34    *Ibid.*, 39.

35    Eliot, "Four Elizabethan Dramatists," *Selected Essays*, 96: he wants, somehow, to have an indirect expression of the actor's personality. His function should be like a carpenter's making a table leg.

36    T. S. Eliot, "*The Duchess of Malfy*," *Listener* (December 18, 1941), 825.

37    *Ibid.*

38    *Ibid.*, 826.

39    Earlier, Eliot had noted another kind of unity of tone. Writing on Cyril Tourneur in 1931, he stated that "Webster, in his greatest tragedies, has a kind of pity for all his characters, an attitude toward good and bad alike which helps to unify the Webster pattern." Eliot, *Selected Essays*, 161.

40    Eliot, "*The Duchess of Malfy*," 286.

41    Eliot, "The Metaphysical Poets," *Selected Essays*, 248.

42    See Chapter V.

43    F. R. Leavis, "*Scrutiny*: A Manifesto," reprinted in Eric Bentley (ed.), *The Importance of Scrutiny* (New York, 1948), 1.

44    F. R. Leavis (ed.), *Determinations* (London, 1934), 44. We might compare this statement with another look at that of his coworker L. C. Knights in his review of Eliot's *Elizabethan Essays*, in *Scrutiny*, III (December, 1934), 314:

Shakespearean criticism (including scholarship) has . . . a double function. It has to make the Shakespeare experience available to each reader to the fullest possible extent, and it has to relate that experience to the possibilities of living at the present time, and therefore, at the time when Shakespeare wrote. All that does not perform one or either of these functions is lumber, and at a time when it is becoming more and more difficult to keep abreast of living issues—to find some answer to the question, *How to live*—it had better be recognized as such.

45    Wrote Leavis in his *Revaluations* (London, 1936), 4, on the business of the critic: "He endeavors to see the poetry of the present as continuation and development; that is, as the decisive, the most significant, contemporary life of tradition. He endeavors, where the poetry of the past is concerned, to realize to the full the implications of the truism that its life is in the present or nowhere; it is alive insofar as it is alive for us."

46    F. R. Leavis, *The Great Tradition* (London, 1948), 29.

47    *Ibid.*, 2.

48    Thus in Leavis, *Revaluations*, 206, 211, we learn that Shelley had a "weak grasp upon the actual"; as the feeling was divorced from his thought, "The effect is of vanity and emptiness (Arnold was right) as well as monotony."

49    F. R. Leavis, *New Bearings in English Poetry* (2nd ed.; London, 1950), 13.

50    *Ibid.*, 78.

51    J. B. Priestley, letter to the *New Statesman* (November 10, 1956), 580.

52  *Ibid.* Stephen Spender reviewed Leavis' *Revaluations* and agreed: "I have come to believe that such critics as Leavis live in projected spheres of fantasy about their own unwritten or unachieved poetry. . . . Poetry . . . exists simply in the minds of the critics, and poets become 'dislodged' or unreadable (Shelley) if Dr. Leavis and his colleagues think badly about them." Stephen Spender, review in *Criterion*, XVI (January, 1937), 350.

53  W. A. Edwards, "John Webster," *Scrutiny*, II (June, 1933), 16.

54  *Ibid.*

55  *Ibid.* 17. Cf. Denys Thompson, another *Scrutiny* critic, and his attack on Charles Lamb: Lamb is unable to say a plain thing plainly, because of his "assumed and easily assimilable bag of tricks, little literary touches which give the illiterate something predigested to mumble, and cheat him into believing he is in contact with great thoughts." Leavis (ed.), *Determinations*, 207.

56  Edwards, "John Webster," 21.

57  *Ibid.*, 23.

58  Ian Jack, "The Case of John Webster," *Scrutiny*, XVI (March, 1949), 38.

59  *Ibid.*, 39.

60  *Ibid.*, 41.

61  *Ibid.*, 42.

62  *Ibid.*, 43.

63  L. G. Salingar, "Tourneur and the Tragedy of Revenge," in Boris Ford (ed.), *The Pelican Guide to English Literature* (London, 1956), 349–52.

64  James Smith, "The Tragedy of Blood," *Scrutiny*, VIII (September, 1939), 270.

65  *Ibid.*, 280.

66  F. R. Leavis, "Jonathan Swift," *Scrutiny*, II (March, 1934), 366, 378.

67  E. W. Hendy, "John Webster, Playwright and Naturalist," *Nineteenth Century*, CIII (January, 1928), 111–23.

68  Walter P. Eaton, *The Drama in English* (New York, 1930), 120.

69  *Ibid.*, 133.

70  Muriel Bradbrook, *Themes and Conventions of Elizabethan Tragedy* (2nd ed.; Cambridge, 1952), 1.

71  *Ibid.*, 4.

72  *Ibid.*, 5.

73  *Ibid.*, 31.

74  *Ibid.*, 8. Robert Ornstein writes later in his *The Moral Vision of Jacobean Tragedy*, 13, that in the interpretation of dramatic art, "the appeal to convention can become like the Renaissance appeal to authority—merely a substitute for critical thinking."

75  Bradbrook, *Themes and Conventions of Elizabethan Tragedy*, 186.

76  *Ibid.*

77  *Ibid.*, 186–87.

78  *Ibid.*, 92.

79  *Ibid.*, 194.

80  *Ibid.*, 209. Years later, Frank W. Wadsworth and Clifford Leech debated whether the Duchess had violated decorum by her marriage to Antonio. Wadsworth in "Webster's *Duchess of Malfi* and Some Contemporary Ideas on Marriage and Remarriage," *Philological Quarterly*, XXXV (October, 1956), 394–407, argues that Webster's audience would not have condemned her for marrying beneath herself; Leech in "An Addendum to Webster's Duchess," *Philological Quarterly*, XXXVII (April, 1958), 253–56, replies that we must recognize her human weakness, her inferior mar-

riage, her disregard of responsibility, in order that we may sympathize with her sufferings.

81  Bradbrook, *Themes and Conventions of Elizabethan Tragedy*, 210. She adds that Webster had "exhausted himself" after the fourth act. Thomas Marc Parrott and R. H. Ball's popular *A Short History of Elizabethan Drama* (New York, 1943), 227, noted similarly that Webster "insists on padding his dialogue with moral maxims often voiced incongruously by other than moral characters. Even worse perhaps is his trick of holding up the action to insert an irrelevant or moral epilogue. . . ." The authors do feel that Act V has a place in *The Duchess of Malfi;* otherwise their criticism is familiar.

82  Bradbrook, *Themes and Conventions of Elizabethan Tragedy*, 212.

83  Una Ellis-Fermor, *The Jacobean Drama* (London, 1936), 18.

84  *Ibid.*, 30.

85  *Ibid.*, 38.

86  *Ibid.*, 170.

87  *Ibid.*, 171, 172–73.

88  *Ibid.*, 175.

89  *Ibid.*, 187.

90  Moody E. Prior, *The Language of Tragedy* (New York, 1947), 121.

91  *Ibid.*, 134.

92  Leavis, *The Great Tradition*, 2; Leavis, "*Scrutiny:* A Manifesto," in Bentley (ed.), *The Importance of Scrutiny*, 1.

93  Eliot, "The Function of Criticism," *Selected Essays*, 18.

NOTES TO CHAPTER 6

1  Clifford Leech, *John Webster* (London, 1951), 65.

2  *Ibid.*, 31.

3  *Ibid.*, 33.

4  *Ibid.*, 52.

5  *Ibid.*, 57.

6  *Ibid.*, 59.

7  *Ibid.*, 78.

8  *Ibid.*, 83.

9  *Ibid.*, 89.

10  *Ibid.*, 103.

11  *Ibid.*, 106.

12  *Ibid.*, 115–16.

13  *Ibid.*, 119.

14  Eliot, "John Ford," *Selected Essays*, 179.

15  Ornstein, *The Moral Vision of Jacobean Tragedy*, 141.

16  *Ibid.*, 13.

17  *Ibid.*, 274–75.

18  *Ibid.*, 21.

19  *Ibid.*, 129. His book is dedicated to Madeline Doran, his former teacher at Wisconsin (he also studied in England with Professor Ellis-Fermor). Professor Doran earlier, in *Endeavors of Art* (Madison, 1954), 298, had also noted that "the tendency to organize events around several episodic centers, with the connections falling slack between them curses such otherwise fine plays as those of Chapman, Tourneur, Webster, and Ford." Like many others, she feels that Webster emphasized in *The White Devil* "the immediate striking effect even at the expense of total design," 355. It is a question of good theater as opposed to artistic consistency. She

notes how the evil creatures of *The White Devil* shine in darkness with simple vitality, and feels that they are to be pitied; yet Vittoria and the Duchess both "exhibit a kind of passivity," 334. We are surer about things, she writes, in the death of Shakespeare's heroes. She finds in *The Duchess of Malfi* a profound ethical implication, but the play is marred by "excessive looseness of time and place," 361. The play belongs in a great tragic tradition of man struggling against the evil in the world; but Webster betrays a conflict "between the Christian ethics that lie on the surface of his tragedies, and a deeper, hardly definable, more defiant and more despairing response to the human condition," 357.

20 Ornstein, *The Moral Vision of Jacobean Tragedy*, 131.
21 *Ibid.*, 132.
22 *Ibid.*, 133.
23 *Ibid.*, 140.
24 *Ibid.*
25 *Ibid.*, 146.
26 *Ibid.*, 148.
27 *Ibid.*, 150.
28 *Ibid.*, 276.
29 Travis Bogard, *The Tragic Satire of John Webster* (Berkeley, 1955), 79.
30 *Ibid.*, 99.
31 *Ibid.*, 101.
32 *Ibid.*, 117.
33 *Ibid.*, 118.
34 *Ibid.*, 55.
35 *Ibid.*, 40, 42–43.
36 *Ibid.*, 147.
37 B. J. Layman, "The Equilibrium of Opposites in *The White Devil*: A Reinterpretation," *PMLA*, LXXIV (September, 1959), 337.
38 J. R. Mulryne, "*The White Devil* and *The Duchess of Malfi*," in J. R. Brown and B. Harris (eds.), *Jacobean Theatre*, (London, 1960), 203.
39 *Ibid.*, 207.
40 *Ibid.*, 219.
41 *Ibid.*, 222.
42 John Webster, *The White Devil*, ed. by J. R. Brown (Cambridge, 1960), xliv. We may mention here Gunnar Boklund's *The Sources* of *The White Devil* (Upsala, 1957), an interesting work concerned not so much with criticism as with Webster's sources. But he too feels that Webster, in his inheritance of the spotty technique of Marston and Tourneur, had his vision impaired. For Boklund, there is too much satire, too much shifting of focus even though Webster's consistent irony is a unifying factor. R. W. Dent's *John Webster's Borrowing* concentrates on Webster's art of pilfering his sources.
43 Brown (ed.), *The White Devil*, li.
44 *Ibid.*, lvii.
45 *Ibid.*
46 Gunnar Boklund, *The Duchess of Malfi: Sources, Themes, Characters* (Cambridge, 1962), 99.
47 *Ibid.*, 108.
48 *Ibid.*, 129–30, 132.
49 *Ibid.*, 135.
50 *Ibid.*, 137.
51 *Ibid.*, 146, 147.

# 184 NOTES

52 *Ibid.*, 169.
53 Clifford Leech, *The Duchess of Malfi* (London, 1963), 39.
54 *Ibid.*, 25.
55 *Ibid.*, 27.
56 Elizabeth Brennan, "The Relationship of Brother and Sister in the Plays of John Webster," *Modern Language Review,* LVIII (October, 1963), 488–94, feels likewise that "Webster was interested not so much in honour or revenge for honour as in their disguises for other passions." In *The Duchess of Malfi,* Ferdinand's concern with honor is a cloak for his incestuous passion. She notes that in each of the two tragedies there is a certain pattern of behavior for a brother with regard to his sister's honor. And in Ferdinand's case, his actions "do not constitute a brother's revenge for his sister's dishonour but the revenge of a husband for his wife's adultery."
57 Leech, *The Duchess of Malfi,* 62.
58 Jane Marie Luecke, "*The Duchess of Malfi*: Comic and Satiric Confusion in a Tragedy," *Studies in English Literature,* IV (Spring, 1964), 276.
59 *Ibid.*, 288. She quotes Alvin Kernan.
60 *Ibid.*
61 *Ibid.*, 289.

NOTES TO CHAPTER 7

1 T. M. Parrott (ed.), *The Tragedies of George Chapman* (2 vols.; New York, 1961), I, 77.
2 Noted by F. P. Wilson in *Elizabethan and Jacobean* (Oxford, 1945), 100.
3 Lucas (ed.), *Works of Webster,* I, 107–108.
4 Wilson, *Elizabethan and Jacobean,* 7.
5 *Ibid.*, 120.
6 *Ibid.*, 7.
7 *Ibid.*, 100.
8 *Ibid.*, 101–102.
9 *Ibid.*, 105.
10 *Ibid.*, 108.
11 Lord David Cecil, *Poets and Storytellers* (London, 1949), 27. Henry Wells, *Elizabethan and Jacobean Playwrights* (New York, 1939), 46, had already expressed the idea that the Elizabethan stage was like a confession booth, and that Webster "uncovers a nest of villains in the spirit of his predecessors and in the severest tradition of Christian morality."
12 Cecil, *Poets and Storytellers,* 29–30.
13 *Ibid.*, 32.
14 *Ibid.*, 33–34.
15 *Ibid.*, 34.
16 *Ibid.*, 37.
17 *Ibid.*, 39.
18 *Ibid.*, 40.
19 R. J. Kaufmann, review of Brown's edition of *The White Devil,* in *Modern Language Review,* LXVI (October, 1961), 586.
20 Irving Ribner, *Jacobean Tragedy: The Quest for Moral Order* (London, 1962), 7.
21 *Ibid.*, 97. See also H. T. Price's excellent study, "The Function of Imagery in Webster," *PMLA,* LXX (September, 1955), 717–39. Much of the imagery of pandarism, poison, infection in *The White Devil* is vitally linked with the essential theme of the difference between deceptive

appearance and bitter reality, a theme Ribner discusses in his treatment of *The White Devil*, and an approach taken by J. R. Brown in his 1960 edition of the play. Price considers the effect of "figures in words" and particularly "figures in action," *i.e.*, the deceptive seduction, the use of the dumb show, the dream of the yew tree, the killing by "monks." The theme is inherent in the title of the play and in its idea of the "relation between fair show and foul truth." James R. Hurt added to Price's approach in his article "Inverted Rituals in Webster's The White Devil," *Journal of English and Germanic Philology*, LXI (January, 1962), 42–47. He emphasizes three parodies of religious rituals introduced in the play as dramatically effective "figures in action." He notes a Black Mass parody in II, i (a parody of a wedding service), a parody of the confessional in IV, iii (the revelation of the murder plot), and in V, the parody of the ritual of extreme unction. ". . . the lost souls of *The White Devil* invert the ceremonies . . . as symbols of their worship of the devil."

22  Ribner, *Jacobean Tragedy*, 97.
23  *Ibid.*, 98.
24  *Ibid.*, 99.
25  *Ibid.*, 106.
26  *Ibid.*, 109.
27  *Ibid.*
28  *Ibid.*, 111.
29  *Ibid.*, 114.
30  *Ibid.*, 119.
31  *Ibid.*, 122.
32  Alexander W. Allison, "Ethical Themes in *The Duchess of Malfi*," *Studies in English Literature*, IV (Spring, 1964), 264.
33  *Ibid.*, 267.
34  *Ibid.*
35  *Ibid.*, 272.
36  T. B. Tomlinson, *A Study of Elizabethan and Jacobean Tragedy* (Cambridge, 1964), 235.
37  *Ibid.*, 133.
38  *Ibid.*, 142.
39  *Ibid.*, 146.
40  *Ibid.*, 146–47.
41  *Ibid.*, 149.
42  *Ibid.*, 154, 156.
43  John Webster, *The Duchess of Malfi*, ed. by J. R. Brown (London, 1964), xli.
44  *Ibid.*, xlii.
45  *Ibid.*, xlvii.
46  *Ibid.*, xlix-1
47  *Ibid.*
48  *Ibid.*, lv.

NOTES TO CHAPTER 8

1  Clifford Leech, "Recent Studies in the Elizabethan and Jacobean Drama," *Studies in English Literature*, III (Spring, 1963), 276–77.
2  Mulryne, "*The White Devil* and *The Duchess of Malfi*," in Brown and Harris (eds.), *The Jacobean Theatre*, 201. Professor Mulryne does not distinguish between amateur and professional productions. (I note with regret

the omission of a professional staging of *The Duchess* by the Dublin Gate Theatre in 1937.)

3   Jack, "The Case of John Webster," 43.

4   H. A. L. Craig, review in the *New Statesman*, December 24, 1960, p. 1002.

5   Review in the *London Times*, November 25, 1919, p. 10.

6   Review in the *Spectator*, November 29, 1919, p. 720.

7   E. M. Forster, review in the *New Statesman*, March 20, 1920, p. 709.

8   James Agate, *Brief Chronicles* (London, 1943), 144ff.

9   F. L. Lucas, review in the *New Statesman*, October 17, 1925, p. 13.

10  Review in the London *Mercury*, XIII (November 25, 1925), 6.

11  Review in the *Nation*, October 17, 1925, p. 116.

12  Review in the *Times*, January 14, 1935, p. 10.

13  Agate, *Brief Chronicles*, 147ff.

14  Review in the *New Statesman*, January 19, 1935, p. 75.

15  Review in the London *Mercury*, XXXI (April, 1935), 409.

16  Ivor Brown, review in the *Observer*, January 20, 1935, p. 13.

17  Review in the *Times*, March 18, 1935, p. 13.

18  Review in the *Observer*, March 24, 1935, p. 17.

19  Grace Goldie, review in the *Listener*, February 2, 1938, p. 240.

20  See Edmund Wilson, "Notes at the End of a War." Wilson found the production powerful, and the more believable for the revelation of German atrocities.

21  Review in the *Times*, April 19, 1945, p. 6.

22  Review in the *Spectator*, April 27, 1945, p. 383.

23  J. C. Trewin, review in *Punch*, March 2, 1945, p. 382.

24  Kenneth Tynan, *He That Plays the King* (London, 1950), 42.

25  Review in the *Times*, March 3, 1947, p. 6.

26  Stephen Potter, review in the *New Statesman*, March 15, 1947, p. 174.

27  Tynan, *He That Plays the King*, 69.

28  Eric Keown, review in *Punch*, March 19, 1947, pp. 246–47.

29  All New York newspaper critics' commentaries are found in Rachel Coffin (ed.), *New York Theatre Critics' Reviews*, VII (1945), 304–306.

30  Brooks Atkinson, review in the *New York Times*, March 3, 1955, p. 32.

31  Henry Hewes, review in the *Saturday Review*, March 4, 1955, p. 30.

32  Jack Landau, "Elizabethan Art in a Mickey Spillane Setting," *Theatre Arts*, XXXIX (August, 1955), 87.

33  Coffin (ed.), *New York Theatre Critics' Reviews*, XVIII (1957), 313–16.

34  Review in *Time Magazine*, April 1, 1957, p. 61.

35  Review in the *Times*, December 16, 1960, p. 5.

36  H. A. L. Craig, review in the *New Statesman*, December 24, 1960, p. 1002.

37  Eric Keown, review in *Punch*, December 28, 1960, p. 946.

38  Alan Brien, review in the *Spectator*, December 12, 1960, p. 1017. As this book goes to press the Circle-in-the Square is staging what the New York *Times* and *Herald Tribune* considered a highly effective *White Devil*, directed again by Jack Landau. It is done in modern dress on what is for the most part a bare stage. Both reviews hailed the vivid and robust acting which helped the drama to grasp the spectator firmly. Otherwise, the *Times* notes, one might be tempted tó smile. But, we gather, there are very few smiles resulting from this energetic staging. The play opened December 6, 1965, and had run for over four months at the off-Broadway theater. It is an important production.

NOTES TO CONCLUSION

1  Louis B. Wright and Virginia A. Lamar (eds.), *The Tragedy of the Duchess of Malfi*, (New York, 1959).
2  David Stacton, *A Dancer in Darkness* (Pantheon, 1962).
3  Eliot, "John Ford," *Selected Essays*, 179.
4  John Mason Brown, *Still Seeing Things* (New York, 1950), 190.
5  Eliot, "The Function of Criticism," *Selected Essays*, 18.
6  Gosse, *Seventeenth Century Studies*, 38.
7  Cecil, *Poets and Storytellers*, 33.
8  Edna St. Vincent Millay, "Spring," *Collected Lyrics* (New York, 1939), 53.
9  Saintsbury, *History of Elizabethan Literature*, 278.
10  C. G. Thayer, "The Ambiguity of Bosola," *Studies in Philology*, LIV (April, 1957), 162.
11  There should be a study of the number of similes beginning with the word *like* in Webster. The amount surely would be staggering.
12  Leavis, *The Great Tradition*, 2.
13  Maxwell Anderson, "Winterset," in his *Eleven Verse Plays* (New York, 1940), 133.

# SELECTED BIBLIOGRAPHY

Abrams, M. H. *The Mirror and the Lamp.* New York, 1953.
Allibone, S. A. *A Critical Dictionary of English Literature.* Philadelphia, 1882.
Allison, Alexander W. "Ethical Themes in *The Duchess of Malfi*," *Studies in English Literature,* IV (Spring, 1964), 263–73.
Archer, William. "*The Duchess of Malfi*," *Nineteenth Century,* LXXXVII (January, 1920), 126–32.
———. *The Old Drama and the New.* Boston, 1924.
———. "Webster, Lamb, and Swinburne," *The New Review,* VIII (January, 1893), 96–106.
Avery, Emmett, ed. *The London Stage, 1700–1729.* 2 vols. Carbondale, 1960.

Baker, David Erskine. *Biographia Dramatica, or A companion to the playhouse.* London, 1764.
Baldini, Gabriele. *John Webster e il linguaggio della tragedia.* Rome, 1953.
Bastiaenen, J. A. *The Moral Tone of Jacobean and Caroline Drama.* Amsterdam, 1930.
Bates, E. S. *A Study of Shelley's The Cenci.* New York, 1908.
Bentley, Eric, *The Importance of Scrutiny.* New York, 1948.
Bentley, G. E. *The Jacobean and Caroline Stage.* 5 vols. Oxford, 1941–56.
———. "John Cotgrave's 'English Treasury of Wit and Language' and the Elizabethan Drama," *Studies in Philology,* XL (April, 1943), 186–203.
———. *Shakespeare and Jonson.* Chicago, 1945.
Bogard, Travis. *The Tragic Satire of John Webster.* Berkeley, 1955.
Boklund, Gunnar. *The Sources of The White Devil.* Upsala, 1957.
———. *The Duchess of Malfi: Sources, Themes, Characters.* Cambridge, 1962.

189

Bowers, Fredson T. *Elizabethan Revenge Tragedy.* Princeton, 1940.

Boyer, C. V. *The Villain as Hero in Elizabethan Tragedy.* London, 1914.

Bradbrook, M. C. *Themes and Conventions of Elizabethan Tragedy.* Cambridge, 1952.

——. "Two Notes Upon Webster," *Modern Language Review,* XLII (July, 1947) 281–94.

Brennan, Elizabeth. "The Relationship Between Brother and Sister in the Plays of John Webster," *Modern Language Review,* LVIII (October, 1963), 488–94.

Brereton, J. Le Gay. *Elizabethan Drama.* Sydney, 1909.

Brooke, Rupert. *John Webster and the Elizabethan Drama.* London, 1916.

Brown, John M. *The Modern Theatre in Revolt.* New York, 1929.

Buckley, Vincent. *Poetry and Morality.* London, 1959.

Carpenter, Frederick I. *Metaphor and Simile in the Minor Elizabethan Drama.* Chicago, 1895.

Cecil, David. *Poets and Storytellers.* London, 1949.

Chambers, E. K. *The Elizabethan Stage.* 4 vols. Oxford, 1923.

Cook, Grace L. "English Tragedy in the Reign of King James I," *Wellesley Magazine,* VIII (February, 1899), 233–43.

Corbin, John. *The Elizabethan Hamlet.* London, 1895.

Courthope, W. J. *A History of English Poetry.* 6 vols. London, 1910.

Crawford, Charles. *Collectanea, First Series.* Stratford, 1906.

——. *Collectanea, Second Series.* Stratford, 1907.

Davies, Cecil. "The Structure of *The Duchess of Malfi*," *English,* XII (Fall, 1958), 89–93.

Dent, R. W. *John Webster's Borrowing.* Berkeley, 1960.

Dibdin, Charles. *History of the Stage.* London, 1800.

Dillon, Arthur. "*The Duchess of Malfi*–A Note," *Library Review,* I (October, 1892), 519–21.

Doran, Madeline. *Endeavors of Art: A Study of Form in Elizabethan Drama.* Madison, 1954.

Downes, John. *Roscius Anglicanus,* ed. Montague Summers. London, 1928.

Drake, Nathan. *Shakespeare and His Times.* London, 1838.

Eaton, Walter P. *The Drama in English.* New York, 1930.

Edwards, W. A. "John Webster," *Scrutiny,* II (June, 1933), 12–23.

Ekeblad, Inga-Stina. "The 'Impure Art' of John Webster," *Review of English Studies,* IX (August, 1958), 253–67.

Eliot, T. S. *After Strange Gods.* London, 1934.

——. "*The Duchess of Malfy*," *Listener,* December 18, 1941, pp. 825–26.

——. "*The Duchess of Malfi* at the Lyric: and Poetic Drama," *Art and Letters,* III (Winter, 1920), 36–39.

——. "Mr. Lucas' Webster," *Criterion,* VIII (June, 1928), 155–58.

————. *The Sacred Wood*. New York, 1928.

————. *Selected Essays*. New York, 1932.

"The Elizabethan Dramatists," *The European Magazine*, LXXVIII (1820), 301–304, 420–24.

Elledge, Scott, ed. *Eighteenth Century Essays*. Ithaca, 1961.

Ellis-Fermor, Una. *The Jacobean Drama*. London, 1936.

Emslie, McD. "Motives in Malfi," *Essays in Criticism*, IX (1959), 391–405.

Franklin, H. Bruce. "The Trial Scene of Webster's *The White Devil* Examined in Terms of Renaissance Rhetoric," *Studies in English Literature*, I (Spring, 1961), 35–51.

Genest, John. *Some Account of the English Stage*. 10 vols. Bath, 1832.

Gildon, Charles. *The Lives and Characters of the English Dramatic Poets*. London, 1699.

Goldie, Grace W. "*The Duchess of Malfi*," *Listener*, February 2, 1938, p. 240.

Gosse, Edmund. *The Jacobean Poets*. London, 1899.

————. *Seventeenth Century Studies*. London, 1897.

Greg, W. W. "*The White Devil*: An Essay in Formal Criticism," *Modern Language Quarterly*, III (December, 1900), 112–15.

Grierson, H. J. C. *The First Half of the Seventeenth Century*. New York, 1906.

"H. M." "*The Duchess of Malfi*," *Blackwood's Magazine*, III (March, 1818), 656–62.

————. "*The White Devil*," *Blackwood's Magazine*, III (August, 1818), 556–62.

Hallam, Henry. *Introduction to the Literature of Europe*. 3 vols. London, 1839.

Hamilton, Clayton M. "*The Duchess of Malfi* Considered as a Tragedy of Blood," *Sewanee Review*, IX (October, 1901), 410–34.

Hazlitt, William. *The Literature of the Age of Elizabeth*. London, 1901.

Hendy, E. W. "John Webster—Playwright and Naturalist," *Nineteenth Century*, CIII (January, 1928), 111–23.

Holmes, Elizabeth. *Aspects of Elizabethan Imagery*. Oxford, 1929.

Hulme, T. E. *Speculations*, ed. Herbert Read. New York, 1924.

Hurd, Richard. *Letters on Chivalry and Romance*, ed. Edith Morley. London, 1911.

Hurt, James R. "Inverted Rituals in Webster's *The White Devil*," *Journal of English and Germanic Philology*, LXI (January, 1962), 41–47.

"J. M." "The Early English Drama," *The Gentleman's Magazine*, CII (May, 1833), 414–17.

Jack, Ian. "The Case of John Webster," *Scrutiny*, XVI (March, 1949), 38–43.

Jones, Richard F. *Lewis Theobald*. New York, 1919.

Kingsley, Charles. *Plays and Puritans*. London, 1885.
Knights, L. C. Review of Eliot's *Elizabethan Essays, Scrutiny*, III (December, 1934), 306–14.

Lamb, Charles. *The Works of Charles and Mary Lamb*, ed. E. V. Lucas. 7 vols. London, 1904.
Langbaine, Gerard. *An Account of the English Dramatic Poets*. London, 1691.
Layman, B. J. "The Equilibrium of Opposites in *The White Devil*: A Reinterpretation," *PMLA*, LXXIV (September, 1959), 336–47.
Leavis, F. R. ed. *Determinations*. London, 1934.
————. *The Great Tradition*. London, 1948.
————. *New Bearings in English Poetry*. London, 1950.
————. *Revaluations*. London, 1936.
Lee, Sidney. "John Webster," *Dictionary of National Biography*, XX (1921–22), 1032–1035.
Leech, Clifford, *John Webster*. London, 1951.
————. *Webster: The Duchess of Malfi*. London, 1963.
————. "An Addendum to Webster's Duchess," *Philological Quarterly*, XXXV (April, 1958), 253–56.
Lewes, G. H. *Dramatic Essays*, ed. William Archer and Robert Lowe. London, 1896.
Lowell, James R. *The Old English Dramatists*. New York, 1893.
Luecke, Jane Marie. "*The Duchess of Malfi*: Comic and Satiric Confusion in a Tragedy," *Studies in English Literature*, IV (Spring, 1964), 275–90.

Minton, William. *Characteristics of English Poets*. Boston, 1889.
Morris, J. E. "John Webster," *Fortnightly Review*, LXXVII (June, 1902), 1065–1078.
Mulryne, J. R. "*The White Devil* and *The Duchess of Malfi*," in J. R. Brown and B. Harris, eds. *The Jacobean Theatre*. London, 1960.

Nicoll, Allardyce. *A History of Restoration Drama, 1660–1700*. Cambridge, 1928.

Odell, George C. D. *Annals of the New York Stage*, VII. New York, 1931.
Ornstein, Robert. *The Moral Vision of Jacobean Tragedy*. Madison, 1960.

Parrott, Thomas M. and R. H. Ball. *A Short View of Elizabethan Drama*. New York, 1943.
Pepys, Samuel. *The Diary of Samuel Pepys*, ed. H. B. Wheatley. 8 vols. London, 1928.
Phillips, Edward. *Theatrum Poetarium*. London, 1675.
Price, H. T. "The Function of Imagery in Webster," *PMLA*, LXX (September, 1955), 717–39.
Prior, Moody E. *The Language of Tragedy*. New York, 1947.

Ribner, Irving. *Jacobean Tragedy: The Quest for Moral Order.* London, 1962.

Rollins, Hyder E. "Samuel Sheppard and his Praise of Poets," *Studies in Philology*, XXIV (April, 1927), 509–55.

Saintsbury, George. *A History of Elizabethan Literature.* London, 1887.

Salingar, L. G. "Tourneur and the Tragedy of Revenge," in Boris Ford, ed., *The Age of Shakespeare.* London, 1956.

Scott, Walter. *Letters of Sir Walter Scott,* ed. H. J. C. Grierson. 12 vols. London, 1937.

Scouten, Arthur H., ed. *The London Stage, 1729–1747.* 2 vols. Carbondale, 1961.

Seccombe, Thomas, and J. W. Allen. *The Age of Shakespeare.* London, 1903.

Shaw, G. B. *Our Theatre in the Nineties.* 3 vols. London, 1932.

Smith, James. "The Tragedy of Blood," *Scrutiny*, VIII September, 1939), 265–80.

Spencer, Hazelton. "Nahum Tate and *The White Devil,*" *Journal of English Literary History*, I (1934), 235–49.

Stedman, Edmund C. *The Nature and Elements of Poetry.* New York, 1892.

Stoll, E. E. *John Webster.* Boston, 1905.

Swinburne, A. C. "John Webster," *Nineteenth Century*, XIX (June, 1886), 861–81.

––––––. *Studies in Prose and Poetry.* London, 1894.

Taine, H. A. *History of English Literature.* Trans. H. Van Laune. New York, 1871.

Tannenbaum, S. A. *John Webster (A Concise Bibliography).* New York, 1941.

Tate, Nahum. *Injured Love, or the Cruel Husband. A Tragedy Design'd to be Acted at the Theatre Royal.* London, 1707. In the Readex Microprint Series *Three Centuries of English Drama,* ed. H. W. Wells. New York, 1952.

Thayer, C. G. "The Ambiguity of Bosola," *Studies in Philology*, LIV (April, 1957), 162–71.

Theobald, Lewis. *The Fatal Secret.* In the Readex Microprint Series *Three Centuries of English Drama,* ed. H. W. Wells. New York, 1952.

Thorndike, A. H. *Tragedy.* Boston, 1908.

Tomlinson, T. B. *A Study of Elizabethan and Jacobean Tragedy.* Cambridge, 1964.

Vaughan, C. E. "Tourneur and Webster," in A. W. Ward and A. R. Waller, eds. *Cambridge History of English Literature.* 15 vols. Cambridge, 1910.

Vernon, P. F. "The Duchess of Malfi's Guilt," *Notes and Queries*, X (1963), 335–38.

Wadsworth, Frank W. "Webster's Duchess of Malfi and Some Contemporary Ideas on Marriage and Remarriage," *Philological Quarterly*, XXV (October, 1956), 394–407.

Ward, A. W. *A History of English Dramatic Literature.* 3 vols. London, 1875.

Wasserman, Earl. "The Scholarly Origin of the Elizabethan Revival," *Journal of English Literary History*, IV (September, 1937), 213–44.

Watson, William. *Excursions in Criticism.* London, 1893.

Webster, John. *The Complete Works of John Webster*, ed. F. L. Lucas. 4 vols. London, 1927.

———. *The Duchess of Malfi*, ed. E. M. Brennan. London, 1964.

———. *The White Devil* and *The Duchess of Malfi*, ed. F. L. Lucas. Rev. ed., London, 1958.

———. *Webster and Tourneur*, ed. J. A. Symonds. New York, 1888.

———. *The White Devil*, ed. J. R. Brown. London, 1960.

———. *The Duchess of Malfi*, ed. J. R. Brown. London, 1964.

———. *The White Devil and The Duchess of Malfy*, ed. M. W. Sampson. Boston, 1906.

———. *The Works of John Webster*, ed. Alexander Dyce. 4 vols. London, 1830.

"Webster's Plays." *The Retrospective Review*, VII (1823), 87–120.

Weisinger, Herbert. "The Seventeenth Century Reputation of the Elizabethans," *Modern Language Quarterly*, VI (March, 1945), 13–21.

Wellek, Rene. *A History of Modern Criticism.* 2 vols. New Haven, 1955.

Wells, Henry W. *Elizabethan and Jacobean Playwrights.* New York, 1939.

Wendell, Barrett. *The Temper of the Seventeenth Century in England.* New York, 1904.

Whipple, Edwin P. *Essays and Reviews.* 2 vols. New York, 1853.

———. *The Literature of the Age of Elizabeth.* Boston, 1895.

Williams, Robert D. "Antiquarian Interest in Elizabethan Drama Before Lamb," *PMLA*, LIII (June, 1938), 434–44.

Wilson, F. P. *Elizabethan and Jacobean.* Oxford, 1945.

Wimsatt, W. K., and Cleanth Brooks. *Literary Criticism, A Short History.* New York, 1957.

SELECTED REVIEWS OF WEBSTER PRODUCTIONS, 1850–1960:

*The Duchess of Malfi*

*Athenaeum*, November 23, 1850, pp. 1225–26.
*The Illustrated London News*, November 23, 1850, p. 409.
*The London Literary Gazette*, November 23, 1850, p. 890.
*The Illustrated London News*, April 18, 1868, p. 319.
*Athenaeum*, October 29, 1892, pp. 599–600.
The *Graphic*, October 29, 1892, p. 522.
*The Illustrated London News*, October 29, 1892, p. 539.
The London *Times*, October 22, 1892, p. 6.

The *Nation*, November 10, 1892, pp. 348–49.
*Athenaeum*, November 28, 1919, pp. 1266–67.
*The London Mercury*, I (January, 1920), 368–70.
The London *Times*, November 25, 1919, p. 10.
*The New Witness*, November 28, 1919, p. 37.
The *Spectator*, November 29, 1919, pp. 720–21.
The *New Statesman*, March 15, 1924, p. 666.
*The Illustrated London News*, February 2, 1935, p. 168.
*The London Mercury*, XXI (April, 1935), 409–410.
The London *Times*, January 14, 1935, p. 10.
The *New Statesman*, January 19, 1935, p. 75.
The *Observer*, January 20, 1935, p. 13.
The London *Times*, April 19, 1945, p. 6.
The *New Statesman*, April 28, 1945, p. 271.
*Punch*, May 2, 1945, p. 382.
The *Spectator*, April 27, 1945, p. 383.
*New York Theatre Critics' Reviews*, ed. Rachel Coffin. VII (1946), 304–
    306. XVIII (1957), 313–316.
*Time*, April 1, 1957, p. 61.
*The Illustrated London News*, December 24, 1960, p. 1150.
The London *Times*, December 16, 1960, p. 5.
The *New Statesman*, December 24, 1960, pp. 1104–1105.
*Punch*, December 28, 1960, p. 946.
The *Spectator*, December 23, 1960, p. 1017.
Agate, James. *Brief Chronicles*. London, 1943.
Tynan, Kenneth. *He That Plays the King*. London, 1950.
Walkley, A. B. *Pastiche and Prejudice*. London, 1921.
Wedmore, Francis. *On Books and Arts*. London, 1899.
Williamson, Audrey. *Theatre of Two Decades*. New York, 1951.

*The White Devil*

The *New Statesman*, March 20, 1920, pp. 708–709.
The *London Mercury*, XIII (November, 1925), 6.
The *Nation and Anthenaeum*, October 17, 1925, p. 116.
The *New Statesman*, October 17, 1925, pp. 11–13.
The London *Times*, March 18, 1935, p. 10.
The *Observer*, March 24, 1935, p. 17.
The London *Times*, March 7, 1947, p. 6.
The *New Statesman*, March 15, 1947, p. 174.
*Punch*, March 19, 1947, pp. 246–47.
The *New York Times*, March 15, 1955, p. 32.
*The Saturday Review*, April 2, 1955, p. 30.
Agate, James. *Brief Chronicles*. London, 1943.
Landau, Jack. "Elizabethan Art in a Mickey Spillane Setting," *Theatre
    Arts*, XXXIX (August, 1955), 25, 87.
Tynan, Kenneth. *He That Plays the King*. London, 1950.
Williamson, Audrey. *Theatre of Two Decades*. New York, 1951.

# INDEX

# LOUISIANA STATE UNIVERSITY STUDIES

The Studies was established to publish the results of research by faculty members, staff, and graduate students of the University. Manuscripts of exceptional merit from sources other than aforementioned are considered for publication provided they deal with subjects of particular interest to Louisiana.

The Studies originally appeared as a unified series consisting of forty-two numbers, published between the years 1931 and 1941. In 1951 the Studies was reactivated, and is now being issued in the following series: Social Sciences, Humanities, Biological Sciences, Physical Sciences, and Coastal Studies. Other series may be established as the need arises.